CASE NO

-75-2035

AUTOPSY REPORT

ME-8 9 72

STATE OF CONNECTICUT

OFFICE OF THE MEDICAL EXAMINER

THIS IS TO CERTIFY THAT I (Name and Title)

Elliot M. Gross, M.D., Chief Medical Examiner

PERFO[illegible] Morn[illegible] BEGINNING AT 12:30 P.M. ON November 1, 1975

AT

the Greenwich Hospital

IN THE PRESENCE OF

Doctor J. Colman Kelly, Assistant Medical Examiner; Detective Daniel Pendergast, and Detective Thomas Sorenson, Greenwich Police Department, and Trooper David Page, Badge No. 189, Crime Laboratory, Connecticut State Police. Also present, Juvenile Officer Daniel

AND SAID AUTOPSY REVEALED:

Hickman, Greenwich Police Department who first saw deceased lying prone at Walsh Lane, Belle Haven area, Greenwich, Connecticut on October 31, 1975 at approximately 12:30 p.m. Autopsy also performed in the presence of Doctor James Spencer, Certified Pathologist.

**********************

The body is removed from the mortuary compartment and from two hospital grayish-green sheets which were covering the body removed and given to Detective Pendergast. Also given in the same folded condition as lying atop the body to Detective Pendergast is a yellow and white plastic sheet. This is not unfolded. The body is lying on its back with a plastic evidence bag lying loosely on the right hand and a red tag with the label, "Coroner's Case" signed J. Colman Kelly, M.D. affixed by a rubber band to the left wrist. This is cut and removed.

The body is lying on its back with an unzippered quilted nylon jacket with the right sleeve in place at the right wrist and the left sleeve pulled down to approximately the left wrist. Dried grass, leaves, and twigs are present about the face, trunk, and lower extremities. The body is clothed in a golden-yellow and blue horizontal stripe long-sleeved blouse which in front is just above the level of the umbilicus. The lower torso and the lower extremities including the thighs and the lower border of the left patella and the junction of the middle and upper thirds of the right leg are exposed and naked. On both feet are brown rubber-soled leather moccasins which have a leather lace, both shoes which are tied. The left side of the face has a distinctly flattened appearance and the anterior surface of the thighs also has a distinctly flattened appearance. The thighs sh[illegible]tis[illegible]rin[illegible]

# CONVICTION

The pla[illegible]ic bag [illegible] photographing the anterior surfa[illegible] [illegible] Under ul[illegible] lig[illegible] [illegible]escence in the pubic region. [illegible] turned o[illegible] to the prone position with [illegible] upper ext[illegible]ity at the side. The back shows the buttocks exposed [illegible] exposed with the unbelted blue jeans and panties with the edge and inner aspect of th[illegible] waist of the blue jeans everted (turned out). It is lowered to the level of the popliteal fossa. The left side of the jacket lies to the right of the head and obliquely over the left scapula to the lower chest area. The body is turned to the position in which it was first observed by Officer Hickman. The jacket and the shirt in back as well as the posterior thighs and the clothing in back are relatively free of leaves and twigs and grass. A few scattered small pine needles are present over the buttocks. A plastic bag from the right hand is again removed prior to photographing. The moccasins are removed by slipping them over the heel. Both moccasins have a double knot and the laces are leather. On the feet are a pair of blue socks with a green and blue argyle pattern. The right one is rolled down and lies just above the right ankle. The height of the left is not noted. After the socks and the moccasins are removed, the blue jeans are then further pulled down without cutting. Only the fifth button is fastened, the upper four are unfastened. The pants have all of their pockets in place. In the left front pocket is a round, pumpkin-shaped golden-yellow invitation to a Halloween Party, the other pockets all of which are in place, are emtpy. The panties are yellow with a green leaf design, bikinis. The panties are intact.

The fingernails of the right hand are short, irregular, with no lacquer and are unbroken. The tips of the nails are cut and along with the original plastic bag are given to Detective Pendergast. The nylon quilted outer jacket is then removed then pulled over the right wrist. There is no jewelry on the right hand. There is jewelry present consisting of an indian-type silver ring with a turquoise stone on the left fourth finger. The clippings from the left hand as well as the ring from the left fourth finger are given to Detective Pendergast.

When the quilted jacket is removed, the deceased is wearing as described golden-blue long-sleeved shirt, the sleeves in the back are intact. The shirt has a white collar with a blue dickey. There is one button at the neckline and this is opened with the button intact.

**Also by Leonard Levitt**

*An African Season*

*The Long Way Round*

*The Brothers of Attica* by Richard X. Clark,
edited by Leonard Levitt

*The Healer*

"Mbeya Dreaming"
in *Going Up Country*

# CONVICTION

## SOLVING THE MOXLEY MURDER

ISBN# 0-06-054430-9

A reporter and a detective's twenty-year search for justice

LEONARD LEVITT

ReganBooks
*An Imprint of* HarperCollins*Publishers*

Photography Credits
Interior: Photographs on page 2 courtesy of Dorthy Moxley; page 94 courtesy of Frank Garr; page 132 by Susan Levitt; page 196 courtesy of the Greenwich Library; page 230 by the State's Attorney's Office, Judicial District of Fairfield.

Insert: Photographs on pages 1–5 courtesy of Dorthy Moxley; pages 6–7 courtesy of the Greenwich Library; pages 8 and 9 (top) courtesy of Tim Dumas; pages 9 (bottom) and 12 (top) courtesy of Frank Garr; pages 10, 11, and 14 (top) by the Greenwich Police Department; pages 12 (bottom) and 13 by Susan Levitt; pages 14 (bottom) and 15 (bottom) courtesy of the State's Attorney's Office, Judicial District of Fairfield; page 14 (top) courtesy of the *Connecticut Post*; page 16 by Southern Connecticut Newspapers, Inc. Copyright © 2002.

A hardcover edition of this book was published in 2004 by ReganBooks, an imprint of HarperCollins Publishers.



FIRST PAPERBACK EDITION PUBLISHED 2005

*Designed by Kris Tobiassen / Richard Ljoenes*

---

The Library of Congress has cataloged the hardcover edition as follows:

Levitt, Leonard, 1941–
Conviction : solving the Moxley murder : a reporter and a detective's twenty-year search for justice / Leonard Levitt.— 1st ed.
p. cm.
Includes index.
ISBN 0-06-054430-9 (acid-free paper)
1. Moxley, Martha. 2. Levitt, Leonard, 1941– 3. Garr, Frank. 4. Skakel, Michael. 5. Murder—Connecticut—Greenwich—Case studies. 6. Murder—Investigation—Connecticut—Greenwich—Case studies. I. Title.

HV6534.G765L48 2004
364.152'3'097469—dc22

2004051114

---

ISBN 13: 978-0-06-054431-7
ISBN 10: 0-06-054431-7

05 06 07 08 09 WBC/RRD 10 9 8 7 6 5 4 3 2 1

To S, J, and M—as always.

# Contents

# Foreword

During the more than twenty years I was involved in the Martha Moxley murder investigation, people asked me why I hadn't written a book about the case, which I probably know as well as anyone. My answer was that I felt I couldn't write a book without knowing the ending.

This proved to be both a strength and a weakness. The strength was that when I decided to write the book, I knew it would be the complete story, the real deal. The weakness was that during those twenty years, three other books about the case were written. After Michael Skakel's indictment in 2000, I presented my proposal but I was unable to interest a publisher. All those I approached told me the same thing: I offered little about the case that hadn't already been written.

Then, after Michael was convicted in June 2002, Joe Pisani, the editor of the *Stamford Advocate* and *Greenwich Time*, asked me to write an article about what the conviction meant to me personally after all this time. As I wrote, I realized what had been lacking in my proposal of two years before. As Judith Regan said to me when I told her of the book I wanted to write: "This is your story. You are not merely retelling the events of Martha Moxley's murder, of the investigation, or how Michael was convicted. This is the story of your unique role, with your insights and your voice."

Indeed, it is the story of my struggle to do my job as a reporter when the editor who hired me refused to run my story about the case. It is the story of my relationship with Dorthy Moxley and how over twenty years we developed a bond that will last our lifetimes. Finally, it is the story of my relationship with Frank Garr, who, more than any other person, was responsible for Michael's arrest and whose struggles with his bosses came to mirror mine.

At our lowest ebb, we made a pact to tell our story. Here it is.

# Acknowledgments

I would like to acknowledge the following people, whose help was invaluable to me over the years in fitting the pieces together:

First, Dorthy Moxley, who became an inspiration to me and others. Our lives will be forever intertwined.

Frank Garr, my mirror image, whose struggles and personality I saw reflected in my own.

The late Steve Carroll, whose remorse over what had occurred allowed me to see that there was no cover-up by the Greenwich police.

John McCreight, who recognized from the outset there was a problem and provided my first lead.

Chief Jerry Hale of the Detroit PD: It really happened, as you said it could.

Tony Insolia, whose honesty on reading my first article gave the lie to the claim that "legal problems" prevented it from being published.

Joe Pisani, who always tried to do the right thing.

Don Forst, who was there when it counted.

The unnamed source who provided me with the Sutton report: The world should know how important you were to solving this case.

Jimmy Breslin for his encouragement.

Dominick Dunne, who shared the same goal and whose disagreements with me I hope are in the past.

Cissy Ix, who was kind enough to share her insights about the Skakels with me.

Tom Sheridan: Ditto, although we'll never agree on who was responsible for Martha's murder.

Sean Crowley, who planted the seed.

Bernie Kerik, who brought me to Judith Regan.

Alice McQuillan, who gives new meaning to the term "undying devotion" and whose literary tough love salvaged this manuscript. Although I knew what I had to do in writing this book, I couldn't shake off thirty years of journalism that had taught me to keep myself out of my stories. Alice struggled for months to force me to unlearn those old habits. I finally got the message.

Editor Aliza Fogelson took it from there. Aliza got so deep into this story she was right there inside my head.

John Mancini, who allowed me some slack.

Sean Gardiner and Rocco Parascandola, who covered for me. I will make it up to you guys.

Susan, Mike, and Jennifer Levitt for tolerating an author's self-centeredness. This last year was rough.

# Introduction

I couldn't let go of it.

I wouldn't let go of it.

The editor who hired me stopped taking my calls.

The publisher told me the story would never appear—not just in Connecticut but in any other newspaper the company owned, including *New York Newsday*, where I worked.

The story was the murder of Martha Moxley. At age fifteen on Halloween eve, 1975, she had been beaten to death with a golf club after leaving the home of her teenage neighbors, Tommy and Michael Skakel. The Skakels were heir to the Great Lakes Carbon fortune and related to the Kennedys. Tommy and Michael's aunt—their father Rushton's sister Ethel—was the widow of the late Senator Robert Kennedy.

Tommy was the last person seen with Martha. The day her body was found, the police discovered two clubs that matched the murder weapon inside the Skakel house. Yet no one was ever arrested. My story, which took me two years to prepare, described how the Greenwich police had bungled the investigation.

But the *Greenwich Time* and *Stamford Advocate* newspapers refused to print it. When they did, nearly a decade later in 1991, after I had badgered, pressured, and embarrassed them, the Connecticut authorities announced they were restarting their investigation.

Again, it went nowhere. It wasn't merely the newspapers that had failed. So had Connecticut's criminal justice system. For two decades it appeared that money, power, and influence had trumped justice.

People say I'm like a dog with my teeth in someone's ankle when I'm on a story. But pursuing the Moxley murder required more than tenacity or even courage. It required stealth, guile, and, most important, patience.

I did not solve Martha's murder. What I did was prevent the Skakel family from getting away with it. I was that unexpected force that created enough of a stir to keep the case alive until someone smarter than me appeared and put it all together.

No, that person was not the notorious former Los Angeles detective Mark Fuhrman, whose claim of solving the murder was trumpeted by the national media. Nor was it the celebrity writer Dominick Dunne, whose claims the media also accepted. Rather, the person who solved the Moxley murder was an unheralded local detective named Frank Garr, who pursued his investigation for eleven years and whose work and life became intertwined with mine.

I had battled the *Stamford Advocate* and *Greenwich Time* and later *Newsday*, which balked at publishing a second round of my stories. Frank battled his bosses at the Fairfield County state's attorney's office, which had taken jurisdiction of the case from the Greenwich police. My bosses were willful. His were blind. My actions ensured me lasting enemies within the Times-Mirror media conglomerate, which had owned both Connecticut papers and *Newsday*. Frank's led to his ridicule and ostracism within Connecticut's criminal justice system.

Both of us found ourselves underdogs and outcasts and naturally formed a bond. We were an odd couple, a detective and a newspaper reporter. It was like the lion lying down not with a lamb but with a crocodile. Except that as we grew closer, I wasn't sure which of us was which.

Nearly thirty years after Martha's murder, Frank and I are still haunted by questions of who might have helped Michael the night of the murder, or afterward, by keeping quiet something they'd seen or heard. We will probably never find out, and because of the statute of limitations, no one will ever be prosecuted. Still, it is enough for us to know that for a story that could never really have a happy ending, the Moxley family has finally found a measure of peace.

# PART I

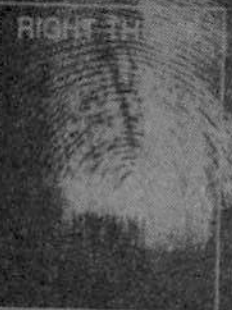

1

PART ONE / CHAPTER ONE

# East Coast O.J.

NORWALK, CONNECTICUT
June 2002

I never thought Michael would be convicted.

I only hoped for Frank's sake the jury would deliberate longer than the few hours it had in the O. J. Simpson case. That way Frank wouldn't be embarrassed.

This was East Coast O.J., involving one of America's richest families with a bloodline to the Kennedys, and the case was all Frank's. He had found all the witnesses. Many hadn't wanted to testify. Frank Garr, they related, had pursued, cajoled, harassed, or threatened them.

Walking about the courtroom in his black pinstriped suit with his air of professional gravitas, Frank reminded me of an undertaker. His hair—all white and formerly worn in a ponytail—curled up the back of his neck. While working as a narcotics detective two decades before, he had taken an acting course in Manhattan. Like all actors, there was a touch of vanity to his appearance.

As Michael's trial begins, Frank is fifty-seven years old, a twenty-seven-year veteran of the Greenwich, Connecticut, police department. For the past seven years, he has been an inspector with the Fairfield

*Martha Moxley at age ten.*

County state's attorney's office. He has investigated the Moxley murder for eleven years and come to know it like no one else. He understands Michael better than Michael's own family and probably better than his numerous psychiatrists.

Frank also knows the Skakel family. Despite the image of forthrightness and generosity they present to the world, Frank says they have no morals or conscience. He calls them habitual liars and says their loyalty is only to each other.

Frank has no more regard for their friends, neighbors, and attorneys—even their family priest. All of them, he says, knew about Michael but looked away.

"Genetic hedonism: the desire for immediate pleasure or instant gratification." That was the term for the Skakels coined by one of those psychiatrists, Dr. Stanley Lesse. He had been hired by Rushton Skakel Sr. the year after the murder when Rushton realized his son Tommy was a suspect.

But "genetic hedonism" falls short of describing them. Tom Sheridan, the Skakel family lawyer, would later offer his own term for them—"histrionic sociopaths."

"Their interest is only self-interest," Sheridan says. "They lack empathy for anyone but themselves." And after the Skakels turned against him—as they did to virtually everyone they used to protect them in the Moxley case—Sheridan added, "And if you disagree with them, you are their enemy."

And here they all are, the Skakels and their supporters, filling the far right section of the courtroom in a calculated display of familial unity. They are a clannish crowd, unbowed and unrepentant. Both inside and outside the courtroom, they speak only to each other. They dress casually as only the rich can, in khaki pants, sports jackets, and loafers. The youngest brother Stephen wears alligator cowboy boots. They begin every morning with smiles and handshakes. Every afternoon they lunch together at the Ash Creek Saloon a few blocks away.

Rush Jr., the eldest of the seven children, has flown in from Bogota, Colombia. David, the second youngest, has come from Oregon. Their cousin, Bobby Kennedy Jr., appears unannounced late in the trial. He'd attended Michael's first court hearing in nearby Stamford two years before but has not been seen since.

Tommy—Michael's older brother, boyhood rival, and tormentor—also turns up, if only for a day. He is in his mid-forties now, balding and wearing glasses. Like Michael, he has admitted lying to the police about his whereabouts the night of the murder.

The family matriarch is Ann McCooey, Michael's aunt, Rushton's sister, known as Big Ann. A stout woman with bleached blonde hair, Big Ann sits in the same seat in the first row every day of the trial, next to her daughter, whose name is also Ann. During the trial, Michael is said to be staying with Big Ann, as his wife Margo—Tom Sheridan's niece—has begun divorce proceedings. The strain from his murder charge has been too much for them.

And there at the center is Michael. Now forty-one years old, portly and blowzy with thinning hair and a florid face, he does not or cannot close his shirt's top button beneath his tie. Each morning before testimony begins, he stands in the courtroom well, accepting his family's chucks of support, chatting with his lawyers and his bodyguard, a huge, bald black man. The bodyguard is not merely Michael's protector. He is his silencer. Michael can't keep his mouth shut.

Two years before at his first court appearance in Stamford, he had lurched from the defense table and made for Martha's mother Dorthy, seated in the first row of spectators. His voice loud enough to make the six o'clock news and even the next day's *New York Times*, he had blurted, "Dorthy, I feel your pain. But you've got the wrong guy."

She had turned to me in tears. Michael had sounded so aggressive, so arrogant. He'd presumed he could address her by her first name, as though they were equals. After twenty years, I still called her Mrs. Moxley.

During a break in that day's testimony, Frank caught my eye. "Did you notice Michael staring at me?" he asked. "Watch him when we go back. He tries to stare me down."

Better than anyone, Frank knows Michael can't control himself. He's blabbed about Martha's murder for years, releasing thoughts that weighed upon him, like steam escaping from a pressure cooker. Indeed, it was Michael's own words—confided to friends, then to private investigators, and to the ghostwriter of his unpublished autobiography—that led to his arrest.

I am one of nearly 100 reporters who have covered every day of Michael's month-long trial here in Norwalk. Unseen by the rest of them, a second drama is occurring.

I notice that Frank does not sit at the table with the prosecution team. Instead, each day, he places himself a few feet apart, in a wooden chair by the railing. This is his personal statement of disgust against his own office, which for years ignored the case, then at the eleventh hour pandered to Mark Fuhrman.

In his book *Murder in Greenwich*, published in 1998 (New York: HarperCollins), Fuhrman named Michael as Martha's probable killer, then claimed he had solved the murder. Frank had named Michael as Martha's killer in 1992, the year after he began investigating it.

"Only I couldn't say it aloud then," Frank has told me more than once. "I am working for a guy who wouldn't even listen to me so there was no sense talking."

I am the only person inside the courtroom who has supported Frank through his eleven-year ordeal. Even Dorthy Moxley has doubted him, although she has maintained a diplomat's silence. Each time I see her, I marvel at how different she is from the woman I met twenty years before. Then, she was the mousy housewife whose husband made the decisions. She says his premature death allowed her to take charge.

Now, passersby stop her on the street. People recognize her in restaurants. Strangers ask for her autograph. Much of this is due to Fuhrman and Dominick Dunne. Grant them that. They made Martha's murder a national story.

Dorthy has steeled herself so that she can sit in the courtroom and hear the details of her daughter's murder. Still, some details remain too difficult to bear. When pictures of the crime scene are introduced, she escapes to the state's office in the courthouse basement.

She is also the consummate hostess, balancing the case's rival interests and personalities. She has been given the courtroom's first three rows of the center section and sits in the first with her son John, his wife Kara, and friends and relatives who have come in from around the country.

Her first courtroom crisis involves Fuhrman. Having pled no contest to charges of perjury in the O. J. Simpson trial for denying he'd used the word "nigger," ABC hired him for the Moxley trial but his "nigger" remark infuriated the network's black journalists and it dropped him. Court TV picked him up but it was too late for him to obtain press credentials.

Dorthy rescued him. She knew what he was and what he was doing. She understood he was using Martha's murder to achieve a kind of redemption. But she refused to criticize him. More than once she has said, "I will not abandon Mark."

So she invites him to sit with her. Because she fears angering Frank, she asks my advice. I tell her to place Fuhrman in the third row, so there will be a space between Fuhrman and herself. Instead, she compromises, and allows him to sit behind her in the second.

She even befriends one of the Skakels. Late in the trial, she tells me she struck up a conversation in the ladies' room with Michael's aunt Ann McCooey, "Big Ann." "I blame this all on Rush," Dorthy says to Big Ann of her brother. Big Ann agrees. "Yes, he fell apart when his wife died."

"I'll pray for you," says Dorthy.

"And I'll pray for you," Big Ann answers, though when the verdict comes, she runs from the courtroom in tears.

There is another man in the courtroom who maintains he solved the Moxley murder—Dominick Dunne. Seventy-six years old, short, stocky, and smiling like a cherub, his passion is celebrity murder. Like Frank and me, he has been around the Moxley case for over a decade. Despite his age, he has lost none of his verve. He sits with reporters young enough to be his grandchildren, charming them—as he had me a decade before—with his informality and apparent lack of pretension. "Just call me Dominick," he says to them.

Like me, neither Fuhrman nor Dominick believes Michael will be convicted. Fuhrman has even prepared Dorthy for an acquittal. Merely bringing him to trial after twenty-seven years, he has told her, is victory enough.

Only Frank believes. He professes total confidence in his witnesses. "They are all telling the truth," he says. "The jury will see this."

As in the O.J. case, where the jury acquitted after only a few hours, I fear a quick verdict means not guilty. So when the jury gets the case on a Tuesday morning, I pray they will remain out the rest of the day.

My prayer is answered. Tuesday passes with no decision. Thank God, I find myself thinking. Thank God for Frank.

Again on Wednesday, the jury deliberates through the day. Again, there is no decision. But now the momentum is shifting. Michael and his family can't understand what is happening.

The announcement comes at eleven o'clock Friday morning—the jury has reached a verdict. I slip into the second row behind Dorthy. Seeing me, she touches my hand and smiles. Our twenty years together have brought us to this moment.

2

PART ONE / CHAPTER TWO

# My Second Half

LONG ISLAND
January 1982

My involvement in the Moxley case began two decades before with a phone call from my friend Ken Brief. Ken and I worked together at *Newsday* on Long Island. His wife was a publicist for Viking Press, which had recently published a book I'd written about another murder.

I knew Ken was bored at *Newsday*. He was the national editor and there wasn't much national news on Long Island. When Times-Mirror, *Newsday*'s parent company, bought two small papers in Connecticut, the *Stamford Advocate* and *Greenwich Time*, I urged him to apply for the editor's job. Sure enough, he was hired.

A year later, he telephoned me. He said he loved his new job and Greenwich, where he and his wife had purchased a house. But something was nagging at him. Wherever he went, he said, people still talked about the unsolved Moxley murder and the Skakels.

"Why don't you spend a few months up here and look into this for me?" he said.

I think back to that conversation that was to alter the next twenty years of my life and ask myself how the murder of Martha Moxley became my obsession. Dominick, I would learn, had been drawn to it because of a tragedy in his own life. Fuhrman sought redemption from it because of his perjury charge. Frank was assigned to it as his job.

But my motives changed over time. I began the case because it looked like someone from a rich and influential family had gotten away with murdering a fifteen-year-old girl and the police had covered it up.

Then, it got personal.

The lives of the rich and famous held no allure for me. On the contrary, I seemed to have spent much of my life escaping from what I perceived as my privileged past. I had grown up in the Five Towns in Nassau County on Long Island, where Jewish families moved from New York City after coming into money. Ours came from my maternal grandfather, a turn-of-the-century immigrant who as a teenager fled the yeshiva in Poland to sell pots and pans on the Lower East Side.

He started his own business and was successful enough that he brought over his brothers. He bought a house in the Bronx and sent his son to medical school and his daughter to Hunter College, where she became a high school English teacher. That was my mother.

My father's family fled Russia and the Communists after my grandfather, for whom I am named, was released from a Bolshevik prison. They crossed the border at night, traveled west through Europe—at one point reduced to sleeping in the barn of my grandmother's sister in Romania because she refused to allow them to sleep inside her house—before ending up, penniless, in Winnipeg, Canada. The uprooting broke my grandfather. He could find work only as the principal of a poor Hebrew school and suffered from depression the rest of his short life.

My own childhood was prototypically American. I played baseball, football, and basketball until I dropped. I read everything I could about sports. My heroes were not just the ballplayers but the bylines: Arthur Daily of the *Times*; Jimmy Cannon of the *Post*; Roger Kahn, Ed Fitzgerald, and Shirley Povich of *Sport* magazine; and years later, as my interests widened, Dick Schaap and Jimmy Breslin in the *International Herald Tribune*.

My reading habits so disturbed my mother that she asked our pediatrician if there was something wrong with me. The doctor assured her I was no different from most American males.

I was also transfixed by *The Big Story*, a television program about crusading newspaper reporters. Each was a solitary figure who, like the Western sheriffs of frontier towns, walked the streets alone, poking into the dark crevices of a city that more sensible people feared.

I suppose it was in part this Lone Ranger–like image that made journalism my calling. How better to right wrongs and help the less fortunate, those unable to help themselves?

Yet it was a quality of my mother's that sustained me through three decades of journalism. She possessed a blind and reckless optimism, a belief that in the end things turn out as they are supposed to. An unpublished writer, she penned novels and short stories into her nineties while taking creative writing courses and arguing with teachers one third her age.

In the Five Towns, she was an oddity—the rare college graduate, unconcerned with Cadillacs, beach clubs, bar mitzvahs at the Plaza, and the Pierre and Del Monaco hotels in New York City, to which we as thirteen-year-olds were driven in chauffeured limousines. I, however, was very concerned. Even at thirteen, I knew something was all wrong with these displays of ostentation. One star-filled night I poured out my lament to my teenage girlfriend, proclaiming as we wandered our school's grounds, "This is not how I want to live my life." Only in retrospect did I understand that I was harsher than I had a right to be about people who'd overcome hardships I never knew.

My escape from the Five Towns came when I was accepted at Dartmouth College, which I imagined as a rural Eden in the green mountains of New Hampshire. It was that. But Dartmouth in the 1960s was also anti-Semitic, anti-black, anti-female, anti-intellectual, and anti-just-about-everything else. Its founding mission had been to educate the American Indian. In 200 years, Dartmouth had graduated seventeen Indians.

Still, there were plenty of people like me who cared nothing for the luxuries that money could buy. Like a number of them, after graduating

I joined the Peace Corps, which President John F. Kennedy had started a few years before. In fact, I felt I owed the Kennedys a debt, for it was the Peace Corps that led me—hell, catapulted me—into journalism.

I taught at what was called an upper primary school in Tanzania, East Africa. The school was in a mountain village where daily rains left wisps of white clouds atop the blue hills, a setting as pristine as my idealism. While there, I wrote a book. It was a sunny book about my students, the school's African teachers, and its headmaster, who taught me far more than I did him. My book was accepted by the first publisher I approached. "The first book which truly conveys the flavor of Peace Corps work, the realities of it, the challenges, the frustrations. . . . an extraordinarily fine book," Sargent Shriver, the Peace Corps's director and brother-in-law of JFK, wrote on the jacket cover.

The book received a full-page review in the *New York Times*. It was excerpted in *Harper's* magazine and published in England. It led me to a big-time literary agent with the awesome name Sterling Lord. Miraculously, he represented not only my boyhood sports-writing idols but also Schaap and Breslin.

"You're in the big leagues now," he said. I was twenty-four. I was so scared I called him Mr. Lord. It took me about five years to work up the courage to call him Sterling.

He arranged my admittance into the Columbia School of Journalism, which—published author or not—had placed me on the waiting list. Mr. Lord knew the dean. When everyone went home for the summer, I went to the top of the list.

And who was teaching there but Dick Schaap, now a city-side columnist. During our week of in-service training, he allowed me to accompany him. One evening, he made a speech in Long Island and wrote his column in longhand on the train back to New York. He allowed me to proofread it and even to alter a word. Then he typed it up at the *New York Times*, of all places, where a friend of his directed us to a desk in the barren city room. Observing such insouciance and derring-do, how could I not want to be like him?

Mr. Lord also arranged my first job at the *Detroit News*, a newspaper that, like the city itself, never recovered from the 1967 race riots. Like all rookie reporters, I was assigned to police headquarters at 1300 Beaubien Street. I was instructed to telephone the outlying counties and ask their police chiefs what crimes had been committed. The chiefs never told you what happened in their counties but blabbed about all the others. That's how I learned police reporting.

Fortunately for me, Detroit's police commissioner, Ray Girardin, had been a newspaperman. He appeared to be in his late sixties or early seventies, slim, stooped, and pockmarked. He took a look at me, saw that I knew nothing about the police, and arranged for me to ride in a patrol car on the four-to-midnight tours. It was my first appreciation of the dangers cops face and of their courage. I saw stabbing and shooting victims, furious husbands and cowering wives, scores of drunks, and plenty of racial hate—all directed at the police.

It was also my first appreciation of why the quality a cop prizes most is loyalty. A partner's loyalty can save a cop's life.

While in Detroit, I covered all sorts of crime—white merchants shot and stabbed by black teenagers during robberies; domestic stabbings and shootings that knew no distinction of color; even a serial killer in Ann Arbor, a darkly handsome young man who offered girls rides on his motorbike, then strangled and buried them in a relative's basement.

After two years, I completed a novel, which the *Times* also reviewed, albeit in two paragraphs south of page thirty-five. Meanwhile, I'd returned to New York as a correspondent for *Time* magazine. I was like a reporter in a television movie: every week, a new story; every story, a new adventure.

And I played the part. The first time I visited the old police headquarters on Center Street, a young cop at the information desk scanned my identification, looked up at me, and said, "Yeah, I really believe everything the newspapers say."

"Yeah," I answered, "and I really believe everything the police say."

*Time* magazine was starting a New York bureau and I was the first reporter hired. But there was a problem. Actually, two problems. The first was that I was in over my head. I'd left newspapering too soon. The second was that after I was hired, *Time* began trimming costs and firing people. I survived only because of my boss, Frank McCulloch. Either he felt I had potential or took pity on me.

An ex-marine, McCulloch joined *Time* as a stringer out West after World War II and caught the attention of its founder, Henry Luce. He left briefly to become a managing editor at the *Los Angeles Times*, then, to Luce's delight, returned to *Time* as Saigon bureau chief during the Vietnam War.

He had been the last reporter to interview Howard Hughes and told a hilarious story of being directed to drive to an abandoned airstrip in the Nevada desert, where a plane mysteriously appeared and flew him to a secret rendezvous with the reclusive billionaire. When he was returned to the airstrip, he found a note from Hughes that one of his minions had somehow placed on the dashboard of McCulloch's locked car.

Then in his fifties, he was an imposing figure with a shaved head, thirty years ahead of fashion. His door across the hallway from my cubicle was always open and I watched a procession of *Time* correspondents and other journalistic luminaries from Vietnam pass through it.

They told amazing stories of war. One spoke of covering a massacre where he saw hundreds of bodies floating down a river. Although some were alive, a British journalist, an older man, announced that a reporter's job was merely to describe what had happened, not to offer help. I wasn't sure where I stood on that. Reporters still belong to the human race.

For the first few months, until other correspondents settled into the bureau, it was just McCulloch and me. I became the sole beneficiary of his instruction.

"What are the qualities a journalist should possess?" I asked.

"Honesty, accuracy, and integrity," he answered, "the same qualities one should practice in daily life." Obvious as this might seem, when articulated by him, it sounded like a revelation.

"Never lie when reporting a story," he added. "You don't have to tell people you interview the full truth. But a reporter must never lie. In the end, you are left with only two things—your byline and your credibility."

Two decades later, I would read in the *New York Times* that Phan

Xuan An, *Time*'s office manager in Saigon during the war, admitted he had been a North Vietnamese spy and a colonel in the North Vietnamese army. Though unrepentant, he stated in an interview with CBS's Morley Safer that he wanted to send his regards to McCulloch.

In words I might have uttered, Phan Xuan An said of him, "He taught me everything about honest journalism. He taught me about 'getting it right.' Tell him whatever I did, I did not let him down on that."

I remained at *Time* for three years. Heady as the experience was, there was something unreal about it. I felt I was only playing at being a reporter. The reason was that *Time*'s editors in New York rewrote every story correspondents filed. Richard Reeves, then a political reporter, with the *New York Times*, said that one *Times* reporter equaled three *Time* correspondents because *Times* reporters wrote their own stories.

While in Detroit I had heard of a group of Jewish gangsters, known as the Purple Gang. From the 1920s to the 1940s, they controlled the rackets and terrorized the city. Sterling (by then I'd worked up the courage to call him that) arranged a book contract and I left *Time* to write their story.

For the next year, I traveled to Detroit in search of them. Many had been killed or had served long prison terms. Those who were still alive were in their sixties and seventies. Their families were embarrassed and ashamed. I couldn't get near any of them. Too late, I realized I was in over my head again. This time, there was no McCulloch to bail me out. The book blew itself out somewhere around page twenty-seven.

I prayed for a second chance to return to journalism. By then, McCulloch had left *Time*. He had never succeeded to its highest editorial positions, either as managing editor or chief of correspondents. While his abilities were recognized throughout Time-Life, its executives understood that his first loyalty was not to the company but to the craft of journalism. That was another life lesson for me: The best people don't always rise to the top.

But a recession was in the wind and nobody was hiring. Ironically, the only place to make an exception for me was *Newsday* on Long Island.

I may have traveled half the world to escape the Five Towns, but I didn't seem to have come very far.

I landed there through Don Forst. He had edited Schaap at the *Trib* and was one of *Newsday*'s three managing editors. At my interview, I listed my bona fides, including having grown up in the Five Towns.

"To the manor born," Forst replied.

With him was a second managing editor, Tony Insolia. He opposed hiring me, distrusting reporters from New York City, no matter where they'd grown up. He was a man of old-fashioned values and virtue, and I became as close to him as I did to Don.

We agreed to a weeklong tryout, which stretched into a month. My second chance had begun.

In some ways, *Newsday* was a step down from *Time*. Whereas *Time* straddled the world, my universe at *Newsday* was bounded by eastern Queens and the western Suffolk County line. But my experience there proved richer and fuller. Bill Moyers had left as publisher a few years before, but the place still rocked. The editor-in-chief, Dave Laventhol, also from the *Trib*, had been a Moyers guy. Erudite and shy, he rarely emerged from his office. Ken Brief was the national editor. Forst ran the newsroom. He said he wanted stories not merely about events but about people—not just what they did but what they thought and felt.

"Just remember," he said, "reporting isn't about you. It's about them."

One of my first interviews was with Meir Kahane, the rabbi who founded the Jewish Defense League. He was holding a news conference and was seated on a podium next to a bearded man with a British accent who insisted on making a speech while Kahane sat glumly beside him. In the midst of it, Kahane cut him off, then stormed off the podium toward me.

"Rich people," he muttered, "I despise them."

He then asked me where I was from.

"The Five Towns," I answered.

"Oh, a rich boy," he said.

"Yes, rabbi," I answered, "but I have overcome it."

Perhaps because *Newsday* was a liberal paper and no one else seemed comfortable doing it, or perhaps because I had done it before, I fell into covering crime and the police. I started small: Kids in a gang fight at a junior high. A gambling ring in a school cafeteria. A middle-aged secretary embezzling from her company. A fifteen-year-old girl named Dawn who beat her alcoholic mother to death. A Vietnam vet, shot and killed by cops after a robbery, who as he fled discarded the women's clothing he was wearing.

And they or their friends or families all talked to me. Dawn's stepfather told me Dawn killed her mother because she'd prevented Dawn from seeing her boyfriend. The Vietnam vet's aunt told me he was a transvestite and was discarding his clothes because he feared being discovered dressed as a woman. "His last act," said the aunt, "was to die as a man."

At the embezzling secretary's office, her coworkers told me she was incapable of stealing and that the police had mistakenly arrested her. We pulled up chairs and I sat them in a circle and led them in a discussion about her. Details emerged that her co-workers had never realized.

I seemed to have found my rhythm as a reporter, although I still had plenty to learn. I wrote a story about Frank Steiner, a shady private eye. Two decades before as a Nassau County detective, he'd supposedly solved the murder of millionaire horseman and socialite William Woodward, who was shot by his wife. She claimed to have mistaken him for a burglar.

As a private eye, Steiner had two partners. One was Walter Cox, a brilliant and bitter ex-con. To prompt Cox to open up to me, I spoke disparagingly of Steiner, unaware Cox was taping our conversation. Cox then excised his voice and presented Steiner with the tape, saying my derogatory remarks had been prompted by their third partner.

From that experience, I learned two lessons. Lesson number one: Never underestimate anyone you interview.

Lesson number two: I wasn't as smart as thought I was.

A surgeon, Charles Friedgood, murdered his wife by injecting her with Demerol. One of his four daughters hid the needle. Another daughter alerted the police after he'd looted their mother's safe deposit box and bought an airline ticket to join his girlfriend in Denmark. Police pulled him off a plane on the runway of Kennedy airport.

Before his arrest, I visited him at his home. His daughter, blonde and in her twenties, answered the door. I wasn't carrying a pad and she asked if I were "a real reporter." I realized she was flirting.

Then I visited the daughter who'd alerted the cops. She told me that the daughter I'd met at the door had hidden the needle used to kill their mother.

I wrote a four-part series that became the book that Viking published. It became a book club selection and was optioned for a movie. I was a natural, a pro, or so I imagined. I didn't realize that as a journalist I was only half-formed. The Moxley story would form my second half.

3

PART ONE / CHAPTER THREE

# "Then, the Sadness Came"

STAMFORD, CONNECTICUT
1982

When Ken Brief called me about the Moxley case in 1982, I had left *Newsday*. By then I had married Susan, the younger sister of my best friend at Dartmouth. She, too, had been in the Peace Corps, and our romance went something like this: Susan told me she'd decided to marry me because she loved my book about Africa. I told Susan I'd wanted to marry her since I first saw her as a high school sophomore wearing braces. Susan said she never wore braces.

When Ken called, we had just returned from Tanzania, where, with a grant from the Rockefeller Foundation for the Humanities, I had set out to find the students from my Peace Corps days of fifteen years before. I did find many of them. But the country was such a mess they were broken and dispirited, their dream of the better life I'd help foster, shattered. My grant money spent, unemployed, and Susan pregnant after repeated miscarriages, I told her I thought Ken's offer to investigate the Moxley murder sounded pretty good.

He sent me a packet of news clips so I could familiarize myself with the case, but they contained scant information. Martha had last been seen with seventeen-year-old Tommy Skakel outside his house in the Belle Haven section of Greenwich, Connecticut, around 9:30 P.M. on October 30, 1975. In Greenwich, Halloween Eve was known as Mischief Night, where kids played pranks. Within weeks Tommy became the prime suspect.

The Greenwich police, however, did not immediately focus on him. Instead, they initially pursued the theory that a transient, perhaps a hitchhiker off the Connecticut Turnpike, had eluded the two manned patrols at Belle Haven's entrance, then attacked Martha as she walked home. I was struck by a remark of Greenwich police chief Stephen Baran on November 2, two days after her body was discovered, which seemed to support the transient theory.

"Kids are always leaving bicycles, tennis rackets, and golf clubs outdoors, after playing with them on the lawn," he said.

It was a bizarre suggestion: A hitchhiker had wandered in off the turnpike, picked up a golf club lying on the ground, then for no apparent reason beaten Martha to death. I wondered whether Baran had said this to deflect attention from the Skakels.

A second clip also drew my attention. In March 1976, five months after the murder, Fairfield County State's Attorney Donald Browne told the Associated Press that "a particular family" had "clearly impeded" the police investigation. Although Browne refused to identify them, he was obviously referring to the Skakels.

There was a third clip I noted, dated June 24, 1977, from the *New York Times*. It reported that the Greenwich police believed they had traced the murder weapon to a set of golf clubs belonging to the Skakels. By then, however, the case had taken a twist. The summer after the murder, Ken Littleton had been arrested for a series of burglaries in Nantucket, Massachusetts. A Williams College graduate on an athletic scholarship, Littleton had taught science at the tony Brunswick school that Tommy and Michael attended. Rushton Skakel had hired him as a live-in tutor for his sons. His first night at the Skakels had been October 30, 1975—Mischief Night.

Questioned by Connecticut authorities after his arrest, Littleton failed a lie detector test and became the second known suspect after Tommy. By the time I arrived, Littleton had long since left Greenwich.

So had Tommy. The Moxley murder investigation was dead. Short of a confession, Browne told the Associated Press in March 1976, a solution seemed unlikely.

"So what do you think?" Ken Brief asked.

"Ken," I answered, "it looks like someone has gotten away with murder."

•

While at *Time*, I'd learned how treacherous it was to enter into the middle of an investigation. The victim then had been my boss, Frank McCulloch.

At the time, *Life* magazine was preparing to excerpt a book on Howard Hughes by Clifford Irving. The book was based on what Irving claimed were exclusive interviews he'd had with Hughes. Irving convinced *Life*'s editors not to contact Hughes, warning they might spook him into reneging on the project. The editors accepted his claims until the publication date approached and Hughes began telephoning McCulloch, saying Irving had never interviewed him.

*Life*'s editors—who had until then ignored McCulloch—now sought his help. Never having met Irving but knowing the mercurial Hughes, he surmised that Hughes had at the last minute developed second thoughts.

That was the only time since I'd known him that McCulloch was wrong. Because he had been kept out at the start and not been permitted to interview Irving, he came to the wrong conclusion. At least in this case, Hughes was telling the truth. Irving had pulled a gigantic hoax on *Life* magazine.

Now here I was entering the Moxley case seven years after it had occurred. Go slowly, I told myself. Take nothing for granted. Rely on your instincts. Do not become personally involved. And form no alliances with sources.

Ken gave me a desk in the city room of the *Stamford Advocate*. The room was open and bright. The reporters were young. Most were in their twenties and afraid to approach me.

I didn't know anyone in Greenwich and began by calling people likely to talk to me. The first was Martha's father, David Moxley. He headed the New York office of the international accounting firm Touche Ross. But he refused to see me. I didn't get it. The police investigation had died years ago. I was perhaps the only person who could help him.

Ken's publisher, Jay Shaw, said he would contact a friend of his, a neighbor of the Moxleys and Skakels. Jay was a knock-around guy who'd come up from the garment district. As much as Ken, he had pushed for the story. But Jay was too rough for the suits at Times-Mirror. Within the year, he was gone.

His friend was Bob Ix, the president of the Stamford-based Cadbury-Schweppes corporation. Ix and his wife Cissy lived adjacent to the Skakels in Belle Haven, on a piece of property Rushton had sold them. Their daughter Helen was Martha's age and had been with her the night she was killed. But Ix, too, refused to see me. He said the Greenwich police had asked everyone to keep silent so as not jeopardize the investigation.

I knew what that was about. By now I knew enough to recognize that the last thing the Greenwich police wanted was a reporter coming around asking why after seven years no one had been arrested.

That meant I had no choice but to call Martha's mother, Dorthy. In the beginning I had hoped to avoid her. I dreaded weepy mothers. At least, I told myself, the murder had occurred seven years ago. I wasn't yet a parent and didn't understand you could live a thousand years and never get over the death of your child.

Although Dorthy agreed to see me, she was wary. "Why, seven years later," she asked, "is a newspaper interested in Martha?"

I didn't want to say, "Because the police let the murderer get away." That would have produced tears and I didn't want to deal with a teary mother, not at the beginning.

Never lie, McCulloch had taught. Instead, I told her the *Stamford Advocate* and *Greenwich Time* had asked me to take a fresh look at the case. This may not have been the full truth but it wasn't a lie.

Still, I found myself wondering why she, like her husband—wealthy, educated, and presumably sophisticated people—failed to recognize that seven years later, with the police investigation dead, I was their last chance.

We met at their apartment in New York City, where the Moxleys had moved a year after the murder. More recently, they had moved into the Carlyle Hotel on the Upper East Side. John F. Kennedy had stayed at the Carlyle when he visited the city as President. I wonder if the Moxleys knew that or cared.

I placed Dorthy Moxley in her late forties or early fifties, maybe ten years older than me. She seemed fragile and bewildered like a frightened bird. I had the sense she was barely holding herself together.

She began describing her problems decorating. Perhaps she wanted to put me at ease. Perhaps she wanted to hide her feelings. My presence was obviously upsetting her.

She led me into the living room. There, a portrait of Martha, with long blonde hair, freckles, and hazel eyes, filled an entire wall. This is probably what she'd looked like the last year of her life.

"No, no," Dorthy said, as though speaking to herself, shaking her head to hold back tears. "I want to talk about Martha. I want to talk about my daughter. People in Greenwich don't talk to us about Martha anymore, as though they are protecting us, as though we never had a daughter, as though she never lived."

She began telling me how she and her husband, with Martha and their older son John, had moved to Greenwich from Piedmont, California, the year before the murder. They'd bought a large, dilapidated house on two acres at 58 Walsh Lane across from the Ixes in Greenwich's Belle Haven section on Long Island Sound, where gothic-like mansions lined Field Point Road with lawns that ran on and on.

Besides the Ixes, the Moxleys' neighbors included the entertainer Victor Borge, *Beetle Bailey* cartoonist Mort Walker, and Rushton Skakel. Rushton lived diagonally across Walsh Lane at 71 Otter Rock Drive with his seven children—six boys and a girl—each, except the last, born nine months apart—"stepping stones," as Cissy Ix called them. The previous few years had been tragic for the Skakels. In 1973, Rushton's wife Anne had died a slow, agonizing death from cancer. She was forty-two.

Though he barely knew the Moxleys, Rushton sponsored them at the local Belle Haven Club on the Sound. He also sponsored David Moxley at the University Club in Manhattan. Such generosity to strangers was characteristic of him. A benefactor of the Catholic church, he volunteered at the nearby Hill House nursing home and allowed groups of the elderly to tour his house and remain for dinner. In the summer, he opened his swimming pool to a camp for the mentally retarded.

Friends and family said he did not know how to say no. "Mi casa es su casa [My house is your house]," appeared to be his unspoken directive, his friend Victor Ziminsky would say of him at his funeral. At the family ski lodge on Windham Mountain in upstate New York, which had been developed by Rushton's attorney friend Tom Sheridan and where the family skied each weekend in the winter, he insisted visitors warm themselves in his ski boots.

While fishing in Long Island Sound, he threw bluefish he caught to the drawbridge attendants. Years later when he and his second wife Anna Mae moved to Hobe Sound in Florida, he gave away twenty-dollar bills after church. His family tried to deter him from driving through the town's poorer sections for fear he would give away whatever money he carried.

To Sheridan, his friend "Rucky," as he called Rushton, was "the most loyal person in the world. The person I'd most want to be stranded with on a desert island."

"Why is that?" I asked him.

"He'd never take advantage of you," Sheridan answered. "He'd never double-cross you."

As generous as Rushton appeared, he and his family remained separate and apart from everyone, including their wealthy Belle Haven neighbors. "We knew about them as Kennedys," said Andy Pugh, Michael's best friend as a teenager and a key prosecution witness against him.

"You understood very quickly they were different from you, that they were superior," said Pugh, whose family had moved to Belle Haven from what he called the "regular" part of Greenwich after his father, a Justice Department lawyer under Attorney General Ramsey Clark, relocated to New York. "It wasn't just their money but the authority with which they used it."

Pugh and Michael were inseparable and played together every day after school. "Once you were his friend he would take care of you," Pugh said. "Michael was charismatic, generous, and welcoming, almost maniacally so. He had a driver take us to stores in town. They had charge accounts everywhere. Michael would say, 'Pick out something,' like a mitt. I thought it was incredible."

The Skakel money had come from Rushton's father, George Skakel Sr., who after World War I founded the Great Lakes Coal and Coke Company in Chicago with two partners and $1,000 between them. According to Jerry Oppenheimer's *The Other Mrs. Kennedy* (New York: St. Martin's Press, 1994), a biography of Ethel Skakel Kennedy, George Skakel's genius lay in exploiting the coal companies' sandlike waste-product residue, known as "fines." Mine owners, Oppenheimer wrote, dumped it in rivers but George Skakel purchased the "fines" for a nickel a ton. Some years later, when coal strikes swept the country and the waste-product residue was in demand, Great Lakes Coal and Coke had cornered the market.

Later, as his company expanded, Skakel did the same thing with the oil refineries' waste by-product, the petroleum coke residue, which he sold to utilities and to steel and aluminum companies. The money, Sheridan explained, financed his purchase of hop-cars, which Skakel sent into the refineries to load the petroleum coke and transport it, so that he invested none of his own money. By the late 1940s, he headed what was believed to be the largest privately held company in America after Ford Motor Company.

During the depression, George moved his business to New York City and resettled his family—his wife Ann Brannack, who'd been his former secretary and was known as Big Ann, and their seven children. First, they moved to a Catholic community in Larchmont, New York, then to Lake Avenue in WASPy back-country Greenwich. It was an area of woods, lakes, and estates, where the Skakels were disdained both as Catholics and as nouveaux riches.

Life on Lake Avenue for the Skakels was chaotic and booze-filled, the parents away for weeks or months, the children unsupervised, managed by friends, servants, and a coterie of priests and nuns, a pattern that would repeat itself during the next generation.

None of George Sr.'s children showed any of his business acumen. When he and Big Ann died in a company plane that crashed over Kansas City in the 1950s, his eldest sons, George Jr. and Jimmy, took over the business and, according to people familiar with the company, ran it into the ground.

At one point, Robert Kennedy—angered because the two were appropriating company perks denied to his wife, the Skakels' sister, Ethel—made a run at the business with his brother-in-law, Steve Smith, infuriating George Jr. and Jimmy, and widening a rift between Ethel and her Skakel siblings.

Ten years after his father was killed, George Jr. died in a plane crash while elk hunting in Idaho. Robert Kennedy served as a pallbearer. Six months after Martha's murder, when Rushton discovered Tommy was a suspect, Ethel rushed secretly to Belle Haven to comfort him. Yet her estrangement from the family never healed. She attended not a day of Michael's trial.

In fact, Sheridan pointed out, the relationship between the Skakels and the Kennedys was never as cozy as it has been portrayed. Rushton was a Goldwater Republican. And all the Skakels despised Robert Kennedy.

Rushton joined Great Lakes Carbon, as the company had been renamed, in the sales department, which required little business acumen but plenty of entertaining for oil refinery executives. "He was a born salesman," Sheridan said of Rushton, whom he had known since their college days after World War II.

"His job was giving parties and playing golf. He excelled at entertaining. He had contacts with all the major oil companies and was also a winer and diner of oil company executives. No one could do it better."

Right after the war, the family purchased an old DC-3 and refurbished it as the company plane. Rushton was always offering key oil executives rides on it.

At his funeral, his friend Ziminsky told of a ride on the family plane. He and Rushton were playing gin rummy when, twenty minutes out of Miami, Ziminsky noticed the left prop had cut out. He pointed this out to Rushton, who put down his hand, ambled forward to the pilot, then made three stops, engaging in conversation with the plane's other guests.

Returning to his seat, he told Ziminsky not to worry. He had discussed the situation with the pilot. Although the plane had two engines, it needed only one to land. Rushton then picked up his cards and announced he was knocking with three points.

Besides their money, something else separated the Skakels from their Belle Haven neighbors. It was alcoholism, which ravaged every branch of their family.

"There was booze everywhere," Pugh recalled. "Periodically, Rushton would try to stop drinking. Periodically, Cissy Ix would clean out the house to straighten him up."

Once, Pugh said, "Rushton came to my house looking for a drink. He sat on the couch, begging my mother for one. When she refused, he began to cry."

Anne Skakel had been the family disciplinarian, and without her, Rushton seemed lost—especially as a parent. Executives at Great Lakes Carbon asked Sheridan, who supervised Rushton's personal finances, to keep an eye on him because he was neglecting the children.

Both Sheridan and Cissy Ix realized Rucky knew nothing about being a father. He seemed unable to communicate with his children. Instead, he indulged their every whim. He gave them golf, tennis, and squash lessons. He denied them nothing but he couldn't talk to them.

His generosity to strangers belied his rigidity toward his children. He had a temper that bordered on self-destructiveness. Once while visiting the

Atlanta Braves, of which the Skakels were part owners, he became so agitated trying to open a door, he kicked it and broke his foot.

"I never saw him touch anyone when he became angered," Cissy recalled. "He might put his hand through a window but he would never touch anyone."

Often away on business or on sporting or hunting trips, Rushton left the care of his children to the cook, Ethel Jones; an elderly housekeeper, Margaret Sweeney, who owned a small house nearby but lived with the Skakels; a governess whom Cissy helped secure; the coterie of priests and nuns; and a live-in tutor Rushton hired each fall.

"He had children that he never should have had," said Sheridan. "It was a sad, sad scene. Rucky was in trouble. I didn't know how deeply. The more I looked, I viewed them as a very sick family."

Years later, Cissy would recall the first Father's Day after Anne had died. "None of the children gave him a Father's Day present," she remembered. "None of them had even thought of it." She took aside Tommy, who she said was something of a painter, and had him draw a picture for his father. Cissy had it framed and placed it in the den.

With no parental supervision, the Skakel home became a place of booze, drugs, and violence. Fights between the boys erupted daily.

"They were vicious fights," Pugh recalled. "The worst I saw occurred between Michael and his older brother Johnny outside in their driveway. It was a serious fist fight, punching in the face, lots of blood. I thought they would have killed each other. At one point Johnny grabbed Michael's hair—he wore it long—and kneed him in the face."

Nor was the recklessness and lack of parental supervision confined to the immediate Skakel family. Their first cousins, John and Jimmy Terrien, also went unsupervised.

In his autobiographical memoir, Michael described Jimmy, who was two years older than he, as "the captain of mayhem." Michael added that he loved spending time at the Terriens', as he did the night of Martha's murder, because Terrien's parents were alcoholics and left him and Jimmy alone.

Describing the night of the murder, Michael would write that he tried to persuade Martha to come with him to his cousin's house, which was in Greenwich's back-country, perhaps ten miles from the Skakel home. At the Terriens', Michael said, "You never had to worry about anything"—meaning, among other activities, drinking liquor and smoking pot.

Terrien's biological father, Jack Dowdle, had drunk himself to death the day Jimmy was born. Jimmy Terrien's mother, Georgeann, was Rushton's sister, and his stepfather George Terrien was Robert Kennedy's University of Virginia law school roommate. Both Jimmy and his older brother John had troubled relationships with their stepfather. Years later George Terrien claimed to the police that his stepson John had beaten him up in a dispute over money after Georgeann's death.

Cissy Ix claimed that as a teenager, Jimmy Terrien appeared to be entirely on his own. Having left one school, he appeared before the priest at another, St. Mary's, and told him he wanted to attend it.

"Where are your parents?" the priest, Father Gay, asked him.

"I'll handle it on my own," Terrien answered.

Of the seven Skakel children, Michael and Tommy seemed the most troubled. Both were two years behind in school and missed classes for weeks on end. Their problems had surfaced long before their mother died. Psychiatrist Stanley Lesse—who after Martha's murder secretly tested Tommy and interviewed the other Skakel children—described both boys as "exceptionally difficult children who suffered from remarkably similar behavior disorders."

In 1971, four years before the murder, both had been sent to a psychologist, Dr. Ellen Blumingdale, because of temper tantrums and constant battles with each other. At the time, Tommy was twelve, Michael, ten.

Some years later, Sheridan (paraphrasing Blumingdale's assessment) wrote in a report by private investigators hired by the Skakels: "Both boys are impulsive personalities. Both have very poor ego development and a bad self-image. Both are sexually immature and blocked emotionally. Both have an alcohol and possibly drug problems. Both are very likable and outstanding athletes. Both are lost, personally disorganized, and have no life plan. Their only point of departure is in the fact that Tommy feels loved by his family and Michael does not." The investigators quoted

Sheridan as noting he had been "informed by Mr. Skakel that Julie is frightened to death of Michael and that Michael suffers from enuresis [bed-wetting] and has engaged in some transsexual behavior."

Doctors believed Tommy's difficulties stemmed from an accident at age four, when he was thrown from a car and suffered head injuries. He was unconscious for ten hours and remained in Greenwich Hospital for two weeks.

A neurologist who treated him at the time noted that his personality had changed and that he'd throw temper tantrums and have violent outbursts. "He would rant and rave . . . and on one occasion put his fist through a door," neurologist Dr. Walter Camp was cited in the private investigator's reports as having written. "On another occasion, he was said to have pulled a telephone out of the wall."

His eldest brother, Rush Jr., told Lesse: "Mom had no control over Tom. If he got mad, there was nothing she could do about it. At times I think Tom brought Mother to tears."

Lesse, whose report was also cited by the investigators, wrote that Tommy "was responsive only to a man who was large in size," adding that when Rushton was away, the family often threatened to call his friend Robert Phelps, a towering ex-marine, to make him behave.

Michael was described as even more out of control, although people also noted his unsparing generosity. When the elderly visited from the nursing home, it was Michael who welcomed them. When Cissy's father visited, Michael spent hours with him.

"He insisted they play golf together," she recalled. "When my father protested that he wasn't very good, Michael said it didn't matter, that he would take him to the Greenwich Country Club, where his parents belonged, and give him tips."

Perhaps because Anne Skakel was so burdened caring for her brood of older children, Michael was raised by the housekeeper Margaret Sweeney, who was known as Nanny. He became devoted to her, and she to him.

When his brothers spilled milk, he would not allow her to clean it up, Cissy said. "I'll do that, Nanny," he would say. In a sad and touching gesture when she died, she left her small home to him.

In his unpublished autobiographical memoir, titled "The Obvious," which was changed to "Dead Man Talking: A Kennedy Cousin Comes Clean," Michael described his childhood: "Family servants, private boats and planes, a private ski area in Windham, N.Y. Our own baseball team [the Atlanta Braves, which the Skakels partially owned]. Meeting Hank Aaron . . . Jean Claude Killy presides over my sister's birthday party in Windham. Touring NASA with Sen. John Glenn."

But he also described his despair, self-loathing, and terror of his father. Michael's first cousin, Bobby Kennedy Jr., would write in *Atlantic Monthly* magazine that Rushton often hit Michael and on a hunting trip fired a gun in his direction. To escape his father, Kennedy wrote, Michael sometimes slept in a closet.

Michael's memoir also described how at age ten he brought home a cache of *Playboy* magazines. When Rushton came upon him reading them, he began choking Michael, slamming him against a wall and shouting, "You little slime."

"I think that was the moment when rage took root in me," Michael wrote. "I hated him. And because I was his son and felt he hated me, I hated us both."

Alcoholism. Violence. Neglect. Abuse. Repeated injuries, his memoir continued. "Hiding in my closet, looking for safety, needing the darkness and the quiet."

He also recounted the family's return in their plane from RFK's memorial at Arlington National Cemetery in 1968 when he was eight, although he misstated the date as 1969. "My father insists over the pilot's objections that we fly back from Washington in a thunderstorm. . . . While praying silently I hear my mother saying in a frightened voice that this is how my grandparents and later my uncle George died."

In school, he had difficulty reading, which decades later would be diagnosed as dyslexia. "The shame," he wrote. "It's obvious I'm stupid. My father's lectures become spankings, become beatings. My brother Tommy follows suit, bullying and terrorizing me with my father's tacit consent."

Then, his mother became ill. "I learn my mother is dying. We pray in vain for her recovery. Relics are brought from all over the world."

Rushton couldn't cope with bad news and as Anne lingered, he made the children say the rosary each afternoon at her bedside with a priest, praying for a miracle. He was in such denial, said Cissy, he never discussed her illness with them and restricted their visits to her in the hospital.

Nor, apparently, did they discuss Anne's illness with each other. Cissy recalled an incident at the country club when Anne played in a tennis tournament and lost in the finals. Afterwards, she broke down in tears. Rushton had never seen her cry before and thought it was because she had lost the match. But that was not the reason. Anne later told Cissy she had missed a number of lobs and realized she'd lost her peripheral vision. That meant the cancer had gotten behind her eyes into her brain.

In a letter of support for Michael at his sentencing, Tommy offered a moving look at life in the Skakel household during their mother's illness.

"When our mother was ill, we had a series of masses called novenas," he wrote. "Mass was once a day, every day for a week, dedicated to our mother. We had countless novenas over the last two years of her life. I remember the priests telling us that we must pray for our mother to get well and if we didn't, then she would die."

Tommy's letter also described a visit to his mother's hospital bedside in her final months. "When entering her hospital room, mother would say, 'It's so nice to see you,' and upon reaching her bedside we'd look into her lifeless eyes always trying to comprehend the words, 'It's so nice to see you' from something that was so contrary to our vibrant, caring mother. She no longer resembled the mother I once new [sic], the eternal athlete. I could have lifted her off the bed with one hand."

More than his siblings, Michael suffered tremendous guilt when his mother died. "Just after my twelfth birthday," he wrote in his memoir "she dies and to my frightened, guilty mind it is obvious that I killed her."

"I killed her, I killed her," Cissy recalled his saying. She became so concerned she told Rushton that Michael needed to see a psychiatrist. Rushton's response, she said, was, "Psychiatrists don't believe in God."

He changed his mind, however, when he visited Michael's bedroom and discovered him dressed in women's clothing.

Susan Wallington Quinlan, a psychiatrist, whose report was also cited by the private investigators, diagnosed him as suffering from a "depression possibly of psychotic proportions."

"The core of the depression is the feeling of being helpless, of being buffeted and brutalized by external forces," she wrote. "There is also great fury inside him focused primarily in hatred for his father. This anger is very frightening and he has inadequate defenses to deal with it." She told Rushton she considered him "a menace to himself and others."

By then Michael had failed out of half a dozen schools. In his memoir, he describes himself as "my family's scapegoat, ashamed of what I took to be my stupidity, wondering if I was crazy."

He took to going out alone at night, peeping into neighbors' windows. There was an older woman he regularly spied upon, watching her in varying states of undress.

Even before his mother died, he was using downers, pot, cocaine, and LSD. By age 13, the year after her death, he wrote, "I became a full-blown, daily-drinking alcoholic."

Rushton kept his liquor—cases of vodka and Old Grand Dad—in a cabinet in the basement. "There was a lock on it," said Andy Pugh. "Michael would take a hammer and screwdriver and remove the hinges."

One night, he and Pugh were in Field Point Park with their skateboards. Michael had a bottle of Old Grand Dad. It was about 5:00 P.M., cold and dark, and they built a fire under a tree. There was a steep hill on the edge of the park. Michael rode down it on his skateboard. Drunk, he crashed and hit the back of his head. There was so much blood that Pugh took him inside a neighbor's house to be treated.

Pugh and Michael regularly used a shed on the Skakel property as a clubhouse until Pugh said, Michael set it on fire. They had slingshots and shot at squirrels. Michael also shot Pugh's dog with a pellet gun. "It wouldn't go into Michael's yard so I knew it was him."

Michael also shot his gun at people, said Pugh. "He'd count to ten and give you a chance to run away. He thought it was funny."

One day Pugh discovered Michael inside the darkened shed, where the gardener kept lawn equipment. "Michael said 'Shh, shh.' He was grinning, with a demonic look in his eye. I didn't know what he was doing."

Then Pugh noticed a burlap bag on the ground filled with leaves that the gardener had raked. Michael lifted it up, revealing four or five dead birds that had been shot. On the driveway Pugh saw a trail of breadcrumbs Michael had spread to lure them to their death. As Michael showed this to him, he began to laugh.

This was a year before Martha Moxley was murdered.

"Then," said Cissy, "the sadness came and it never went away."

# 4

PART ONE / CHAPTER FOUR

# Doing Things by the Rules

GREENWICH, CONNECTICUT
1982

The Moxleys knew none of this. They knew nothing of what lurked next door.

"We felt comfortable in Greenwich the day we moved in," Dorthy said in our first meeting. "People were so kind to us. The kids loved the schools. The Ixes welcomed us with open arms. I saw Cissy every day."

Both Martha and John thrived at Greenwich High, where John made the football team and Martha played piano and violin. "She was bright, attractive, and confident," Dorthy said. "She and John made friends so easily. It was all so very positive."

Even after Martha's murder, she and her husband continued to socialize with Rushton and the Ixes.

"The day of Martha's funeral, Rush sent over a ham," Dorthy said. She gratefully accepted what she thought was his generosity. Later, Tommy offered John a summer job with the Atlanta Braves. "At the beginning Cissy couldn't have been nicer," said Dorthy. "After Martha's funeral, the adults all came back to our house. Cissy had all the kids over to hers."

Not long afterward, when the police began focusing on Tommy, Dorthy said she recalled walking down her hallway with Cissy. "Cissy said, 'Tommy is such a sweet child. I can't believe he could have done such a thing but I'd give you Michael in a heartbeat.'" For years Dorthy wondered whether Cissy was protecting Tommy or whether she knew something about Michael she wasn't sharing.

During our first meeting, I asked Dorthy about the Greenwich police and their apparent bungling of the investigation. I was taken aback by her response.

"The police have been good to us," she said. "I have nothing but praise for them. They have been compassionate and kind. I feel they have been loyal to us."

"The newspapers mention a cover-up," I said gently.

"Oh, you know, you do hear those rumors," she answered. "But I know it wasn't Keegan. I know it wasn't Lunney." I knew both those names from the newspapers. Thomas Keegan, Baran's successor as Greenwich police chief, had supervised the investigation into Martha's murder as captain of detectives. James Lunney had been one of the case's two lead detectives.

I was astonished that Dorthy and her husband still accepted what the Greenwich police told them. In seven years, the police had failed to make an arrest. But they had succeeded in convincing the Moxleys to keep silent.

Then, as an afterthought, Dorthy said, "My husband and I are not the kind of people to make noise, to protest. After Martha died and no one was arrested, we accepted what the Greenwich police told us, that they were doing everything they could. We accepted it because we believe in the system. That's the kind of people we are. Doing things by the rules through proper channels is what we have always known.

"But," she said, "maybe in retrospect, we should not have remained silent. Maybe when the rumors started and nothing happened we should have done something. But frankly, we didn't know what we could do."

She had been speaking to me for two hours beneath that portrait of Martha. During the entire time, she had not stopped crying.

There was something cleansing about her tears, both for her and, surprisingly, for me.

•

My interview had apparently gone well enough that Dorthy gave me the names of two people to contact. She was torn, I sensed, about cooperating with me because her husband disapproved.

I viewed that portrait of Martha on their living room wall as symbolic of their differences. Dorthy said David had buried his grief inside himself. Martha's death was so painful he could never speak of it. Yet Martha's portrait so dominated their apartment, how could he forget? Maybe that's what Dorthy had intended.

She needed to talk about Martha, and once she started, she couldn't stop. My appearance had opened the floodgates.

Dorthy suggested I call Marilyn Robertson, a family friend whose husband worked at Touche Ross with David. Not long before the murder, Marilyn told me, she and her husband attended a party at the Moxleys'. Martha met them at the door and took Marilyn's fur wrap. At that moment, David Moxley asked Martha to bring him a cigar. Moments later Martha reappeared, wearing the fur wrap and holding an unlit cigar between her teeth.

I form a portrait of Martha: poised, confident, provocative.

Dorthy also suggested I contact Martha's friend Christy Kalan. Christy showed me a letter Martha had written her shortly before she was murdered.

"I met Rob Somebody," it began. "[He's really cute and supposedly he has a crush on me.] He walked me home the other day. Last Thursday they had a swim team dinner and Helen decided to go. We walked in and got thrown in! . . . Then we were also playing water polo against the life guards. And this guy named Ross, he wasn't too bad, kept telling Helen and me how good we were [as we almost drowned . . . ] He was really nice. . . . Guess who called me and asked me to go to the movies Friday? . . ."

From that letter, I see another dimension in my portrait of Martha. She is boy crazy. Not necessarily teasing or vampish. Just fifteen-year-old boy crazy.

Martha kept a diary that the police would seize and release only at Michael's trial two decades later. It would reveal her as a prototypical, albeit privileged, American teenager.

"Dear Diary," she wrote on December 31, 1974, shortly after moving to Greenwich, nine months before she was murdered, "today is the last day of '74. Boo Hoo. '74 has been one of the best years of my life. . . . LOVED IT! The parties and the people were so fun! Well, hope '75 is as good. Today, I played paddle tennis for the first time. I guess I wasn't too bad. We went to the Keydel's house for dinner. We ate at about 11:00, maybe even 12:00, drank French champagne and gin but didn't get drunk!"

The following month, she wrote: "I got my braces off today!! I am so glad! I am so sick of basketball practice. I can't stand it. Beth is too much to handle too! She is a bragger and she cheats on tests—some of them. I also can't stand sitting with Sue and Christine in bio. It took me 5 or 10 minutes to open my locker after lunch with Buddy, Peter, Danny and Tom all attacking me at the same time. It's kinda fun but I sure am late to O'Brien's class a lot. My teeth feel so queer!"

At another point, she wrote: "Alan found out who both Mei and I like and he told Mark. Jeff wasn't at school today. But Alan has a big mouth so Jeff will probably find out."

Another entry read: "I was waiting for the late bus and Danny and Bob and Joe threw my geometry book into the boys' locker room. So I ended up in the boys' locker room. Then they were carrying me around the locker room. I got a full tour."

She also reported going to "first base" and "second base" with boys and even "third base" but never "all the way."

"I was sitting in this bean bag with Peter," she wrote, "and he bit my nose so I bit him back. Then he bit off all my fingernails and he bit my nose a few more times. Then we were just making out. We had such a good time."

And there was this: "I am writing sloppy because I am drunk. I had 2½ screwdrivers, 1½ Baccardi and Cokes and an aspirin. Then Alan came over for about 3½ hours and I got really drunk. I dropped a butter dish, ate a Pop-Tart. We called Peter. . . . I made an ass of myself in front of Giff. Me and Christy took a walk without our coats. It's about 10 degrees outside. Alan sat on me a long time."

After a doctor's appointment on her fifteenth birthday on August 16, 1975, she wrote, "I weigh 115 and I am in perfect health." Three days later, she reported trying marijuana and meeting the Skakels for the first time. Friends threw her into the Skakel pool.

On September 1, her first day at Greenwich High, she reported she went pool-hopping at night with Michael, Tommy, and David Skakel. On September 7, she visited the Skakels again. Five days later, she went driving with Tommy in his car. When Martha leaned over to steer the car, she wrote that she was "practically sitting in his lap" and that he "kept putting his hand on my knee."

On September 15, she and her friend Jackie Wetenhall visited the Skakels again and "as usual" sat in their mobile home parked in the driveway. On September 17, Michael "was so totally out of it that he was being a real asshole," accusing her of leading Tommy on. Michael and Tommy then started a fight, and she told Jackie they should leave.

She returned to the Skakels on September 21 and hung out with Tommy, who was drinking. She also saw him and Michael at a dance on October 4 and wrote that she bumped into Michael on October 10. It was one of her last entries. Three weeks later she was dead.

•

Dorthy also suggested I speak to John McCreight, who worked at Touche Ross with David Moxley. Waiting for him in Touche Ross's midtown office, I thought how bizarre this was: I am interviewing David Moxley's colleague while David Moxley refuses to see me.

McCreight was in his mid to late forties, short and balding, and as wary of me as Dorthy had been. At the time of Martha's murder, he said, he had been consulting for Detroit's Mayor Roman Gribs to improve the city police department's response time. Detroit was then the country's murder capital, with the highest per capita homicide rate. Yet McCreight had somehow arranged for Detroit's homicide chief, Gerald Hale, to take a week off to come to Connecticut six months after the murder and help the Greenwich police in their murder investigation. If that wasn't influence in high places, I didn't know what was.

"The Greenwich police were extremely receptive to Hale," McCreight began. "They were not at all defensive." McCreight was a pro. He wanted everything to be nice. He wanted everyone to make nice. He did not want to insult or upset the Greenwich police. He wanted to make Hale's involvement seem like a natural, normal law enforcement event. But it was hardly that. Recruiting Hale meant McCreight knew something had gone terribly wrong.

"Did Hale write a report of his visit?" I asked.

McCreight paused. Perhaps he had not anticipated the question. Perhaps he had thought I'd give him the once-over-lightly. That was the phrase New York City police chief Sidney Cooper had used a decade before when I'd interviewed him for *Time* about the Knapp Commission, which in the early 1970s investigated a department corruption scandal.

"Your questions are once-over-lightly," said Cooper, who headed the Internal Affairs Department. I'd never forgotten that. I was a kid then, just beginning to understand police. The chief was telling me I didn't know the subject well enough to ask the right questions.

But that was then and this was now. Now I knew what to look for. I knew what to ask. If Hale had written a report, was there something in it never before made public?

McCreight was a cautious man. I watched him, weighing his response.

"Yes," he finally answered.

So there was a report. Perhaps this is why Dorthy had pointed me to McCreight. Perhaps this was why David Moxley had allowed McCreight to talk to me. Perhaps David Moxley wanted me to know about the report. Or perhaps I was giving him too much credit.

McCreight and I met twice more before he agreed to show the report to me, and only with stipulations. The first was that I could not quote it in my story. The second was that I could reveal its content only to my editor. Third, that the newspapers' lawyers draft a letter confirming our agreement.

"I don't want there to be any 'misunderstandings,'" he said. McCreight apparently knew newspaper reporters.

Years later he would explain why he had given me Hale's report. "You were the only engine for the next leg of the trip," he said elliptically. "Your newspaper was the only road open. And there was something else. I felt I could trust you."

Ken was thrilled. My obtaining Hale's report vindicated his decision to pursue the Moxley story. He called Jim Imbriaco, a Times-Mirror attorney in New York, to draft McCreight's confirmation letter.

And I was right. Hale's report—written on May 10, 1976, six months after Martha's murder—did provide information never before made public. It detailed specific mistakes in the police investigation.

The report began with Martha's walk to the Skakel house with Cissy's daughter Helen and two other friends, Jackie Wetenhall and Geoffrey Byrne, around 9:00 P.M. on Halloween Eve—Mischief Night. Michael was standing outside. He and Martha settled into the front seat of his father's maroon Lincoln, parked in the driveway, while Helen and Geoff sat in the back. The Skakel boys referred to the Lincoln as the "lust mobile" or "love mobile." According to Michael's memoir, Rushton had bought it after Anne had died. He had a machine shop remove the Lincoln logo and replaced it with a $5,000 Lalique eagle head with a light underneath.

A few minutes after nine, Tommy emerged from the house and plunked himself down in the front seat on the other side of Martha. Around 9:15, two Skakel brothers—Rush Jr., nineteen, and John, sixteen—appeared with their cousin, Jimmy Terrien. Hale's report said that Rush, John, Michael, and Terrien drove off to Terrien's home in the back-country. This left Martha, Helen, Byrne, and Tommy outside the Skakel house.

So far, there was nothing in the report I didn't know. Everything so far had been in the newspapers. But the next sentences changed that.

"Jeff [sic] and Helen stated that it appeared as if Martha and Thomas were 'making out.' This, after careful questioning, consisted of Martha pushing Thomas and Thomas pushing Martha. At one point, Thomas pushed Martha down and either fell or got down on her. . . ."

There it was, the sexual undercurrent between them now out in the open. It made me think of a question Dorthy had asked aloud at her apartment: "Did Martha say something? Did she do something to provoke it?"

I had ignored her question, thinking she meant nothing specific. Now I wondered whether Dorthy had sensed her daughter's sexuality. The fur wrap across her shoulder, the cigar between her teeth. I couldn't get that picture of Martha out of my mind. Not that it mattered or rather not that it should have. Not that there was any relevancy to it. Even if Martha were a tease or promiscuous—and there was no indication she was either—she was only fifteen. Even if the killer had misread her signals, only a deranged person would have murdered her for flirting.

Hale's report said that Helen and Byrne left for home shortly afterward. Five minutes or so later, around 9:30, Tommy told the police he also went home. He said he last saw Martha walking across his back lawn toward her house.

Her path would have been across the Skakel backyard to Walsh Lane and then into her driveway. It was there that the killer first attacked her with the golf club, the report noted. She broke free and ran. He chased her forty feet down to the edge of her property under a weeping willow tree, began swinging the golf club at her. Full strokes. Again and again and again. Ten to twelve blows, all to her head. So savage was the beating that the golf club shattered in the attack. Then, with one of the broken pieces, the killer stabbed her through the neck.

Dorthy awoke after midnight. Realizing Martha was not home, she called the Skakels first about 1:15, and again after 3:00. She reached Julie. Julie awakened Tommy and put him on the phone. Tommy said he'd last seen Martha at 9:30 when she walked across his back lawn toward her home.

Julie got back on the phone and said her cousin Jimmy Terrien might know something. Dorthy called there. His mother Georgeann answered and said she would look for him. Minutes later she called back and told Dorthy that Jimmy was not home. Later, Terrien would tell the police he was with a married woman, whose name he would reveal only under subpoena. Questioned by the police, the woman denied Terrien had been with her.

A passing schoolgirl found Martha's body at 12:45 P.M. the next day under a clump of pine trees at the edge of the Moxley property. She was lying on her stomach, her blue jeans and underpants pulled down, exposing her buttocks and legs to the knees. She had not been raped. The killer either had been interrupted or was physically unable.

Inside her pocket police discovered a pumpkin-shaped Halloween party invitation. It was from a friend, Nadine Imus, the daughter of radio talk show host Don Imus.

A small amount of blood had been found in her driveway, indicating the first attack had occurred there. Two large pools were found in the shadow of the weeping willow tree, showing where the killer beat her mercilessly. A drag path of blood from the two large pools through high grass ended under the pine tree where her body lay.

Hale's report described the murder weapon as a #6 Tony Pena iron. Three pieces of the club—its head and two pieces of the shaft—were found nearby. The grip—the handle and a small part of the shaft—were missing.

Hale next focused on the time of death. Although the medical examiner estimated it occurred between 9:30 P.M. on the night of October 30 and 5:30 A.M. the following morning, the Greenwich police had narrowed it to shortly before 10:00 P.M.

"The Ix dog and another neighbor's dog went wild at about this time and began barking violently and both were facing toward the area of the weeping willow tree," Hale wrote.

The report also noted there had been a suspect before Tommy, whose name had never surfaced. "A Mr. Edward Hammond 27/W of 48 Walsh Lane was the main initial suspect but has been eliminated since," Hale wrote.

A Yale graduate and student at the Columbia Business School, Hammond lived with his mother next door to the Moxleys. The report didn't explain how or why the police had focused on him. But Hammond's mother Marianne later said to me, "He happened to be home alone the night of the murder. The police wouldn't believe him. They gave him a very hard time. They searched our house without a warrant. They never read him his rights. They just hauled him off to the police station."

Hale's report also did not explain when or why Hammond was dropped as a suspect. But David Moxley felt convinced enough of his innocence that a year after the murder he recommended Touche Ross hire him in its San Francisco office.

The report then turned to Tommy.

"Thomas Skakel became a suspect after the investigators found two Tony Penna [sic] golf clubs in the Skakel home which were identical to the murder weapon. These had been part of a complete set, which had belonged to Thomas's deceased mother Anne."

That was something else I hadn't known. The *New York Times* story of June 24, 1977, said the police "now believe they have traced the golf club used in the murder to a collection belonging to the Skakels." But the story hadn't said why.

My journalistic antenna was wiggling. Something wasn't right here. Why had the police told the *Times* they "believed" the clubs came from the Skakel house when it was they themselves who had discovered them? I found myself wondering exactly when the police had made this discovery. Hale's report didn't say.

"The officer," Hale's report continued, "confiscated one of these clubs with a Consent to Search form signed by Mr. Rushton Skakel." . . . The confiscated club was a 4 iron. It had a label on the shaft just down from where the grip ends with Thomas's mother's name on it. "The label would be located on the part of the murder weapon which is missing," the report read.

So that was why the club's grip had not been found at the crime scene with the other pieces. Anne Skakel's name on the grip was obviously why the killer had kept or hidden it.

This was a major discovery, another indication the killer was a Skakel. Who but a family member would have cared if the grip with Anne Skakel's name were discovered at the crime scene? And all this time the police had been searching for a transient. What had they been thinking?

The report then discussed Tommy's whereabouts after he left Martha at 9:30.

"Kenneth Littleton stated that Thomas came into the den of the Skakel home where Mr. Littleton was watching television at about 10:30 P.M. Littleton did not notice anything unusual about Thomas at that time," Hale wrote.

"Thomas accounted for his whereabouts by stating that after he left Martha, he went to his room and wrote a report that he had to have for school. However, a check revealed that there was no such report."

So Tommy appeared to have lied to the police.

He was subsequently given two polygraph tests by the Connecticut state police. The first "could not be read because Thomas was all washed out and tired. The second resulted in a finding that he was truthful."

But, Hale added intriguingly, "The validity of this test is in question."

Hale noted Tommy's skull fracture at age four and his history of violence. "[H]e would become violent frequently and quite suddenly.

"He would jump up from the table, begin to throw things about, turn over beds, pull phones from the wall or threaten siblings. He would not lose consciousness and the episodes varied from 15–20 minutes to as long as 2–3 hours. His father was able to control him but only physically. There is evidence that these rage reactions continue to this day."

During one of these recent incidents, "Thomas slashed a picture of himself in the groin area. A witness that works for the Skakel family also stated that Thomas has been seen going for walks carrying a golf club."

Hale's report also noted that the police did not immediately confiscate the clothing or shoes Tommy wore the night of the murder so they could be tested for Martha's blood or clothing fibers. Why not? Could their failure to do so have spawned the rumors of a cover-up?

"Search warrants for clothing, shoes and other golf clubs have been denied by the State's Attorney Mr. Donald Browne," Hale added with no further explanation.

I wondered why. Had there been a dispute between the Greenwich police, who had sought the warrant, and state's attorney Browne, who had refused it? If so, did the rumors of a cover-up refer to him?

•

My next move was obvious. I had to speak to Hale. And not by phone. I had to go to Detroit.

His report had made the Greenwich Police Department's case against Tommy. Not only had he been the last person seen with Martha; their meeting had been charged with a sexual undercurrent that suggested motive. In addition, he had a history of violence. And he had apparently lied to the police.

Ken didn't question the trip's expense, usually a concern at a small paper. "When do you want to go?" was all he said.

It was at 1300 Beaubien Street that I had begun as a police reporter. More than a decade had passed since then. In that time, I had come to know something of police. I knew some of the qualities that differentiated detectives from uniformed officers, homicide detectives in particular because murder is considered "the ultimate." I understood the importance of the first forty-eight hours of a homicide investigation—the time before suspects can concoct their stories and call their lawyers.

The homicide detective in the Charles Friedgood case, Tommy Paladino, had insisted on taking Friedgood's written statement the afternoon he reported his wife's death. In it, Friedgood maintained he had examined his wife and concluded she died of a stroke. It was a blind alley from which he could not escape after an autopsy determined she'd been injected with massive doses of Demerol.

I had called McCreight to smooth the way with Hale. Without his intercession, there was no way Hale would have seen me. His office was two floors above the press room where I had cut my teeth as a reporter, calling chiefs in outlying townships. The building on Beaubien Street hadn't changed. What had changed was me. There would be no once-over-lightlies. Now, I knew what I was doing.

Hale was a burly man in his late fifties, nearing retirement. Perhaps that was why he spoke so candidly. First, he set the scene. "Martha is with Tommy Skakel, the last person to see her alive," he began. "They're making out. Helen Ix and Geoff Byrne are so embarrassed they felt they had to leave.

"But the Greenwich police don't focus on Tommy immediately. They don't get a warrant to search the Skakel house for the killer's bloody clothes and shoes. Instead, they were looking at other people like Hammond, who had no connection to the case. Why was that?"

I half-expected—I half-hoped—Hale would blurt out, "Because there was a cover-up." Instead, he said, "Because when it came to the Skakels the Greenwich police were treading lightly."

Hale then turned to the police's use of the lie detector test. "They attempted to give polygraphs to virtually everyone they questioned," he said. "They even tried to test Dorthy Moxley." Dorthy hadn't mentioned that. Later, she would tell me she had been too nervous to take one.

"I tried to tell the Greenwich police many times that a polygraph is not an investigative tool," Hale continued, "that for it to be effective, investigators must know the suspect and his reactions. A polygraph is just short of voodoo. I've seen them cause a lot of harm in homicide investigations if they are not properly given."

"What do you mean by 'not properly given'?" I asked.

"If, say, they gave the polygraph too soon, too early in the case, before the police knew the details, before they knew the proper questions to ask." As I found out, that was precisely what had occurred.

I asked Hale about Tommy's having passed the polygraph, as the police had said, as he had written in his report.

"I heard the tapes of that [Tommy's] test," Hale said. "Professionally it did not clear anyone of anything."

I then asked about Littleton, who became a suspect after he failed a lie detector test. Hale said there could be many reasons for his failing, including fear, nervousness, and improper questioning by the person giving the test. "There's a difference between asking, 'Do you know something about the case?' " he said, "and 'Did you kill Martha Moxley?' "

Hale was no less critical of State's Attorney Browne, accusing him of "a lack of aggressiveness": "Browne tells the Associated Press a Greenwich family—who everyone knows is the Skakels—was not cooperating and what happens? Nothing.

"So what does Browne do next? Does he hold a news conference and embarrass the Skakels again? Does he pressure them to cooperate? No, he did nothing.

"I've investigated over 1,000 homicides," Hale continued. "I believe the Moxley case is solvable, even at this late date. What the Greenwich police must do now is to question each suspect's friends—their wives, ex-wives, and girlfriends—to determine if such behavior—not necessarily killings but violent behavior—is repeated. It will not be easy. It will take time and money and manpower, but it can be done."

"Keep on with your investigation," Hale urged me. "It might prod the Connecticut authorities into restarting theirs.

"I feel strongly about the Moxley case," he said. "Years later, it still haunts me. Whoever killed Martha Moxley should never have been allowed to get away with it. That is why I am saying these things to a newspaper reporter."

He was passing me the torch.

# 5

PART ONE / CHAPTER FIVE

# "I Believe I Know Who Killed Martha Moxley but I Cannot Prove It"

GREENWICH, CONNECTICUT
June 1982

Two weeks later, I was at Greenwich police headquarters, seated across a table from Chief Thomas Keegan and Detective Jim Lunney. I had just begun to interview them. I had asked Lunney, a bull of a man, over six feet and 200 pounds, what he had been doing since leaving the Moxley case.

"Narcotics," Lunney answered. Then, swift and sudden as a cobra, he leaned forward and grabbed the front of my shirt. His strength took my breath away. For a second, I was inches from his face. "You wanted to know what I've been doing?" he said, releasing me. "This is how we question narcotics suspects."

Keegan did a double-take, then tried to turn Lunney's move into a joke. I said nothing, struggling to regain my composure. Was Lunney a goon, I wondered, or a nut?

I wondered whether he and Keegan planned this routine beforehand. "There's this reporter coming around, asking questions about the Moxley case," I imagined them saying. "Let's show him how we do things."

I had never covered a small-town police department. Even on Long Island, the Nassau and Suffolk County departments each had several thousand officers and covered a population of two million people.

With a population of 60,000, Greenwich had only 150 cops. They shared the town's superior attitude, regarding themselves as a notch above the surrounding departments, even though their most visible work was standing in uniform along Greenwich Avenue—an East Coast version of Hollywood's Rodeo Drive—sometimes in white pith helmets, directing traffic.

Martha's murder had been Greenwich's first homicide in twenty years. It was telling that Keegan's predecessor Stephen Baran, the chief at the time, had played no role in investigating it. The reason Keegan gave was that Baran's expertise was in traffic control.

I didn't know what to make of Keegan, a graduate of Greenwich High School and the Marines, who smoked cigarettes from a long holder, was known to his officers as "the major," and was said to be as comfortable around the town's highest elected official, First Selectwoman Rebecca Breed—whose family had come on the Mayflower—as he was with his cops.

"I'm not closing the book on this," Keegan said to me. "I have every intention of bringing this case to trial."

Maybe he thought all reporters were gullible. By now, in 1982, an arrest seemed out of the question. But I was unprepared for what he said next.

"I believe I know who killed Martha Moxley, but I cannot prove it." Was Keegan serious? Why was he telling me this? Was he trying to impress me by showing he was on top of the case even though it remained unsolved?

"I assume you mean Tommy Skakel," I said nonchalantly, as though I were accustomed to police chiefs I'd just met revealing their cases' secrets.

Keegan nodded, although I noted that he never uttered Tommy's name.

"I told this to the Moxleys," he added. Referring to Dorthy, he said, "As a mother, she has a right to know what people close to the investigation feel. I waited a long time to tell them. They are haunted by this."

Dorthy later confirmed what Keegan had said. "It was in the living room of our apartment." I was shocked when he told me. Not by whom he identified, but that he actually said it."

I also noted that Dorthy had never volunteered this information to me. Her silence on the subject until I asked her directly only confirmed her wariness of me and her loyalty to Keegan and the Greenwich police. I was someone who could help her. Instead, she and her husband continued to rely on people who had failed them seven years before. I didn't get it. No, they didn't get it. They were lost. How lost, I still didn't appreciate.

Keegan refused to provide evidence of his suspicions about Tommy, but Lunney chimed in. "Tommy told us he left Martha to write a school report on Abraham Lincoln. But when we checked with Tommy's teachers at the Brunswick School, none of them had assigned it."

I, too, had interviewed Tommy's teachers at Brunswick. Barbara Train, chairwoman of the history department, told me the police had questioned her about the supposed report. "I told them I hadn't assigned it. I checked with other teachers and none of them had either."

She added that her stepfather, Desmond Fitzgerald, had worked for the CIA and that individual responsibility had been his credo. Fitzgerald's name was familiar, although I had to look him up to learn the specifics. He was a top agency official involved in covert activities in Vietnam and Cuba.

Referring to the Skakels, she said, "Their money and connections have gotten them out of all their difficulties so that they lack personal responsibility."

I then asked Keegan when Tommy had become a suspect. Hale's report said it had been when police discovered the matching golf clubs inside the Skakel home. I was becoming increasingly curious about exactly when that was.

Keegan, however, deflected my question. "We looked at a lesbian couple, a mentally retarded girl, several residents with tempers or drinking problems that had attracted police attention," he said. "There was no shortage of suspects, I'll tell you that."

Because of what Dorthy had told me about Michael, I asked whether he was ever a suspect. Keegan assured me Michael had been investigated and discounted. Michael, he explained, had driven with his brothers at 9:15 P.M. to their cousin Jimmy Terrien's home in back-country Greenwich. That was a fifteen- to twenty-minute drive from the Skakels. If Martha had been murdered around 10:00 P.M., Michael could not have returned in time to have killed her.

I then asked Keegan about Littleton.

"His burglary arrest in Nantucket cried out for attention," Keegan said. He explained that he had focused on Littleton's initial statement about Tommy. Littleton said he had been unpacking while watching *The French Connection* on television when Tommy entered shortly after ten. Littleton said he had noticed nothing unusual about him.

"We felt Littleton was protecting Tommy," Keegan said. "We felt he knew something he wasn't telling us." He paused. "Did Littleton know something? Did Littleton see something?" Keegan paused again. "Did Littleton participate?"

I decided Keegan was a performer, a showman. When he retired a few years later and moved to South Carolina, he was elected to the state legislature. I pictured the Connecticut Yankee sitting back in his chair in the legislature, blowing smoke rings from his cigarette holder.

When Littleton returned to Greenwich that fall and resumed teaching at the Brunswick School, Keegan said he persuaded him to take a lie detector test. "I told him I believed he was innocent and wanted him to clear himself," Keegan said, grinning. He paused again. "Littleton failed. And he failed badly."

Still, Littleton refused to cooperate. "I won't help you build a case against Tommy," he had said to them. So Keegan sent Lunney and his partner, Steve Carroll, over to Brunswick to have a chat with its headmaster. Littleton was fired.

He landed a job at St. Luke's in neighboring New Canaan. Keegan sent Lunney and Carroll over there. Littleton was fired again.

In June 1977, Keegan sent Lunney and Carroll to Nantucket for Littleton's sentencing on the Nantucket burglary. Their plan was to have Massachusetts prosecutors allow him to plead guilty to a misdemeanor and receive a suspended sentence that would allow him to continue teaching. In return, Littleton would cooperate in the Moxley investigation.

But Littleton refused the deal.

"We told him we'd do everything in our power to help him with his burglary case if he agreed to cooperate with us," Keegan said. "We said we would speak in his behalf and help in any legal way we could in return for his cooperation. We are at a loss to explain why he refused.

"Personally," he added, "I don't think he had anything to do with the murder but that he may know something about it." He turned and grinned at Lunney. "But Jim disagrees."

Lunney began to say he believed Littleton may have participated with Tommy. As he spoke, Keegan began pumping his arm up and down in an obscene gesture, indicating Lunney didn't know what he was talking about.

Two jerks, I found myself thinking as I left the office. Two rubes. Keegan, the front man, was Mr. Personality. Lunney, the workhorse, was an ox.

I was sure they viewed me equally disdainfully, as someone to be gotten in and out of their office as quickly as possible, hopefully never to return. But it was one thing to be an oaf. It was another to be corrupt. I wasn't sure if or where the two came together.

•

Ken was so excited by Keegan's identification of Tommy as Martha's killer that he wanted me to return with a hidden tape recorder and have Keegan repeat it. I refused. If we, through the newspaper, were presenting ourselves as shining the light of discovery into the crevices of an unsolved murder, then our actions had to be in the open. Ken reluctantly agreed. As it turned out, Keegan probably realized he'd gone too far and was never as expansive again.

I began my second interview with him and Lunney by exploring the possibility of a cover-up. I asked Keegan why, after discovering the matching golf clubs, he hadn't obtained a warrant to search the Skakel house for the clothing and shoes Tommy wore the night of the murder to test for traces of Martha's blood or clothing fiber.

Keegan answered that Rushton Skakel had signed a Consent to Search form, allowing the police to look inside the house informally without a warrant. "The Skakels were completely cooperative at the beginning," Keegan said. "They gave us carte blanche."

Lunney added, "We were afraid that if we had asked him [Rushton] to conduct a formal search he might have said 'Get out!' and we would lose what access we had."

Then, Lunney offered a second reason. "The ultimate decision came from State's Attorney Browne's office," he said. "They determined the feasibility. We relied on advice from Browne's chief investigator, Jack Solomon. He was with us from the get-go. He was with us every step of the way."

This was the first time I had heard Solomon's name, but it would not be the last.

I relayed Keegan's and Lunney's explanations about the search warrant to Hale. "There should have been a thorough, formal search of the Skakel house," Hale said. "If Rushton Skakel was as cooperative as the Greenwich police say, why not go and do it immediately? Then, if he refused, they could have asked the state's attorney for a search warrant."

He reiterated what he had told me in Detroit: When it came to the Skakels, the Greenwich police were treading lightly.

•

Still pursuing the cover-up angle, I sought out Lunney's former partner, Steve Carroll. He had recently retired and was willing to talk.

Soft-spoken and articulate, Carroll had a craggy face and wavy gray hair. Unlike most Greenwich cops, he lived in town and had raised his children there. His two sons had graduated from Greenwich High and the Naval Academy at Annapolis. On the surface, he seemed more patrician than police officer.

"The initial investigation was disorganized," Carroll said. "Individual teams of detectives began canvassing the neighborhood. Everyone was out to make a collar."

Carroll explained how the police had begun by pursuing the transient theory. Then, they had looked at Belle Haven neighbors. "People with drinking problems and violent tempers, oddballs or loners, a lesbian couple, a retarded girl."

Repeating what Keegan had told me, he said, "There was no shortage of suspects." Apparently, no one had alerted them to the Skakels.

"We were too willing to believe Tommy," he said. "The questioning that first night was too casual, too informal, not thorough enough. One of the detectives who questioned him liked kids and was overly friendly and did not press Tommy on details. For example, we never satisfactorily determined what clothing he wore that night so we could test it for blood stains."

There it was again—the failure to obtain a search warrant for Tommy's clothes.

"Maybe it was the Skakel money," Carroll said. "Maybe it was their position. Maybe I was subconsciously intimidated. But we eliminated rather than zeroing in."

Law enforcement is a macho business. I had never heard a cop speak so candidly of his own and his department's failings. In certain law enforcement circles, talking this frankly to a reporter was regarded not merely as weakness but as disloyalty.

Yet here was Carroll bearing all. I could only conclude he was wracked with guilt over his failure to have made an arrest. But as I replayed his conversation in my mind, I realized his words reflected contrition, not cover-up.

•

I also met Stephen Baran, who had recently retired as chief after twenty years. His wife Nancy was a newspaper reporter in Bridgeport.

She'd learned I was knocking around Greenwich and was concerned for her husband's reputation. She invited me to lunch at their house on the edge of Belle Haven.

Their house, which was either on or next to the estate of the Van Munchings—the family that owned Heineken beer—had become the subject of gossip following the Moxley murder. How could Baran afford to live in Belle Haven on a police chief's salary? people whispered. Was the purchase of his house somehow connected to a cover-up of the Moxley case?

As it turned out, there was nothing untoward about Baran's purchase. He had bought the property from the Van Munchings' neighbor, Alice P. Thayer, a widow in her nineties who had outlived her money and subdivided, Nancy Baran explained to me two decades later after her husband had died.

"We were one of the lucky ones who bid," she said. "It was Steve's dream when he retired to build a house of his own. We put it up ourselves with friends and relatives."

With a trace of bitterness, she added, "I am certain the speculation contributed to my husband's early death."

But the problem in Greenwich wasn't Baran's integrity, or Keegan's, for that matter. Rather, it was the cozy relationship between the Greenwich police and the town's wealthiest residents.

A police chief from a nearby city put it this way: Crimes involving Greenwich's more prominent citizens were sometimes ignored because detectives did not know how much freedom they would be allowed before a call was made to higher-ups to stop them. Because of this, he said, there was an undercurrent of resentment.

Baran had been chief at the time of another death involving the Skakels. In 1966, Rushton's niece—his brother George's seventeen-year-old daughter Kathleen, known as Kick—had driven her convertible over a speed-bump in the back-country. A six-year-old neighbor, Hopey O'Brien, seated on the rear fender was thrown to her death. Kick was never charged.

According to Jerry Oppenheimer's *The Other Mrs. Kennedy*, Baran investigated the case as a traffic fatality but never interviewed Hopey's siblings, who had been with her in the car. He subsequently told the *Greenwich Time* he did not believe negligence was involved.

It seemed to me the Greenwich police had investigated the Moxley murder as they had the death of Hopey O'Brien. Instinctively, they had shied away from the Skakels. Instead, they had sought the transient off the turnpike. I recalled Baran's quote the day after the murder, which seemed to justify that theory: "Kids are always leaving bicycles, tennis rackets, and golf clubs outdoors, after playing with them on the lawn." Again, I asked myself when the police had discovered the matching club inside the Skakel home—the clue that made Tommy a suspect.

I was also sensing the contempt many Greenwich residents felt toward the police. Many cops like Carroll worked second jobs as drivers, taking people to the airports. Others worked as bartenders at private parties. Some Greenwich residents viewed the police as servants.

Carroll said detectives had scoured Belle Haven in the days following Martha's murder, asking residents about neighbors with tempers or drinking problems. No one apparently told them about the Skakels. Cissy Ix, who knew all of it, said the police never asked.

Years later, after the grand jury was called and prosecutors attempted to reexamine the crime scene, Susan Henze, who had purchased the Skakel home on Otter Rock Drive refused to let Frank Garr on her property. "I hold you personally responsible for bringing this all back and bringing it out in the newspapers," she screamed at him, rushing outside where he and the prosecution team had assembled.

And the contempt was returned in kind. The day Martha's body was found, Lunney said to another detective about the Moxley's Belle Haven neighbors: "It seemed that no one wore a watch. No one could tell you where he was or what he was doing at any particular time that night. You would have thought a dog had been run over. That was about the level of concern we were getting from people."

As for Frank, he bit his tongue when Henze rushed out to upbraid him. "I never said what I wanted to," he told me. "I never said what I felt I should have. I never said to her, 'How would you have felt if it were your own daughter who had been murdered?' "

•

Next, I sought an interview with Fairfield County State's Attorney Donald Browne in Bridgeport. He refused to see me. Repeated phone calls to his office didn't soften him up, so I called Dorthy.

She and her husband had hired their own criminal attorney as a liaison with the authorities. God only knows what the Moxleys were paying him. And for what? God only knows what they expected from him. To me, this was a further indication that they didn't know who to turn to for help.

Nonetheless, he did call Browne. Reluctantly, Browne consented to see me. He was one of Connecticut's five appointed state's attorneys, a career prosecutor, middle-aged, of medium height with a saturnine expression. He offered only the briefest responses to my questions. Unlike Keegan, he showed no interest in impressing me.

Still on the cover-up track, I began by asking whether Jack Solomon, Browne's chief investigator, had prevented the Greenwich police from obtaining a search warrant, as Lunney had suggested.

"It was Greenwich's investigation," Browne answered. "We only advise. Unless it's an organized crime investigation, we don't supervise."

"Why did you reject the Greenwich police's attempt to obtain a warrant to search the Skakel house?" I asked. Browne said he couldn't remember.

"Probably too much time had elapsed," he said. He seemed disinterested in what I regarded as a key facet of the case. How could he not remember?

But as I came to learn, what Browne said was probably true. It was not until Hale suggested the search warrant to the Greenwich police that they requested it of Browne. That had been six months after the murder.

Unlike Browne, his boss—the chief state's attorney Austin Mc-

Guigan—seemed eager to speak to me. Whereas Browne was cautious, McGuigan was brash. The first thing he said was that he didn't trust cops—a bizarre opinion from the state's chief law enforcement official.

What McGuigan said he did trust—what he said Browne trusted—was the polygraph, the lie detector test, what he called "the box."

"The fact is Tommy Skakel passed the box and Littleton failed," McGuigan said.

I recalled Hale's saying there could be numerous reasons for failing the polygraph but McGuigan appeared to have no doubts about the test's reliability.

"Does that mean you think Littleton murdered Martha?" I asked.

That would be going too far, he said. "Failing the box means Littleton had 'guilty knowledge' of the murder," McGuigan said. "If you know who did it and you refuse to say, you flunk the box."

"What indications are there that Littleton had knowledge of the murder?" I persisted.

"The indication," said McGuigan, "is that he flunked the box."

The rift between the Greenwich police and the state's attorney's office ran deeper than Browne's refusal to grant the search warrant. It sounded like the two agencies disagreed about who had killed Martha Moxley.

# 6

PART ONE / CHAPTER SIX

# The Case File

I was now so troubled about how the investigation had been conducted that I felt we had no choice but to take the next step. The cover-up theory wasn't holding up. Rather, it seemed that in the beginning of the investigation, the police had instinctively shied away from the Skakels.

Dorthy Moxley knew her daughter had gone to their house the night she was murdered. She repeatedly called them during the night, even speaking with Tommy. Yet the police hadn't focused on him until they found the golf clubs inside their house, presumably at some later date. They had wasted the crucial first forty-eight hours investigating Hammond, other neighbors, and the imaginary hitchhiker.

Meanwhile, Browne and Solomon seemed to have relied exclusively on the polygraph. Never having investigated a homicide, the Greenwich police had gone along, polygraphing everyone they could.

Yet these were merely my hunches. I lacked documentation. I needed to see the Greenwich department's case file, which Keegan refused to show me. The only way to get it was to make a formal complaint with the state's Freedom of Information Commission.

I knew Keegan and Browne would oppose us. Although seven years had passed since the murder and no detective was even assigned to it anymore, I knew what both agencies would claim. They'd argue that the file's release would harm a future prosecution. I'd been around long enough to know what their real reason was. It was to hide their mistakes—or worse.

While I respected cops individually for their courage and their loyalty, I'd come to distrust police departments as institutions. A decade before, during the Knapp Commission hearings in New York City, I'd seen how loyalty to an institution could lead to cover-up and corruption.

During those hearings, I learned how important it was for the police to be scrutinized and why police departments fear a reporter more than a reporter fears the police. I understood how much trouble a reporter can cause a police department. By obtaining that file, I'd be causing lots of trouble.

Ken couldn't have been more supportive. "This is great," he said. "What better way to serve the community?" As the local newspaper, he said, we had a responsibility to inform readers about an unsolved crime and to hold the police department accountable in explaining why an investigation has produced no arrest.

Once again he contacted Imbriaco, the paper's lawyer, this time to write to Browne, explaining the newspaper's position.

"Considering your . . . statements to the effect that you are not optimistic about solving the Moxley murder . . . any news article which might arise out of the [newspapers'] investigation of this crime might actually help in the arrest of a suspect," he wrote. "It is also clear that given the history of the state's investigation of this matter there is absolutely no concrete prospect of any individual being prosecuted for this crime."

In mid-July, Keegan telephoned Ken to dissuade him from filing our complaint. "I have the impression that Keegan was intent on convincing me that he has nothing to hide or cover up and that he is serious about pursuing this case," Ken wrote in a memo. "I told him our only interest was informing our readers of what had transpired since the murder in 1975 and laying out for them what we had learned."

Some months later, Keegan wrote Ken again, asking that before we published our story, he be able to vet it.

"I have been informed that prior to publication of the article on the murder of Martha Moxley, attorneys employed by your newspaper will review and/or edit the article to reduce or eliminate the likelihood of civil action against Mr. Leonard Levitt or the newspaper," he wrote.

Keegan requested that he and Lunney be afforded what he termed "the same courtesy."

I knew what Keegan was worried about: his having said to me he had told the Moxleys that Tommy had killed Martha but that he couldn't prove it. Perhaps in the past, he had been able to pressure the *Greenwich Time*, which had not had the resources to counter them before Times-Mirror purchased it. But no longer. He was now dealing with Times-Mirror, one of the nation's most powerful media conglomerates.

"The freedom of the press embraces within it a newspaper's right to publish in a society free from the constraining influences of government or of other third parties who seek to limit that which a newspaper has the constitutional right to publish," Ken wrote back to him.

"To grant your request would, in my opinion, establish a most dangerous precedent not only because it would represent the creation of a constitutionally objectionable relationship between government and the press but also because of the adverse affect such an action would have on the credibility of the *Greenwich Time* and *Stamford Advocate* as responsible newspapers in this community. . . ."

Five months later, on December 9, 1982, in a small room in the state's capitol in Hartford, our Freedom of Information complaint was heard before a lone Connecticut FOI commissioner. Keegan appeared to testify, resplendent in full police regalia with all his medals. I testified for the newspapers.

The following month, the commissioner made his recommendation to the state's five-member panel. He had sided with us. Seven years had passed since the murder. The Moxley investigation was dormant, he ruled.

He ordered Keegan to release 400 pages of documents and provide an inventory for those he maintained were confidential.

We had won.

•

The file detailed a pattern of missteps, worse than I had imagined.

Not only had the police searched for an unknown hitchhiker, but they'd wasted the crucial first forty-eight hours focusing on the Moxleys' next door neighbor, an innocent man. The file did not explain what had piqued their interest in Hammond, although it did state he had had blood on his clothing from a household accident. He was asked to accompany the officers to police headquarters to provide a statement and to leave several items of clothing he said he'd worn the night of the murder.

"Mr. Hammond also gave freely and voluntarily the above items . . ." the report read. "Fingerprint samples, fingernail scrapings and hair samples [were taken] from head."

I noted that Hammond's "free and voluntary cooperation" contrasted with what his mother had told me—that the police had violated her son's rights and hauled him off to headquarters.

But when it came to the Skakels, the police sounded deferential.

At 3:00 P.M. the day Martha's body was found, Keegan instructed Lunney and his partner to interview members of the Skakel family.

"Interviewed Julie Skakel, age 18," wrote Lunney, "and she related the following: she and her family and friends—brothers Rushton [age nineteen], Thomas [age seventeen], John [age sixteen], Michael [age fifteen], David [age twelve] and Steven [age nine], cousin James Terrien, [Julie's friend] Andrea Shakespeare and a house guest Ken Littleton had returned to the house at approximately 9 P.M. on 10/30/75 after having dinner at the Belle Haven Beach Club.

"Miss Skakel stated that her father Rushton is presently away and Mr. Littleton was at the house to keep an eye on the family."

I pictured Lunney questioning "Miss Skakel" and the other Skakel children. I was sure he was on his best behavior, not grabbing any of them as he supposedly did his narcotics suspects—or me.

Apparently, nothing the Skakels told him raised suspicion because later that afternoon, the police were back at Hammond's, interviewing his mother Marianna. Over the next two weeks, detectives interviewed Hammond's neighbors, college and prep school roommates, and teachers at Yale and the Columbia Business School.

Amidst these interviews, I found what I was searching for. It was just a four-line entry but one that said it all: "5:30 P.M.—October 30, 1975—Dets. Brosko and Lunney," it was captioned. I noted that the date was incorrect. The writer obviously meant October 31, the day Martha's body was discovered.

"At about 5:45," the entry began, "the investigators had an occasion to be in Rushton Skakel's home . . . and observed the following described golf club located in a storage bin in a room located on the north side of the house, first floor."

I had wondered at exactly what point in the investigation the Greenwich police had found the matching clubs and began focusing on Tommy. I had assumed it had been days or weeks after the murder.

Now I saw that Lunney had discovered the first matching club the afternoon Martha's body was found!

Yet no warning bell had gone off, indicating the killer had come from the Skakel house or that the reason that the piece of shaft with Anne Skakel's name was missing was because the killer did not want attention drawn to the Skakels.

Nothing in the file indicated that Lunney or Brosko had immediately reinterviewed the Skakel children, Littleton, Andrea Shakespeare, or anybody else at the Skakel house the night of the murder, separately and more closely, or taken written statements from them.

Instead, the next entry read, "At this time Mr. Rushton Skakel was away on a hunting trip in Vermont and the investigators were unable to obtain permissions to remove the golf club from his home."

So the police had just left it there. Just as they had left everyone in the Skakel home alone while they searched for a transient and questioned Hammond.

Not until two days later did Lunney return for it.

The next entry in the file, dated 10:00 A.M., November 2, read: "Since the golf club, which was still at the Skakel home, was similar to the one that caused the death of Martha Moxley, the investigators proceeded to the Skakel home in an attempt to obtain the golf club.

"The investigators met Mr. Rushton Skakel [who had cut short his hunting trip] and informed him of this investigation and asked Mr. Skakel if we could take possession of the golf club which was still in his home.

"Mr. Skakel further related that the aforementioned golf club was the possession of his wife, who passed away several years ago. [He agreed to let them take the club.]

"Mr. Skakel added he then gave the whole set of clubs to his daughter Julie.

"Interviewed Julie and she related that she last used the set of golf clubs this past summer.

"Julie made a quick search of the house and was unable to locate the set of clubs.

"Mr. Skakel and Julie advised the investigators that they would make a thorough search of the house in an attempt to locate the golf clubs and advise the department of their findings."

So, there it was. They had wasted two days—the crucial forty-eight hours—searching for a transient and browbeating Hammond while the killer was someone under their noses at the Skakels'.

Not only had they failed to confiscate the club immediately, they hadn't sought a warrant to immediately search the house for the missing shaft/handle or for the bloody clothes and shoes the killer had worn.

There was Lunney—the tough guy with his lowlife narcotics suspects—standing before Rushton and Julie, asking them to search the house for him.

By the time he realized what had happened, it was too late.

# 7

PART ONE / CHAPTER SEVEN

# Our Mutual Tragedy

NEW YORK CITY
1982–1984

I was standing in the corridor outside the maternity ward at North Shore University Hospital on Long Island. It was a Saturday night, the week before Christmas, 1982.

Susan's obstetrician had just told me they could not stop her contractions. She was in her thirty-first week of pregnancy and had been rushed to the hospital the night before. The obstetrician had attempted a drug to slow the contractions and gain a precious few more weeks. When twenty-four hours later the contractions had not abated, he said he felt there was no other course but to deliver by cesarean section.

And so our daughter Jennifer was born nine weeks early at three and a half pounds—not a bad weight for a preemie, as the obstetrician pointed out. She spent her first few days in a neonatal ward incubator with tubes protruding from her, next to babies with spina bifida or holes in their hearts, at whose sides their grieving parents sat silently for hours. We were the fortunate ones. Jennifer was healthy. She was merely small.

A nurse taught me how to lift the incubator's bottom flap so that I could reach in and touch her. As I brushed my hand against her tiny fist, she grabbed my finger.

Yet so involved was I in the Moxley story that the following afternoon I left her and Susan to interview David Moxley. Dorthy had finally persuaded him to see me.

I had kept her abreast of my investigation, from my discovery of Hale's report to our Freedom of Information lawsuit. We spoke every couple of weeks and lunched in the city every few months. The Moxleys had moved to the River House, to a grand apartment on the East River, and we would go around the corner to a restaurant she liked on First Avenue.

The change of scenery from the Carlyle hadn't helped her state of mind, however. When we'd meet, she seemed listless, resigned, almost in a state of depression.

"This is your old friend, Len Levitt," I would say whenever I called her, seeking to boost her spirits.

Not only did her husband refuse to discuss the murder with her, she said. He even refused to talk about Martha. Ditto her son John.

"My brother would say to me, 'Why don't you just stop all this and move on?' My sister-in-law said she didn't want to hear about it anymore."

More than I ever realized, Dorthy was alone.

I also realized she was coming to trust me and believed I was there to help her. What I brought her was hope.

"It was that someone cared," she said years later. "I was just so glad that someone was interested. It was so important to me because my family wouldn't talk about it. When no one cares, you feel despair.

"Until you came, no one encouraged me. Not the police. Not a soul. It wasn't that you were going to solve Martha's murder." Dorthy couldn't let herself even imagine that possibility any more than I could. "I didn't want to hurt myself by thinking that," she said. "But it was that you wanted to talk about Martha and I needed that."

Early on, I had informed her of Susan's pregnancy. She never failed to ask about her condition. I was coming to view her not merely as the subject of a story or the victim of a horrible crime but as a friend.

As a parent now, I knew that for her, Martha's murder would never end. For her, the case would never be over. What Dorthy understood was that she had to learn to live with it. Without realizing it, I was helping her. She would call me her first angel.

•

David Moxley and I met at his office at Touche Ross. He was a large man with blonde hair like Martha's. He never raised his voice or revealed emotion.

What puzzled me was that he, a wealthy, influential executive, had remained silent all these years. Even now, he was reluctant to acknowledge meeting with me.

"Please make it clear when you write your story," he began, "that the initiative for this meeting did not come from us."

By this point I had learned, through the Greenwich police report, about the department's subsequent attempts to focus on Tommy. In the fall of 1975, they somehow obtained Rushton's written permission for Tommy's medical, school, and psychological records. Only the Whitby School—which had been founded by Georgeann Terrien on the grounds of her estate and which Tommy attended from first through eighth grade—refused to comply.

On January 20, 1976, Christopher Roosevelt, a Whitby board member, told the police he would not release the records without speaking to Rushton and to Tommy. According to the Greenwich police report, Roosevelt said that if Tommy were arrested, a battery of lawyers would claim he was temporarily insane.

The following day, Rushton appeared at police headquarters with a letter addressed to Chief Baran, withdrawing his permission for Tommy's records. It was only then that he realized Tommy was the prime suspect.

The shock was apparently too much for him. An hour later, an ambulance was sent to the home of the Ixes, where he was visiting. Complaining of chest pains, Rushton was rushed to Greenwich Hospital. Doctors feared he'd suffered a heart attack. Instead, he spent two weeks in the High Watch Sanitorium after a drinking bout.

On January 31, 1976, Keegan and Browne met with Rushton and Manny Margolis, a veteran criminal attorney Rushton had hired, seeking permission to test Tommy with sodium Pentothal, the so-called truth drug. Margolis refused. He would stonewall the police for the next twenty-six years.

Two months later, on March 28, Rushton visited Dorthy. He told her he had come to put her mind at rest. His own doctors, he said, had tested Tommy and the results had proved negative: Tommy, said Rushton, had not murdered Martha.

But on Margolis's advice, he refused to show the test results to the police. It was this refusal that led Browne to announce to the Associated Press that a "particular family" had "clearly impeded" the police investigation.

Now in David Moxley's office, Moxley explained a piece of the investigation that had never made sense to me. I recalled Hale's criticism of Browne for his lack of aggressiveness after the Skakels stonewalled the authorities. David Moxley told me what happened next. Unable to obtain the test results from the Skakels, the authorities turned to him.

"I, in effect, brokered an agreement between Rush Skakel and the Greenwich police," he said. "The Greenwich police initiated the idea. They felt I could do more with the Skakels than they."

The poor guy, I found myself thinking. Not only had he lost a daughter; the police had also asked him to do their job.

The agreement turned out to be meaningless, even ridiculous. The criminal attorney the Moxleys had hired in turn hired a doctor. Through Margolis, the Skakels hired their own doctor. He supposedly shared the test results with the Moxleys' doctor.

"The agreement was constructed so that neither the police, the lawyers, nor I would see the results," Moxley said. And none of them did.

So that was it for the police investigation of Tommy. That was the end of the line, five months after the murder. It was also the end of my interview with David Moxley.

As I turned to leave, he said to me, "In hindsight I would have pushed back. I would have gotten aggressive as hell. Within twenty-four hours I would have brought in outside detectives and outside attorneys. I would have offered a reward. There'd have been an uproar, I'll tell you that."

My heart went out to him. For reasons I couldn't explain, tears came to my eyes. Like Lunney, by the time he'd figured this out, it was too late.

•

Two months later, in February 1983, I entered the fourteen-story brown-brick maze called One Police Plaza, the headquarters of the New York City police department. Tony Insolia, who years before had opposed hiring me at *Newsday*, had asked me to open the police bureau for its new city edition, *New York Newsday*.

*New York Newsday* was the brainchild of Dave Laventhol, who had risen from *Newsday*'s editor-in-chief to head all Times-Mirror's East Coast newspapers. He appointed Tony to succeed him at *Newsday*. When he did, Don Forst left the paper, feeling he had been passed over.

Soon after I began working in New York, Laventhol appointed Don as *New York Newsday*'s editor. In the company hierarchy, he reported to Tony on Long Island. Unfortunately, their rivalry came to mirror that of the two sister papers, contributing a decade later to *New York Newsday*'s demise.

Its demise would impact on my investigation of the Moxley murder. I had kept both Don and Tony abreast of the case. Both encouraged me to continue with it while I covered the New York City police department for *Newsday*.

My first problem at police headquarters was that *New York Newsday* didn't circulate in Manhattan, so that no one in the department read my stories. No reporter can function this way, so I arranged with *Newsday*'s circulation department to have a few copies specially delivered.

Meanwhile, the job of covering crime in New York City was all-consuming. The crack epidemic was racing through the ghettos, and crime was exploding. Because I was *New York Newsday*'s only police reporter, I was writing three or four stories a day. One story flowed into the next. A Queens man was arrested for fatally stabbing his sister's boyfriend. Five sanitation workers were charged with stealing cartons of old postage stamps off a conveyor belt in Coney Island. A Manhattan hotel porter shot and killed his manager in the hotel lobby, then shot the victim's wife. In the porter's room, police discovered the bodies of his wife and two others.

A woman who'd joined the army and planned to attend officer candidate school was shot by her drug-dealing boyfriend. A forty-seven-year-year-old remedial teacher, alone in her classroom, was robbed at gunpoint. A pregnant nineteen-year-old woman was shot to death by a mugger. Her purse containing $5 was missing.

A St. John's basketball star who drove a cab at night was killed after he failed to see a flagman at an open drawbridge. A former CIA agent and his son were indicted for conspiring to murder two assistant United States attorneys. An off-duty cop shot a man on crutches who got into a fight with two teenagers who'd walked on wet cement outside his home.

A New Jersey man drove his pickup truck onto Fifth Avenue in the middle of the St. Patrick's Day parade. Spectators said he was laughing as he bore down on the marchers.

Amidst this mayhem, I gathered the last strands of my Moxley story.

From my office at police headquarters, I reached Christopher Roosevelt, the Whitby school attorney, who had refused to turn over Tommy's medical records to the police in 1976. "I gave Mr. Skakel one piece of advice," he said. "To get competent legal advice on this. I told him to put his emotions in the background and to best represent the child's interest."

By phone, I also located Edward Hammond, the case's first suspect. He was in Venezuela, working for Lloyd's of London. His mother had died a year before and he had not been back to Greenwich since.

"It used to be so enjoyable in Belle Haven," he said. "But the way the police treated me changed one's view and coloring."

"One question," I said. "Why did your clothes have bloodstains that night?"

"I cut myself in a household accident."

I asked him if I could use his name in my story. "No problem," he said. "I suppose you're using everyone else's."

Then out of the blue, Julie's friend Andrea Shakespeare, who'd been at the Skakels' the night of the murder, agreed to talk to me. Her father was Frank Shakespeare, a top news executive at CBS, who would later become the ambassador to the Vatican. The police report said Andrea had been with the Skakel children at the Belle Haven Club, returned to their house, and then left at around 9:30. When Julie went to her car, she realized she'd left her keys inside. Andrea went to retrieve them and saw Tommy, who'd just come inside. Her story appeared to support Tommy's alibi that he had left Martha at 9:30 and returned home.

I wasn't sure what she could add. Still, she was an insider, albeit a peripheral one, and worth pursuing.

I met with her one night at a restaurant on Greenwich Avenue but she proved unhelpful. She insisted she be able to vet whatever I wrote about what she told me. When I told her that was out of the question, she said, "My father said you'd never agree."

I wrote her off as a spoiled rich brat, accustomed to having her own way, and forgot about her. Not until two decades later did I learn I'd misjudged her.

•

Three black hospital workers at a Veterans Administration hospital were attacked by whites in the Bath Beach section of Brooklyn. Four people died when a fire swept through adjoining tenements in Chinatown. A customer at a fast-food restaurant was shot to death by robbers who mistook him for the owner and demanded he open the cash register.

A fourteen-year-old Queens boy shot his twelve-year-old brother with a gun found in a vacant lot. A manager at Cartier stole $100,000 in jewelry with her brother, a salesman at Tiffany's. A ninety-two-year-old widow leaped to her death from her tenth-floor Park Avenue apartment, saying she could no longer live in pain.

A Harlem drug kingpin was charged with six members of his "family" for conspiracy to distribute heroin. Federal officials raiding his house discovered $2 million in cash, two Mercedes-Benz automobiles in the driveway, two sawed-off shotguns, and twenty-eight fur coats.

"Real fur?" asked the magistrate as they all entered not guilty pleas.

I also found Tommy Skakel, then twenty-four years old and living on a horse farm across the Connecticut state line near Bedford, New York. Ken had assigned Kevin Donovan, a reporter at the *Advocate*, to work with me on these final interviews around Stamford. I took off a day from One Police Plaza and drove over with Kevin to see Tommy.

We'd hoped our surprise visit might get Tommy talking. Kevin, who was close to Tommy's age, rang the doorbell. I stood a few feet behind him. Tommy opened the door. He wore glasses and was balding—not at all what I had expected.

Kevin began by asking what he had been doing over the years.

"I haven't spent too much time in Greenwich," he said. "I wanted to get it out of the way and live my life and be myself. I would go to a restaurant and go shopping in Greenwich and people would talk about it. Like who the hell are those people to judge me? What gives them the right?"

Kevin asked him about the night of Martha's death and his "making out" with Martha, then falling down on top of her as Hale had described.

"I don't remember anything like that," Tommy answered. "The last thing I remember is saying good-bye to her and going back into my house. I didn't know her. Michael liked her. I didn't."

With that, he closed the door. Kevin and I looked at each other. How could he not remember that? we asked ourselves. Neither of us gave a thought to what he had said about Michael.

•

My last stop on the Moxley story was Ottawa, Canada, where I had traced Ken Littleton through his alma mater, Williams College. The Greenwich police had lost track of him years before.

After losing his teaching jobs in Connecticut, he began a downward spiral. Unable to obtain another teaching position, he began drinking and moved around the East Coast, from Williamstown, Massachusetts, to Saratoga Springs, New York, to Stowe, White River, and Manchester, Vermont.

By 1982 he had moved to Florida and was homeless. He was arrested for a variety of crimes—trespassing, disorderly conduct, drunk driving, public intoxication, shoplifting. He was also in and out of hospitals. He began hallucinating. He believed he could cause a tornado or hurricane by flushing the toilet. He drank toilet water and collected JFK matchbooks.

One night he telephoned David Moxley, leaving a message about "our mutual tragedy." He offered to take sodium Pentothal to help him remember the events of that Halloween night.

Another time, he climbed a sixteen-foot structure and gave President Kennedy's "Ich bin ein Berliner" speech. When arrested, he identified himself to the police as "Kenny Kennedy, the black sheep of the Kennedy family."

When I found him, he was living with Mary Baker, his future wife and the mother of his two children. They had met in an alcoholic recovery program and returned to her home in Ottawa, to the house she had inherited from her father. At least financially, Littleton appeared to have caught a break, since he couldn't find a job.

He was even bigger than Lunney and showed no apparent sign of the depression and mental illness that was to wreck his life. Friendly, even eager to talk, his openness with others would cause him nothing but grief.

With Mary at his side, he maintained his innocence, saying he had been railroaded by the Greenwich police. "I was fully cooperative with them through the end of school at Brunswick," he said. "Even after I got in trouble in Nantucket, I was cooperative."

He told me how he had allowed the police to take him to be tested outside Hartford. "I was naïve. I didn't see any harm," he said. I recalled Keegan's grin when he admitted tricking Littleton into taking the polygraph.

They'd strapped him into the polygraph, Littleton said. A detective told him they would be right back to begin the test, then left him alone for twenty-five minutes. That was standard police procedure. Confessions come just before polygraphs are given because suspects mistakenly believe the lie detectors are infallible. Sure enough, when the detective returned, the first thing he said to Littleton was, "You murdered Martha Moxley."

"Then they brought me into another room where Keegan was waiting," Littleton continued. "The detective said it to me again, 'You murdered Martha Moxley.'

" 'You know I didn't,' " Littleton said he answered. " 'I know I didn't. I'll walk back to Greenwich if I have to.'

"I never knew Martha Moxley," he said to me. "I never saw Martha Moxley. I had nothing to do with her murder. And I didn't think Tommy did either.

"But," he added intriguingly, "when they questioned me in 1976, I did give the police circumstantial evidence about someone else."

"Who was that?" I asked.

"Michael. At fifteen, I would have termed him an alcoholic. I was afraid of him. I thought Tommy was a good kid but I was scared of Michael."

"Why was that?" I asked.

He related an incident in which he was playing golf with Michael and Jimmy Terrien at the Greenwich Country Club. Michael, he said, had been in a threesome ahead of him. When Littleton caught up to him, he saw that Michael had crushed the head of a chipmunk and put a tee through it like a crucifix.

"At the next hole, there was a squirrel with its head crushed in. When we finished the hole, Michael came up to us with a crazed expression and told us how he had run down the animals.

"Up in Windham he used to flush out pheasants from the bushes and shoot them. I saw him run one down before it could get into the air. Another time, he shot a hawk resting in a creek."

"But the police say Michael couldn't have murdered Martha," I told Littleton. "They say if the murder occurred at 10:00 P.M., he was at the Terriens' and couldn't have returned in time."

Littleton shrugged. "I'm just telling you what I told them."

He suggested I telephone his mother in Massachusetts because she might have something to add. I thought he meant about Michael. Instead, when I called, his mother said, "Our family is ruined over this. My son became an alcoholic. His brain was nothing. He couldn't get a job. My husband and I were at each other's throats over what we should do." I was at a loss as to how to respond. "I'm so bitter," she continued. "We were all so naïve. We're poor people, my husband and I. We don't have the money they do to protect ourselves. And they," she said, referring to the Skakels, "they're probably just going on living their lives as though nothing ever happened."

•

I was now ready to put my story together. The focus was not on who had killed Martha Moxley. I didn't know that and, I was convinced, neither did anyone else involved in the investigation.

Rather, I would focus on how the Greenwich police had bungled the case—how their first instincts about the hitchhiker off the turnpike had been wrong; how they had wasted precious time on Hammond; how they'd discovered the matching golf clubs inside the Skakel house the day Martha's body was found but failed to obtain a warrant to search it and had instead allowed Julie to search for them.

For all that, there had been no cover-up, no payoff to Chief Baran or anyone else. Yes, the Greenwich police may have been initially intimidated and may have felt they had to "tread lightly," to use Hale's phrase. But when they did get their bearings and zeroed in on Tommy, they were aggressive enough that Rushton suffered a breakdown and had to be hospitalized.

Of course, the story would address how the Greenwich police had focused on Tommy while the state's attorney suspected Littleton. I wanted to use Keegan's quote—"I believe I know who did it but I can't prove it"—and the fact that he'd shared his belief with the Moxleys. The article would offer the disclaimer that there was no evidence to determine whether Keegan was correct or merely trying to justify having blown the biggest case of his career.

Because of people's damning remarks about him, I wanted to insert a line about Michael, if only to quote Keegan that if Martha had been murdered at 10:00 P.M., Michael could not have returned in time from the Terriens' to have killed her.

When I'd begun the story, I hadn't realized why Dorthy believed so strongly in the police. When I'd asked about a cover-up, she had said, "I know it wasn't Keegan. I know it wasn't Lunney." When I'd asked her why she was so supportive of them, she'd answered, "Because they were so sincere."

And there it was. Although they'd been misguided early on in their investigation, Dorthy understood that Keegan and Lunney genuinely wanted to solve Martha's murder.

I had come to know Lunney. Despite his missteps, I knew how much he wanted to arrest Tommy and perhaps Littleton as well. Whenever he saw Tommy on Greenwich Avenue, he would say to him, "I am going to pursue you to the ends of the earth until you admit you murdered Martha Moxley."

With Lunney everything was out there, on the surface. There was no guile to him. I believed not a moment went by that he didn't regret his mistakes and pray he'd have another chance to get it right.

•

The story was to run on the day before Halloween 1983, the eighth anniversary of Martha's death. I had worked on it for nearly two years.

But as the publication date approached, Ken told me it was not quite ready. He said loose ends remained—trivial things, such as dates, quotes, transitions. I thought nothing of it then. How was I to know what lay ahead?

Ken said he wanted the story to have maximum impact. That meant running it on the anniversary of Martha's death in 1984, a year later.

Okay, I told myself. Let's make sure we have it right. Difficult as it would be to explain this to Dorthy, I knew the story could wait. If we wanted maximum impact, it would have to.

•

Beginning in the fall of 1983, the following events occurred in New York City: Michael Stewart, a black man in his twenties, died of a choke hold while under arrest for marijuana possession at the Union Square subway station in Manhattan. Six white cops were tried and acquitted of his murder. A congressional commission headed by Michigan's John Conyers held hearings on police brutality. Mayor Edward Koch announced the appointment of the city's first black police commissioner, Benjamin Ward.

The knock on Ward was that a decade before he had released a dozen black suspects arrested for the murder of a white cop at a Harlem mosque. The president of the police union, the Patrolmen's Benevolent Association, referred to Ward as "Bubba."

A fellow *Newsday* reporter, Gerald McKelvey, found the transcript of a civil suit in the mosque case. The suit mentioned a confidential police document known as the "Blue Book," which was circulated only among the highest levels of the department. Somehow, Gerry turned up a copy of it. It revealed the suspects at the mosque a decade before had been released not by Ward but by the former Chief of Detectives Al Seedman.

I tracked Seedman to Alexander's department store in Queens, where he was director of security. He acknowledged he had released the suspects.

"Why didn't you ever come forward?" I asked. "Why did you allow Ward to take the blame all these years?"

"What good would it have done?" he answered.

*New York Newsday* ran our story about Ward, Seedman, and the mosque murder on page one. Waving a copy at city hall the next day, Mayor Koch crowed, "Thank God for *New York Newsday*." The paper that six months before I'd had to arrange to be specially delivered to police headquarters had finally arrived.

And Susan was pregnant again.

•

Despite Ken's promise that the Moxley story would appear on the anniversary of Martha's death in 1984, it did not. As we re-edited it, I realized he was asking me questions I had already answered, minor questions such as dates and times. For the first time he mentioned unspecified "legal concerns."

"Ken," I pleaded, "this is why we are on this planet as journalists. To do stories like this. What's wrong? What are you afraid of? What's happened that you can't tell me?"

The year before, when Ken decided to hold the story, I had tried to lift Dorthy's spirits, assuring her that it would eventually run and that the police would restart their investigation. Now, seeing how frustrated I was becoming, she tried to lift mine.

"We'll just have to be patient, Len," she said. "There is a time for everything. You'll see."

# 8

PART ONE / CHAPTER EIGHT

# Poisoning the Well

NEW YORK CITY
1984–1991

To assure Susan's second pregnancy went as long as possible before certain premature delivery, our obstetrician devised a plan. Susan was to take to bed at the beginning of her seventh month. Tony Insolia gave me a leave of absence to play Mr. Mom.

Each night we'd cross off another day on the calendar. We set our first watershed at twenty-six weeks, when we told ourselves the baby stood a fighting chance. We set our next at twenty-eight weeks; then at thirty-one when the baby's gestation would equal Jennifer's. When Susan entered the hospital in February 1985, she had hung on for thirty-four weeks. Whatever would follow, the baby was out of danger.

Again, it was a Saturday night. The plan had called for delivery by cesarean section, but as it was Saturday, the hospital was short-staffed with only one delivery room. A woman lay there ahead of us, her contractions further along. Then, Susan's contractions sped up. Two hours later she had delivered, by natural childbirth, a five-pound boy.

I sensed there was trouble when the doctor ordered me out of the delivery room moments later. They could not control Susan's bleeding.

Transfusions were begun. After midnight, when the bleeding had abated and Susan lay in her darkened room in drugged slumber, our obstetrician, who specialized in high-risk pregnancies, confided to me that he was not certain what to do next. He said he was trying to call an expert in Cleveland. But as it was a Saturday night, he could not reach him.

He suggested that when the uterus contracted, as it would by the next day, he perform a hysterectomy. Given Susan's medical history and the realization now that she should never undergo another pregnancy, he saw this as the most conservative approach.

The doctor slept down the hall through the night to be on hand should her bleeding begin again, while I stayed awake fighting the terror I felt that I might lose her that night in childbirth. As for our son Michael, born at five pounds and never at risk, could I ever have imagined that after all we had gone through to have him, he would become an afterthought?

The following afternoon, the doctor performed Susan's surgery. There were no complications. A few days later, she and Mike came home. Our family was complete.

•

October 30, 1985, marked the tenth anniversary of Martha's death. Surely, I thought, the story would run then. But the date passed with no story in the paper—and no explanation from Ken.

A month later, Ken did call. He asked to meet for dinner. He apologized for not leveling with me and said the story had been held because of objections from the new publisher, Steve Isenberg.

Dave Laventhol, who headed all Times-Mirror's East Coast newspapers, had appointed Isenberg a year after I'd begun my investigation. I had never met him. I knew he had been the former chief of staff to New York's former mayor John Lindsay. I also knew he had little journalistic experience and that although he was a lawyer, he'd practiced for only about six years.

Ken then told me that earlier in the year he had sent the Moxley story to Tony Insolia. "Tony said it was ready to be printed," said Ken, "but that wasn't good enough for Steve."

I called Tony, who confirmed this. "They sent it to me for my opinion. I may have suggested some editing but I said there was no reason not to run it. It was a very tough story. And I remember Ken seemed afraid of it. As an editor, you have to have a lot of self-confidence to go with a story like that. I think someone was putting pressure on him."

"Who?" I asked.

"I don't know," he answered.

At dinner, Ken added something else. Isenberg, he said, was leaving the Connecticut papers. His new job would be Associate Publisher of *New York Newsday*. Ken didn't state the obvious. Isenberg was going to be my boss.

•

By the time Isenberg and I met two years later, I had moved from One Police Plaza and was working out of *New York Newsday*'s main office at 2 Park Avenue.

The year before, I had been sent to the Bronx to open a bureau there. Soon after, I was in a fight with the spokesman for the newly appointed district attorney, who had promised me an exclusive on a murder story if I agreed to hold it a day. I did. Just after my deadline, he called to say he'd decided to give the story to the *Post* and *Daily News*. As payback, I identified him in the story as my source. He cut me off from the district attorney and threatened to run me out of the Bronx.

Well, we'd see about that. That was another lesson I learned, albeit a midlife career lesson—a reporter had to be able to take a punch. Not a physical punch, although I suppose you should learn to take that, too. What you had to do in these circumstances was to have the confidence not to be bullied and the ability to develop sources outside the organization you are covering. Which is what happened.

I befriended the district attorney's enemies. An assistant district attorney had just quit the office to run against him. His supporters gave me documents, showing that the district attorney had used money from the office's confidential witness fund to pay for a champagne brunch for his election campaign. I wrote the story. He dropped out of the race.

Seeing the story's impact, an embittered judge confided in me. He opened a trapdoor that led to a netherworld of corruption beneath the surface of the state's judiciary.

Unknown to me and the general public, the presiding judge of the civil side of the Bronx State Supreme Court, Louis Fusco, controlled the court calendar. While assigning cases to other judges, he kept the biggest ones, against the city's hospitals, for himself. Each year the city paid out hundreds of millions of dollars in negligence claims in cases he heard. Before agreeing to a settlement, he forced the lawyers appearing before him to use his girlfriend's insurance firm to structure the deals.

A system had been set up to protect him. A politically connected Manhattan law firm, Bower and Gardner, had obtained a $25 million, no-bid contract to represent the city in all its medical malpractice cases. The firm had secured the contract through one of its partners, Stanley Fink, the former Speaker of the State Assembly. Meanwhile, the firm's senior partner, John Bower, was a member of the State Commission on Judicial Conduct, the body that disciplines judges.

I started examining the cases before Fusco. Bower and Gardner, it turned out, had used his girlfriend's insurance firm more than any other lawyers. Now I understood why those lawyers were afraid to protest. Until I came around, they had no one to protest to.

I switched from the district attorney and began writing stories about Fusco. After they appeared, the state's chief judge began an investigation. Fusco resigned as administrative judge and then retired.

I did not realize it then, but I had tapped into a vein of corruption that ran from Manhattan through the Bronx to the state capital in Albany. Although *New York Newsday* had existed only a few years, we had unearthed the tip of a judicial corruption scandal.

The more I wrote, the more lawyers and judges contacted me. I had penetrated the wall, cracked the perimeter. Presently, I was back in Manhattan, writing about two other powerful judicial figures, also unknown to the general public. Francis T. Murphy, the son of a Bronx district leader, was the presiding judge of the First Appellate Department, which heard appeals from state courts in Manhattan and the Bronx. Harry Reynolds was his chief clerk. Reynolds, I learned, had placed his wife and children on the appellate payroll. Murphy had worked out a deal with federal judge Charles Brieant to place their children as assistants in each other's offices.

Reynolds thought two of his aides were my sources and fired them. The Brooklyn District Attorney, Joe Hynes, jumped in and hired them. Then, the chief judge began an investigation of Reynolds, who resigned. Murphy hung on until his term ended, then retired.

But this nepotism was but a minor concern compared to what I was learning about Manhattan Surrogate Court Judge Marie Lambert. Also unknown to the general public, surrogates in New York state settle and distribute billions of dollars in estates.

Lambert was awarding millions of dollars in guardianships and receiverships to a small clique of attorney friends. At least three of them were stealing from people she had appointed them to protect. One, Melvyn Altman, whom Lambert had awarded half a million dollars in legal fees, stole $200,000 from the estate of a retarded man and lost it in a Brazilian dance revue.

Another, Lorraine Backal, became a civil court judge in the Bronx after Lambert awarded guardianships to the borough's Democratic county chairman and two of his district leaders. Backal then hired an ex-con as her driver, who allegedly supplied her with drugs.

After my stories appeared, Altman was indicted and convicted in federal court and went to prison. Backal resigned from the bench and was disbarred.

Then, there was Manhattan State Supreme Court Justice Francis Pecora. In a case before him, he seized an office building from its owner, then appointed a receiver to sell the building. The sale took three months. Pecora awarded the receiver a fee of $7.7 million, ten times larger than any ever awarded in state history. The receiver was none other than John Bower, the lawyer whose firm had the lock on the city's medical malpractice cases and who was now the chairman of the State Commission on Judicial Conduct.

And the office building he had sold was *New York Newsday*'s headquarters at 2 Park Avenue.

As I continued writing, Pecora sued me and *Newsday* for libel. *Newsday* refused to settle, or even run an apology, as Pecora had demanded, in return for dropping his suit. (He eventually dropped it after I discovered he had given contradictory testimony in two personal injury suits he had filed in Brooklyn.) Nonetheless, before its deductible kicked in, *Newsday* and Times-Mirror were forced to pay hundreds of thousands of dollars in legal fees to defend me.

Tony Insolia had retired but neither Don Forst nor Tony's successor as *Newsday*'s editor-in-chief, Anthony Marro, ever mentioned those costs to me or suggested that my stories might cause problems for *Newsday* with the new owner of 2 Park Avenue. It was an article of faith at *Newsday* and throughout Times-Mirror that truth is worth a price; that a lawsuit, expensive as it may be, is the cost a major media company pays to do business.

That was what made *Newsday* and *New York Newsday* great newspapers and Times-Mirror a great media conglomerate. In the company's culture, the news and the truth came first. If a reporter's facts were correct, lawsuits would be dealt with later. That was why I'd never accepted Ken's explanation of unspecified legal concerns as the reason for not publishing the Moxley story.

And there was something else. Never while at *Newsday* on Long Island or in New York had I been warned off a story. Never did anyone tell me there was something—a sacred cow or favorite of an editor—that I couldn't cover. Never did anyone tell me to tank a story.

In the midst of my lawsuit with Judge Pecora, Steve Isenberg introduced himself. He was tall and balding, a few years older than I, and he seemed pleasant, even hearty. We chatted about his former boss, Mayor John Lindsay, and about the Knapp police corruption scandal exposed during Lindsay's administration by Frank Serpico. Like me, Isenberg said he had been Serpico's friend.

Then, almost as an afterthought, he said, "You know, Len, your Moxley story will never appear—not just in Connecticut but in any Times-Mirror publication. I poisoned the well." He smiled as though he'd told a joke.

I never for a moment believed that Isenberg, or anyone else at Times-Mirror, had been pressured or paid off by the Skakels or the Kennedys. Nobody had "gotten to him," or to anybody else.

Still, I could not conceive of a valid journalistic or legal reason not to run the story and I was furious that Isenberg, for whatever reason, was standing in the way of a critical piece of investigative reporting. (The fact that the story ultimately ran in much the same way I originally wrote it, without generating any problems, confirmed my earlier conviction.)

Isenberg's comments left me too stunned to speak. It was bad enough, in my view, that Isenberg was telling me he wouldn't run the story in two small papers in Connecticut. For the entire Times-Mirror corporation to ban it from all of its newspapers, as Isenberg was suggesting, was a blatant abdication by a major media company of its responsibilities to its readership. I was offended by the offhand manner in which Isenberg was telling me this, as if he did not realize the import of what he was saying.

I had become a journalist because I dreamed of righting wrongs, of helping those whom everyone else had failed. Here the Moxley family had been lost and alone with nowhere to turn. The local papers—the *Stamford Advocate* and the *Greenwich Time*—had been their last resort.

Ken and Isenberg's predecessor, Jay Shaw, had been prepared to help them. That was why Ken had called me. Now Isenberg was admitting in effect that the newspapers had abandoned them. If he were telling the truth, the Times-Mirror Corporation had abandoned them as well.

I had begun this case believing the police had engaged in a cover-up. I had been wrong. The cover-up was by the newspapers that had hired me in refusing to tell me why they had killed the story.

And what was I expected to do about it? Even my boyhood television heroes on *The Big Story* had never found themselves in this situation. Their pitfalls had all occurred outside their newspapers. None had involved their paper's publisher.

Years later, as I prepared this book, I called Isenberg to ask him to explain his decision to kill the story. He invited me to lunch at his club to discuss it. Instead, I said I would take him to lunch. We agreed to meet at the Oyster Bar at Grand Central Station.

As fate would have it, that morning I received a call from, of all people, Frank Serpico. I had met him three decades before while covering the Knapp Commission police department scandal for *Time* magazine and we had remained friends.

Since Isenberg had said he knew him, I told Serpico to join us for lunch. As Isenberg and I sat down, I informed him Serpico would be joining us. "Great," he said. "I haven't seen Frank in years."

Before Serpico arrived, I asked Isenberg my questions. I told him I was aware that Tony Insolia had proofread a copy of my Moxley story and had no problems with it.

Isenberg didn't dispute this. "Frankly," he said, "I didn't think Tony's comments were thorough enough."

Well, that was rich. Tony had been a journalist for forty years. He had been the editor-in-chief of *Newsday*, one of the country's leading newspapers. Isenberg had had virtually no journalistic experience when Laventhol hired him in Connecticut.

I then asked him about his remark to me years before about "poisoning the well." He denied having said it and suggested I had either imagined it or mistakenly attributed it to him. He had apparently learned over the years how dangerous a remark like that was.

"I would never say anything like that," he said. "And if you write in your book that I did say it, you will be doing me a great disservice."

Isenberg insists that the decision to kill the story stemmed from "adamant advice" he had received from a senior legal counsel for the Times-Mirror, who had advised against publication in the "strongest terms" and told him that he "would be crazy to publish it." No one, including Isenberg, explained these legal objections to me when I was preparing the story.

In the midst of this, Serpico arrived. "Frank," Isenberg said, standing up to greet him. "It's great to see you."

True, Serpico had been to hell and back and thirty years had passed since the Knapp commission hearings. Nonetheless, it was clear he hadn't a clue who Isenberg was.

•

Despite his denial, Isenberg had indeed poisoned the well, at least in Connecticut. So long as he was publisher, the story hadn't appeared. Ken said now it could be published. But when we re-edited it, he began asking the same questions I had answered years before. I would make the changes he requested. A few days later, he would ask them again. Our conversations became more testy. Our relationship, now brittle, snapped.

While preparing this book, I called Ken. He had left the Connecticut papers and joined the faculty of the Columbia School of Journalism. Periodically, he asked me to speak to his classes about police reporting. I refused.

"We won't discuss the Moxley case," he would say. "You can talk about covering the police in New York City."

"Ken, you don't understand," I'd tell him. "The only way I'll do it is if we discuss the Moxley case and you explain to your class why you didn't publish my story."

Nonetheless, when I called him about this book, he shared details he never had before. Perhaps my phone call had caught him off guard. Perhaps he was no longer afraid.

"When Times-Mirror bought the papers in the late 1970s, they had a lot of trouble in Greenwich," he began. "They tried to start a Saturday paper and it bombed. When I was hired in 1981, my mission was to start a Sunday paper. The first day we lost 2,000 in circulation. Here we had one of the richest markets and we were having problems."

In Ken's opinion, the story did not appear because Isenberg did not want to run a piece about a decade-old murder. His claim of journalistic and legal shortcomings had been a cover, an excuse not to run it for fear it would offend Greenwich residents—*Greenwich Time* newspaper readers and advertisers.

"Editors resign over things like this," Ken said. "But that's not me."

He added: "Why didn't I tell you this before? Frankly, I did not want to tell people my publisher had killed the story."

Well, I thought, I suppose I can understand that. But what I couldn't understand was why he didn't publish the story after Isenberg left. By not running the story and remaining at the paper, he had lost his legitimacy. By not leveling with me, he had cost us our friendship.

•

One day in 1988, I read in the *Times* that David Moxley had died. I hadn't seen him since my interview at Touche Ross years before. I felt I owed it to him to attend his funeral.

I arrived late at Frank Campbell's funeral home on Madison Avenue and slipped into a rear pew. Except for Dorthy, I recognized no one. But why should I? I was not a part of the Moxleys' lives. I had presumed too much. My presence here mattered to no one but myself.

I was struck by the minister's eulogy. He never mentioned Martha, referring only to "an unspeakable tragedy." So silent had David been about his pain that his daughter's name was not even spoken at his passing.

At that moment I think I hated Ken and Isenberg more than anyone on earth.

I didn't speak with Dorthy then. I felt I would only be a reminder of all she had lost. Unable to publish the story, I felt I had failed her.

But not long after the funeral, she called. She had discovered a letter from David that she wanted to read to me. The letter was actually a memo, written about the phone call David had received years before from Littleton—the call in which he'd offered to take sodium Pentothal and had used the phrase "our mutual tragedy."

"He [Littleton] went on to explain that he was doing this simply to give himself peace of mind," David had written. "He thought that perhaps things had happened on the night of Martha's death that he would possibly remember under sodium Pentothal. . . . He specifically referred to his intention to try to remember whether or not Tommy Skakel was wearing different clothing at different times during the evening. He made specific references to Tommy stopping in his room at about 10:30 and saying he was going to his room to work on a report on President Lincoln and went on to volunteer that no such report was written."

His memo added that Littleton "rambled quite a bit, and in a fairly dramatic way said that he thought he had been 'framed' and that he thought perhaps Tommy had purposely used him as an alibi. . . . He made reference to how badly the police had 'screwed up the investigation and had hung him out to dry.'

"When I asked him why he wanted to give me the opportunity to listen to the tape of his examination, he said because he knew that I would not screw him."

The memo concluded by saying that Littleton had refused to allow Connecticut authorities to conduct the test and expressed David Moxley's concern that only someone familiar with the case could frame the proper questions for him.

"I suggested that perhaps the reporter who has been actively pursuing the investigation for some period of time had enough information that working with an independent forensic expert they could establish a line of reasoning that would be sufficiently rigorous to be useful."

Dorthy said she wanted me to know that the reporter David was referring to was me.

•

And then it happened. And it had nothing to do with anything I did. At least not then. There is a time for everything, Dorthy had said during our lowest point. Whether it was fate, luck, or coincidence, that time had arrived.

In the spring of 1991, William Kennedy Smith, a son of John F.

Kennedy's sister and first cousin to Tommy and Michael Skakel, went on trial for rape in Palm Beach, Florida. A false story surfaced that on the night of Martha's murder Smith had been at the Skakel house. That rumor led to a flurry of articles on the Moxley murder.

John Cotter, the city editor of the *New York Post*, had worked with me at *New York Newsday* and knew of my problems with the *Stamford Advocate* and *Greenwich Time*. He sent a reporter to interview me. On his instructions, the reporter asked me whether the papers' failure to publish the story was part of a cover-up.

I saw this as an opportunity to shame Isenberg and pressure Ken into publishing the story. I described how he had hired me nine years before to investigate Martha's murder and how we had obtained the Greenwich police report, showing that the Greenwich police had discovered the missing golf club inside the Skakel house the day after the murder yet failed to obtain a warrant to search the house. I described how the newspapers had refused to publish my story.

My interview ran in the *Post* on May 1, 1991, under the headline, "Once again, there are hints of a cover-up."

On June 2, 1991, with no explanation from Ken, my story on Martha Moxley's murder appeared on page one of the *Stamford Advocate* and *Greenwich Time*. It filled four full pages and ran virtually as I had written it years before.

The reaction was electrifying. Dorthy was, of course, thrilled. Far from the negative fallout Isenberg had feared, circulation increased. Although the article pointed out that the police had blundered, Greenwich residents could rest assured that their department was not corrupt and had not engaged in a cover-up.

Even the Skakels did not protest the story. Because it pointed out that they had initially cooperated, they quoted it in defending themselves. Years later, when Robert F. Kennedy Jr. wrote of Michael's innocence in *Atlantic Monthly*, he described the article as the case's most thorough piece of journalism.

On August 8, 1991, Keegan's successor as Greenwich police chief,

Ken Moughty, held a news conference at headquarters. At his side were State's Attorney Donald Browne and his chief investigator Jack Solomon. They announced they had reopened the Moxley investigation.

Next to them stood a Greenwich detective I didn't recognize. Moughty announced that he was the detective assigned to represent the Greenwich Police Department on the case. He was Frank Garr.

# PART II

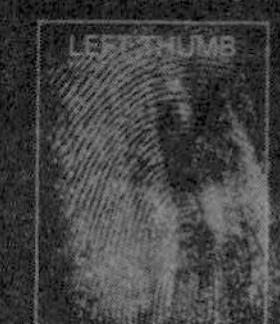

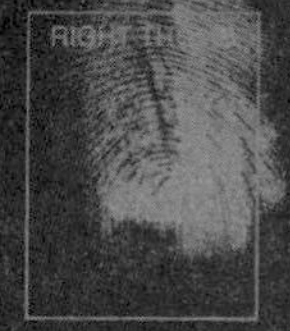

# 9

PART TWO / CHAPTER NINE

# "They Didn't Bungle, Botch, or 'Tread Lightly' "

GREENWICH, CONNECTICUT
1991

When Frank Garr was growing up, he was something of a mama's boy.

His father Tony owned a restaurant on Westchester Avenue in the gritty city of Port Chester, just over the New York state line from Greenwich but light years away. Port Chester was a city of immigrants, and the restaurant, which Tony ran with his brothers and those of his wife Beatrice, consumed his life.

For young Frank there were no games of catch with his dad or trips to the ballpark. The only time he spent with his father was a week each summer when the family vacationed in Spofford Lake in Keene, New Hampshire.

Instead, Frank spent every day after school with his mother. His was the traditional old-world Italian household, where the men worked and the women reared the children. Their house was spotless, with the smells of home-cooked food. All social life revolved around the family. All holidays and celebrations—birthdays, weddings, Thanksgiving, or Christmas—were spent with his aunts, uncles, and cousins.

Yet there were tensions that left his mother in tears and caused her to

***Frank Garr's headshot from his days as an aspiring actor in New York.***

run with little Frankie to her brother's house until tempers settled. Beatrice was one of nine children of Italian immigrants from outside Naples. Because she had had to help support her parents, she never graduated from high school. Port Chester was the center of her world. Once, as a girl, she'd taken a bus to Stamford to visit relatives. The trip had so unnerved her that she never wanted to travel again.

Years later, after Tony moved the family to Greenwich—a step up the social and economic ladder—Beatrice was never comfortable. She hadn't learned to drive and missed her friends and relatives and her Port Chester life. Though it was just a ten-minute car ride, she felt a million miles away.

While Tony worked day and night in the restaurant, Beatrice took Frank shopping after school and to the movies or to amusement parks. Because she didn't drive, they took the bus or taxis. At home, they'd snack together—a piece of Italian bread, a raw onion, and an orange—before Frank went out to play or do his homework. In the evenings, while Tony worked, they watched television together—the 1950s variety shows, Perry Como, Lawrence Welk, Jackie Gleason, and *I Love Lucy*.

Despite her lack of education, his mother was, as Frank put it, "extremely wise to the ways of the world. She taught me lessons not through words but through deeds."

"Frankie," she told him, "never tell people your business. Always be friendly but never intimate with anyone outside of your family."

To Frank, his mother was the most loving person in the world. "But if you wronged her, if you crossed her, you were *fini*."

Frank's grandfather on his father's side had changed his name from Carino to Garr for reasons Frank never learned. Among the family, the subject was never discussed. His paternal grandmother—"Grandma Red," as she was called because of her fiery hair—lived in the Bronx, and as a boy Frank spent weekends at her apartment.

Grandma Red knew New York City and took Frank all around Manhattan. A favorite spot was the automat on Forty-second Street. He loved looking in the little compartments filled with different foods. Grandma

Red gave him coins to select his favorite: a bologna and cheese sandwich and lemon pie for dessert.

Frank became familiar with Manhattan's tourist attractions: Rockefeller Center, Radio City Music Hall, and the Museum of Natural History, where his favorite exhibition was the dinosaurs. Grandma Red even took him to the Metropolitan Museum of Art, where he stared, entranced, at the mummies.

With his dad always at the restaurant, his mother's brother, Frank's Uncle Babe, became a second father. During World War II, Uncle Babe had served in the Air Force. When he returned, he drove a cab for Port Taxi at the train station. Whenever he could, little Frankie accompanied him.

Babe let him answer the dispatcher on the cab's two-way radio. He loved talking on it, answering when they were given a location to pick up a fare or telling the dispatcher they were clear for another call. Years later, Frank would recall this as his first experience of being on patrol.

Uncle Babe promised Frank that if he did well in school, Babe would give him his 1958 Pontiac Bonneville or buy him any car he wanted when Frank was old enough to drive.

"And he would have," Frank said. But on October 30, 1958, exactly seventeen years before the murder of Martha Moxley, Frank experienced his own Halloween tragedy.

Returning from school, he noticed his father's and relatives' cars parked outside. As he drew closer, he heard screaming. It was his mother. He started running and bounded through the front door. His mother was crying hysterically. His father and another uncle were trying to subdue her. They had just told her Uncle Babe had died of a heart attack.

The mourning continued for months. Life seemed as though it would never be the same. And in some ways it never was. "To say that I miss my uncle would be an understatement," Frank said. "His death left an enormous void in my life."

Uncle Babe had worn a yellow-and-white-gold band–type ring with a three-diamond setting. Frank's aunts and uncles all wanted him to have it. When he married, it served as his wedding band. "I wear it to this day and never take it off."

Not a student, Frank struggled to keep up. Even then, in the early 1960s, he realized that without a high school diploma he had no chance of success. Despite poor grades, he managed to graduate in 1964.

He took an office job with an insurance company. It did not take him long to realize this was not how he wanted to spend his life. A year later, the decision to leave was made for him when he was drafted into the Army.

After two months of basic training, he reported to a communications center in Duncanville, Texas, outside Dallas. Three months later he shipped out to Vietnam. He spent the next year there in the Signal Corps.

In March 1967, he returned to the United States—to "the world," as they called it. Four months remained of his military service. He had begun thinking of a career and considered becoming a cop.

"My first inclination was to apply to the NYPD but I allowed myself to be talked out of it by my family," he said. "To this day I have some regrets about that."

His family wanted him closer, at home in Port Chester where they had ties and an in with the police department. Frank didn't want that. Instead, he applied to the Greenwich police department, which was considered a step up from Port Chester's.

While home on leave, he took the police exam, then with other returning Vietnam vets, reported to the White Sands Missile Base in Las Cruces, New Mexico, for his last four months of service. Those four months seemed to take forever while he waited for the test results. He drove a tanker truck, delivering water to troops working in the desert, and lounged in the afternoons by the base swimming pool.

Then, he received a letter from his mother telling him he had passed the exam. On September 10, 1967, he received his honorable discharge. Ten days later, he was sworn in as a Greenwich patrolman. His first detail was directing traffic on Greenwich Avenue. Frank was twenty-two years old.

Most people have one or two individuals who have had an impact on their lives, either positive or negative. For Frank, one of those people was Tom Keegan, the street sergeant his first night on the job.

When Frank's traffic tour ended, Keegan picked him up and drove him around town, explaining about the department and what it expected of its officers. "He demanded loyalty, honesty, and courage of those who worked for and with him," Frank said. "He was generous with his advice, which I have passed on to new officers."

One of those new officers, whom Frank broke in, was the son of a former chief. While on patrol together, the chief's son accidentally fired his gun, shattering their patrol car window. After some discussion, he owned up to it. Police departments being what they are, it was Frank who was transferred.

His new assignment was a nowhere post in the back-country, but Frank never questioned the transfer. "You'll never ask, will you?" said his sergeant a few months later. "Well, I'll tell you. They wanted someone to keep the kid under control, to make sure he didn't get into any more trouble. And you weren't the guy."

Meanwhile, Frank had married Mariann Marconi, a nurse in Greenwich Hospital's emergency room. They'd met while he was driving the two-man "accident car" to all major calls and he'd spend a lot of time in the ER. The place was social, with unwritten rules. When the cops arrived, they brought donuts. The nurses made sure the coffee was hot.

Mariann—"Miss Priss," as Frank called her—had recently arrived from Syracuse and would have none of this socializing. Someone complained about her to the head nurse. Mariann was called in and informed of the facts of Greenwich life.

As things came to pass, seven of eight nurses working in the ER married Greenwich cops. The eighth married a cop from the Port Authority.

Frank and Mariann were one of the lucky couples to buy in Greenwich before the mid-1970s when skyrocketing prices forced cops out of the market. They paid $62,000 for a house in Glenville, the poor man's part of town, if there is such a thing in Greenwich.

"I got in just in time," Frank said.

The house had three bedrooms, a front yard, and a deck for barbecuing. Soon, they had two children, Dave and Angela, both of whom attended Greenwich's public schools. Dave was a natural athlete. At six-foot-four inches, six inches taller than his father, he played hockey and pitched on Greenwich High's baseball team. Angela was artistic, with a flair for drawing and sketching. She would become a graphic designer. Meanwhile, Miss Priss forced Frank to return to college and obtain a college degree—a Bachelor of Science from Iona College.

Like all Greenwich cops, Frank worked second jobs, from driving wealthy Greenwich residents to the airports, to providing security at their parties and serving drinks as a bartender.

"I drove. We all drove. Did I like it? No. But if my son needed a $350 pair of ice skates each year for hockey, I had to work extra for it."

He also provided private security for Enid Haupt, the millionaire sister of philanthropist and ambassador Walter Annenberg. Haupt owned an apartment on Park Avenue in New York that had been robbed. After that, whenever she stayed at her back-country home in Greenwich, she called the detective division.

Frank and Lunney ran the job. At 9:00 P.M., the maid and butler let one of them in. The burglar alarm was turned on and one of them stayed until 7:00 A.M., watching TV and earning $25 an hour. When he arrived, Frank saw Haupt for ten minutes. He was gone before she woke up the next morning. It took him two nights to earn the money for his son's ice skates, money Haupt could write a check for in less than two minutes.

Frank also provided security for Frank and Kathie Lee Gifford, who lived in the back-country. "We just hit it off," said Frank. Whenever the Giffords had a party, he arranged for guys to park cars. When the children, Cody and Cassidy, were born, Gifford, not wanting reporters to bother Kathie Lee at Greenwich Hospital, hired Frank Garr to keep them away.

As Keegan rose through the ranks, he and Frank stayed close. In Greenwich's Irish-dominated department, traces of anti-Italian prejudice remained. When Frank grew a mustache, one of his superiors was heard to grumble, "That's all we need. Another guinea with a mustache." When Keegan was promoted to captain of detectives, he brought Frank into the division as one of the first detectives of Italian origin.

In affluent Greenwich, burglary is the most common crime. Frank soon figured out that most burglars are drug addicts and created the department's first drug unit. He began working undercover, together with counterparts in surrounding departments and the state police, the federal Drug Enforcement Administration, and the FBI.

Frank also acknowledged a secret passion—acting. He enrolled in the Weist Baron acting school in Manhattan. He used his training to play undercover roles in narcotics cases.

From his patrol and detective work, he had learned how to deal with all sorts of people, from bankers in bow ties to heroin addicts with snot running from their noses.

"My job was to get people to talk to me," he explained. "To be effective as a cop, I had to reach all kinds of people. I had to be able to change personalities, to change my style in different situations."

The DEA guys got a kick out of watching him. Frank would go into a bar, cozy up to a dealer, and say he was an advertising guy. He'd make the dealer comfortable, convince him he had money. That way, the dealer would sell him drugs or return to his people, higher up the chain, and tell them he had a live one here, a golden goose. Frank never received public recognition for his drug arrests. He wrote the press releases for them, but because he worked undercover, he always omitted his name.

As the Moxley case wound down and Lunney needed a place to settle, "Double J," as Frank referred to James J. Lunney, joined him in his narcotics squad. As one by one, the detectives who'd worked on the Moxley case retired, Frank inherited it. When in 1987 Lunney retired, Frank was the department's only member with a connection to it.

His mother had taught him to trust no one outside his family. To Frank, that family now included the Greenwich police department. Despite my criticisms of their investigation, Frank defended Keegan and Lunney.

When we met at that news conference at Greenwich police headquarters in August 1991, I was an outsider to him—no different from anyone else who was not part of the official investigation. As I would learn, Frank distrusted outsiders—even those who sought to help.

Years later, after we became friends, he would quote disparagingly from my article in the *Stamford Advocate* and the *Greenwich Time* and say to me, "The Greenwich Police Department was never intimidated by the Skakels."

He was enraged by Detroit Chief Hale's criticism of Keegan and Lunney. Referring to Hale's quote in my article, Frank, teeth clenched, said, "They didn't bungle, botch, or 'tread lightly.'"

He said about Hale: "No one sitting in Detroit or anywhere else for that matter can read a Greenwich police report and know how he would react at any point. Hale didn't have the right to criticize anyone. If he wasn't there, he should keep his mouth shut. No one was afraid of the Skakels."

Then, there was David Moxley's Touche Ross colleague, John McCreight, who had showed me Hale's report, which led to my first break in the case. When Frank began his reinvestigation, McCreight again made a behind-the-scenes move. He wrote to Greenwich's highest elected official, First Selectman John Margenot, seeking to arrange Hale's return, together with a second investigator, former New York City detective Vernon Geberth, author of a homicide textbook.

"We want to be able to assure both Mr. Hale and Mr. Vernon Geberth that they will be welcomed by both the Greenwich and state authorities and that they will be able to function effectively as a team," McCreight wrote to Margenot.

His professionalism notwithstanding, Hale was the last person Frank wanted to work with in the Moxley murder investigation. McCreight was next to last.

Frank complained to Greenwich police chief Moughty. "He was at a clambake in old Greenwich. I said to him, 'Chief, this guy McCreight pushed his way in back in 1975 but it's not happening now. He didn't report to us then. He reported to the Moxleys. If you allow him back in, I'd rather be out.'"

McCreight vanished from the investigation. The first Moxley ally to enter the case who ran afoul of Frank, he would not be the last.

And Frank's loyalty to the Greenwich police was returned in kind. Years later, when his work led to the arrest not of Tommy but of Michael as Martha's killer, he called Chief Keegan in South Carolina.

"There was no defensiveness, no justifying past actions," Frank said. "Keegan couldn't have been more supportive. He simply congratulated me, saying he would be here to testify if I needed him.

"Of Michael, all he said was, 'The little fuck lied to us.' "

# 10

PART TWO / CHAPTER TEN

# Leads, Lies, and Jeans

GREENWICH, CONNECTICUT
1991–1995

How do you begin an investigation into a sixteen-year-old murder, when all the detectives who worked on it retired years before? How do you proceed when the case's prime suspect and his family refuse to be interviewed on the advice of their attorney? How do you avoid the treacheries of entering into the middle of an investigation in which your superiors had committed themselves to a suspect?

"The only thing I had was the case file, the thousands of pages of Greenwich police reports," Frank explained to me years later. "I must have read them twelve times. I became an encyclopedia."

Since 1975, the file had been kept in a locked metal box in Keegan's office. Only Keegan, Lunney, and Carroll had been permitted to see it. All leads had been forwarded to those three—no questions asked. So sensitive was the case that detectives avoided discussing it in idle conversation. Unless you were part of the investigation, the subject was considered taboo.

Frank set up an office in the police library with Jack Solomon, the chief investigator from the state's attorney's office. At the news conference they announced a $50,000 reward and set up a tip line with an answering machine. They agreed to start from scratch—as though the murder had occurred that day.

And from day one, August 8, 1991, said Frank, the phone started ringing. Except for one person who confused the two brothers, no one called about Tommy or Ken Littleton. The only tips concerned Michael.

"Not that anyone said Michael did it," Frank clarified. "No, the callers said things like, 'I just want you to know Michael was out of control.' "

Actually, the phone had rung a few months before. Just as the William Kennedy Smith trial had indirectly precipitated the publication of my story, it also led to Frank's first tip. The tip concerned a place he'd never heard of, the Elan School in Poland Springs, Maine, a drug rehabilitation facility for rich kids. Michael had been sent there, following a drunken driving arrest, in 1978, at age eighteen, three years after Martha's murder.

Frank was aware of the arrest, which had been noted in the Greenwich police file, though it would not be until years later that its relevance to Martha's murder became clear. Driving the Skakels' station wagon without a license, at the Skakels' house in Windham, N.Y., accompanied by twenty-one-year-old Debbie Diehl, whose family were longtime friends, Michael had crashed the car into a telephone pole, then fled, leaving Diehl with a broken leg.

The tip about Elan—where Michael remained for the next two years—had come in around midnight of April 29, 1991, when a Lieutenant Thomas Perry of the Palm Beach Police Department reported that his department had received a telephone call from a David Bowlin of Santa Monica, California.

Bowlin—a convicted felon with a half-dozen aliases and arrests for car theft, drunk driving, assault, burglary, and drug possession—had also been at Elan. He told Lieutenant Perry he had just seen the television program *Hard Copy*, which speculated, falsely, that William Kennedy Smith had been at the Skakel house the night of the Moxley murder. The program had also mentioned earlier news accounts that Tommy Skakel, a member of the Kennedy family, was a suspect.

According to Lieutenant Perry, Bowlin "related that the mention of this murder . . . made him think an acquaintance, Michael Skakel, might be involved." As a teenager in 1977, Bowlin had been sent to Elan when Michael was there.

"Bowlin knew Mike was related to the Kennedy family and stated Michael had told him he had been taken from the ski slopes and delivered to the facility. The relationship to Thomas Skakel and the proximity in time to the murder made Bowlin think Mike Skakel may have been involved and that he was sent to the facility to hide him from investigators," Perry reported. This, three years after the murder.

•

Two ninth-grade classmates of Michael's at Greenwich's St. Mary's Catholic School also called with suspicions about Michael.

Victoria Russell Haigh, of Providence, Rhode Island, said that after the murder, Michael would bring newspaper articles about the case and read them in class.

Diane Birney, of Carmel, New York, remembered that Michael stared at her in speech class. It happened so many times the teacher escorted him from the room.

Two small notes in the file also provided clues.

On a torn napkin, Frank found a mention that Michael's polygraph with the state police had been canceled. This was a surprise. Frank knew from the file that Tommy had taken a lie detector test. He never knew Michael had been scheduled for one.

He called Lunney, who didn't remember any such arrangements. Maybe, he told Frank, Michael was too young. He was only fifteen.

But that made no sense because the state police can polygraph juveniles with their parents' okay. If Rushton had consented, Michael could have been polygraphed.

"I'm thinking maybe it was scheduled but the old man put the kibosh on it," said Frank. "I'm asking myself, Why would he do that since he hadn't objected to Tommy's?"

The second note mentioned a conversation between Dorthy's now-grown son John and their former neighbor, Cissy Ix, about the medical tests Tommy supposedly had taken but whose results had not been given to the police.

In late 1991, Frank drove over to the Ixes in Belle Haven. He was surprised at how cooperative they seemed. "Cissy was very attractive, very proper. She had a faint Massachusetts accent. I liked her." He also described her husband. "He was businesslike, dignified, reserved, and cautious with his words. I liked him too."

While still protective of Tommy, as she had been with Dorthy years before, Cissy had no qualms saying she always felt that Michael and Jimmy Terrien should be looked at. With all his problems, Michael had always been suspect in her mind, and she had even told this to Chief Keegan. Keegan, however, had been dismissive. He had never questioned Michael's story of having gone to the Terriens'. If the murder had occurred at 10:00 P.M., Michael couldn't have returned in time.

Cissy added that two or three weeks after the murder, she had gone to Tommy's room and asked him what had happened that night.

"Why don't you go and ask Jimmy Terrien?" Tommy said to her.

To Frank, this indicated at least two people—Tommy and Jimmy—might have been involved in Martha's murder. If the killer was Michael, that would make three.

•

There was also the caller who misidentified Tommy.

May Stone Versailles of Greenwich reported that the husband of a friend said Tommy had practically admitted to the murder while at an Alcoholics Anonymous meeting at Greenwich Hospital in 1987.

Frank tracked Versailles's friend to Mill Valley, California. Then, he reached her husband. The first thing he told Frank was that it was Michael who attended the meeting.

The husband described Michael's standing before the group of about fifteen to twenty people, red-faced, with five o'clock shadow, his clothes too big for him but wearing brand new cowboy boots.

He said his father had sent him to Windham, New York, and from there to Elan, where he was beaten. He escaped in the winter and nearly froze to death.

Michael also told the group that once he had once put a gun to his head and pulled the trigger but it jammed and wouldn't fire. Michael said he tried to fix it by banging the gun on a table. It went off, a bullet hitting the ceiling. Because the gun hadn't fired when he pointed it at himself, Michael told the group that God did not want him to kill himself.

•

Michael's Alcoholic Anonymous connection provided Frank with another lead—Andy Pugh.

Michael had bumped into Pugh when both turned up at an AA meeting at Greenwich's Christ Church in the mid-1980s. Once best friends, they had been out of touch. After the meeting, Michael called Pugh, asking if he had cut off contact because he believed Michael had killed Martha.

Michael had never been a suspect in the murder. No one in Belle Haven thought it could have been a kid, Pugh said. Everyone had accepted the Greenwich police's theory that it was someone off the turnpike, maybe a loony. When in 1978 Michael had gone off to Elan, the speculation in Belle Haven was still that the killer was either Tommy or Littleton.

But the more Pugh thought about the murder over the years, he told Frank, "The more it pointed to Michael. The killer was not a stranger. It was someone within that household. I found myself thinking, 'Is it possible it was him?' "

Pugh remembered that Michael was bigger and stronger than Martha and was a tremendous athlete. "Pound for pound, he was the strongest kid I had ever met. And he liked her. She liked him but he liked her more." Pugh said he had once seen them wrestling around and kissing. And Michael, Pugh told Frank, was violent and aggressive when he was drinking.

•

Then, there was Julie Skakel's friend Andrea Shakespeare, who had been at the Skakels the night of the murder. I had written her off as a brat when I'd interviewed her in 1984. But Frank saw something else in her—her honesty. She dropped a bombshell—no, a live grenade—in Frank's lap.

Frank found her in Massachusetts, married and the mother of three small children. He and Solomon drove up to see her. "She was smart, brash, a firecracker, and as open as can be," Frank said. "I liked her immediately."

The night of the murder, Andrea told them, she remembered drinking tea with Julie and hearing voices outside the house shortly before 9:30. " 'Oh, that's Martha Moxley,' Julie said to me." They heard another girl's voice. Julie told Andrea it was Helen Ix's.

Andrea said she never saw either one of them. "I am happy now I never did," she said.

Frank tried to jog her memory. He reminded her of the Skakel car pulling out of the driveway with Michael and his brother driving to the Terriens'.

"Michael went to the Terriens'?" Andrea said.

"Yeah," Frank answered, "Michael got in the backseat."

"I was always under the impression Michael was in the house when the car left," she said, "that Michael didn't go."

Frank was stunned. This was the first time he or anyone else connected to the investigation had heard that Michael didn't go to the Terriens'.

"How do you know that?" he said to her.

"I just have this impression," she answered. "I am as sure as I can be."

But no matter how hard he pushed her, Andrea could not explain why she thought Michael did not take that trip. This was June 1991, sixteen years after the murder. "I must have talked to her 165 times between that day and the last day I saw her in court eleven years later," said Frank. "Each time, I would say to her, 'Andrea, just tell me why you are so sure Michael didn't go.' "

Each time she would answer, "All I can tell you, Frank, is that he didn't go. I can't tell you why."

So what do you do with this information? Frank asked himself. Nothing then. You just tuck it away in the back of your mind.

•

In the file, Frank also discovered Dorothy Rogers. She was the first witness he found to whom Michael had made an admission about Martha's murder.

Dated September 10, 1980, from Greenwich detective Rich Haug, a memo in the file said that Rogers, then nineteen years old, had been brought in for questioning about a fire she had set at her parents' house in the back-country. She mentioned that from June 1978 to June 1979, she'd been at Elan, where she and Michael often spoke. Once, she said, he'd brought up Martha Moxley. He'd confessed to her that he was drunk and might have murdered her during a blackout period.

Rogers added that part of their therapy at Elan was a general meeting of patients and staff. Everyone formed a circle around one person, who stood in the middle. One night Michael was in the middle and a staff member asked him, "Why did you crush Martha Moxley's chest with a golf club?" Michael didn't answer.

Reading through the file, Frank found himself thinking that this had occurred in 1978 or 1979—when Michael was not a suspect. Why would anyone—how would anyone know to ask him about Martha's murder?

So Frank went to Haug, the detective who'd investigated the Rogers fire and asked whether anyone had acted on his memo. Haug said he'd passed it on to the captain of detectives.

Frank knew anything regarding the Moxley case went to Lunney. But Lunney said he'd never seen it. He didn't remember it.

So Frank began to search for Dorothy Rogers. He found her date of birth, searched for a record of a driver's license, for any activity regarding her Social Security number or employment history.

He picked up a lead that she might have been in Anaheim, California. He contacted the Anaheim Police Department, which connected him to its vice squad. Detectives there thought they knew her. They remembered a street person with the description Frank had given them. But they hadn't seen her in years. Maybe she was dead.

It bothered Frank so he kept calling around. He called corrections departments in Anaheim and the surrounding areas, then tracked her to, of all places, Graham, North Carolina. She was on probation. Married. Her name was now Dorothy Mickey. She was an alcoholic. Frank found her probation officer. Then he flew to Graham.

On the flight, he wondered how he would get her to talk to him. He assumed she didn't like cops. And if she did talk, how good was her memory, and would she be a credible witness?

"Well, she looked like a drunk," Frank recalled after he saw her. "A lot of hard miles on her. Her teeth were bad. She looked drawn. Here she was, a rich back-country Greenwich girl who anyone could see had once been attractive, and she looked like trailer trash."

But she was willing to talk to him.

She had a southern accent. Frank couldn't believe she came from Greenwich. "She had come from a life of privilege and look what she had done to herself, although I know this happens to a lot of people."

Her memory was foggy but not as bad as he had feared. She remembered Michael and what he had told her.

While in Greenwich, she said she had twice stolen her family car and driven to Maine. Each time she was arrested and returned to Greenwich. Finally, her family sent her to Elan. She stayed eleven months.

Michael, she remembered, was already there when she arrived. At a dance, she asked him about the Moxley murder. He told her the police believed either he or his brother Tommy was responsible.

"So she's telling me this," Frank remembered, "and I am thinking, there is no way Michael was a suspect then. Only Tommy was. For Michael to claim the police thought he might be responsible for this murder or that the police might arrest and charge him with the murder was, in my eyes, an example of what we call 'consciousness of guilt.'"

Rogers said Michael had also told her that on the night of the murder he had gotten drunk. He claimed to have blacked out and couldn't remember what he did but was afraid that he might have committed the murder. He woke up in his house or in a car in a daze, she recalled his saying. A relative or an attorney insisted he stay at Elan or face murder charges.

Michael's story made Frank think of a pressure cooker. It was as though Michael were letting off steam. Frank realized Michael had been blabbing about the murder for years, releasing thoughts that had been weighing on him. Was this his way of coping, Frank wondered, short of admitting he had killed her?

Frank told Rogers to make sure to stay in touch with him. He knew he would use her at some point. Her story was powerful, and it dovetailed with his suspicions.

Sometimes, Frank had to call Rogers's mother to learn her whereabouts, mostly in and out of jail as she battled her addiction. Sometimes, Rogers called him from various prisons.

"Frank," she would say, "I just want you to know where I am. . . ."

•

And there was the Skakel family chauffeur, Larry Zicarelli. He told Frank that Michael said he had done something so bad he felt he had to kill himself.

Zicarelli had been hired six months after the murder in the spring of 1976, replacing the Skakel's longtime caretaker, Franz Wittine, who had lived in a guest room in the basement and recently retired.

Every Friday at 4:00 P.M., Zicarelli said, he drove Michael to a psychiatrist in New York City. One Friday morning, Zicarelli recalled, Michael came downstairs shouting at his father. He raced outside, screaming, "You're not my father." Then he jumped into a car in the driveway and tried to drive it through a fence.

Zicarelli ran outside to the car. Michael pulled out a switchblade knife and pointed it at him.

"Start driving this fucking car or I'll stab you to death," he screamed.

Zicarelli turned to Rushton, who nodded his approval, thinking it might calm Michael down.

Zicarelli talked Michael into putting away the knife, then drove him into the city. But on Park Avenue, Michael jumped out and, without a word, ran off.

Zicarelli didn't know what to do so he drove to Rushton's office at Great Lakes Carbon nearby. There, they told him Michael's appointment with the psychiatrist had been changed from 4:00 to 2:00 P.M. That's where Michael had probably gone.

Zicarelli drove over to the psychiatrist's and waited for Michael to appear. Sure enough, an hour before his appointment, Michael showed up. Zicarelli asked him why he had run off.

"You're the only person I can trust," Michael told him.

Zicarelli bought him lunch, then waited for him to finish his appointment. When Michael came out, he was in tears.

He got into the car and Zicarelli headed back to Greenwich. But driving onto the Triborough Bridge, Michael again jumped from the car.

"I've done something very bad. I'm in a lot of trouble. I've either got to kill myself or leave the country," he shouted as he crossed traffic lanes and began climbing up one of the bridge's spans.

Zicarelli pulled the car over. He jumped out, chased after him, pulled him down.

He drove Michael back to Greenwich and quit the next day.

Lunney and Carroll had been keeping tabs on the Skakels and had gotten to know Zicarelli. They had asked him to keep an eye out and to call them about anything suspicious. Over the years, Zicarelli met with them. But he never told them about the incident on the bridge.

Instead, early in 1992, he mentioned the incident to his friend Edwin Jones. Jones, who'd seen stories in the paper about the reopened investigation, called the Greenwich police.

"Why did you wait so long to tell your story?" Frank asked when he questioned Zicarelli. "I was afraid," Zicarelli explained. "I was so afraid of those people. My wife told me, 'Don't ever say anything to anyone. Don't cause any trouble.'

"Besides," Zicarelli added, "nothing was going on with the investigation all these years."

"It is now," Frank answered.

•

Finally, there were the jeans. For Frank, they cinched the case against Michael.

Early in 1992, he was poring through the case file for what seemed the hundredth time. On November 5, 1975, less than a week after the murder, he read that two sanitation men had found a black plastic garbage bag outside the Skakel home. The bag held a pair of Tretorn sneakers and blue, size 36–30 Wrangler jeans.

Both had stains resembling blood. The stains were on the bottom of the jeans and tops of the sneakers. Inside the jeans' right pocket was a laundry stamp with the name "Matthai-B."

Tests of the stains done at the state lab in 1975 came back negative for blood. But the lab discovered a long blonde hair on the dungarees. The lab report suggested the police compare the hair to Martha's, so the following day the police sent the jeans, sneakers, and the blonde hair to the FBI lab in Washington.

Four days later, at 9:20 P.M., November 9, 1975, Frank read, detectives asked Rushton Skakel about the sneakers and jeans. He said they were Michael's. While in camp the previous summer in New Hampshire, Michael had swapped clothes with another boy, believed to be the "Matthai-B" of the laundry stamp.

Frank knew he couldn't speak to Rushton or any of the Skakels. Margolis had forbidden that. Frank's last conversation with Rushton had occurred six months before, when he and Solomon had come to question Cissy Ix, following up about Tommy's medical tests.

While interviewing Cissy, she had telephoned Rushton, who offered to show them the test results. Frank and Solomon had walked across the street to Rushton's home on Otter Rock Drive but Rushton then said he couldn't find them. He asked them to call him the next day.

*Martha Moxley in kindergarten*

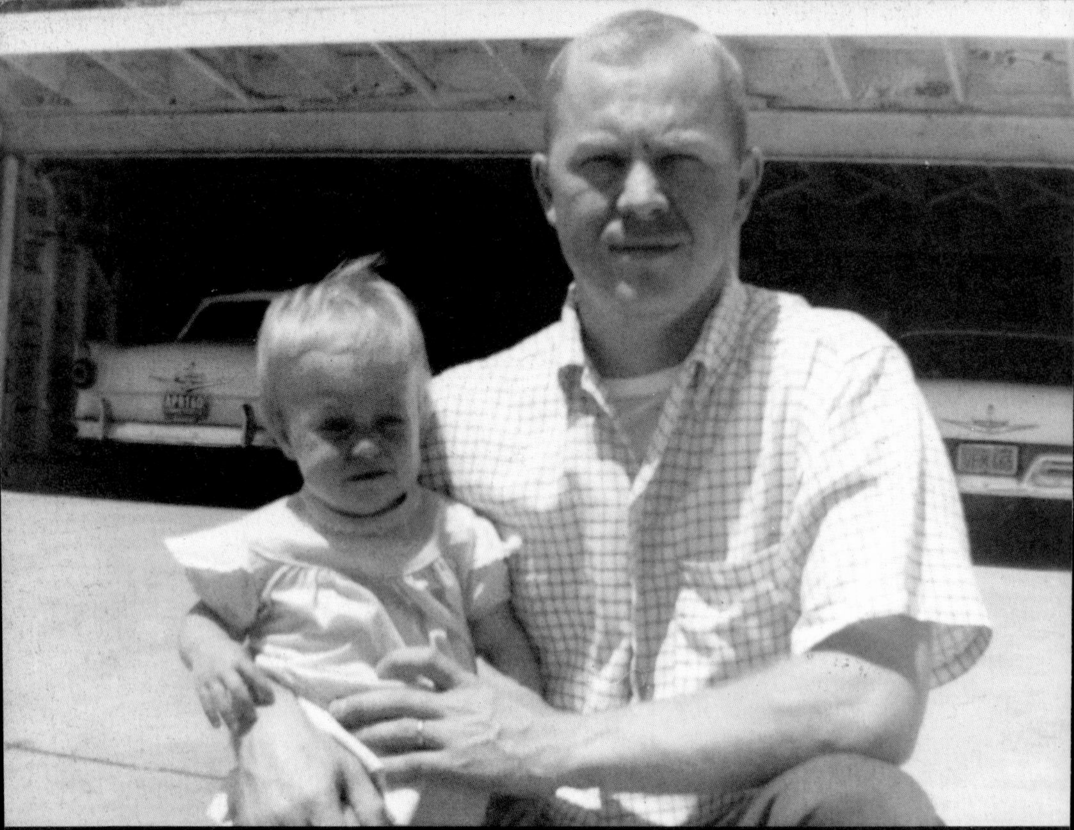

*Martha and her father, David, in July 1961*

*Above: Christmas 1963*
*Right: From an early age, Martha showed her confidence and independence.*

*Martha with her pets, Rowdy and Sundance*

*Martha and her mother, Dorthy Moxley, in 1969*

*At Lake Tahoe in 1969*

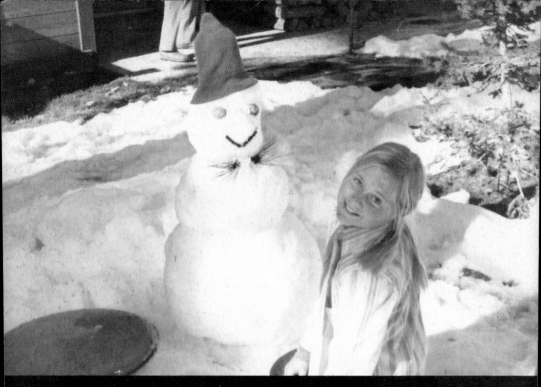

*John, Dorthy, Martha, and David Moxley at Lake Tahoe in the summer of 1974*

*At fourteen*

*Michael Skakel (top row, third from right) in a 1974 yearbook photo*

*Tommy Skakel in a 1975 yearbook photo*

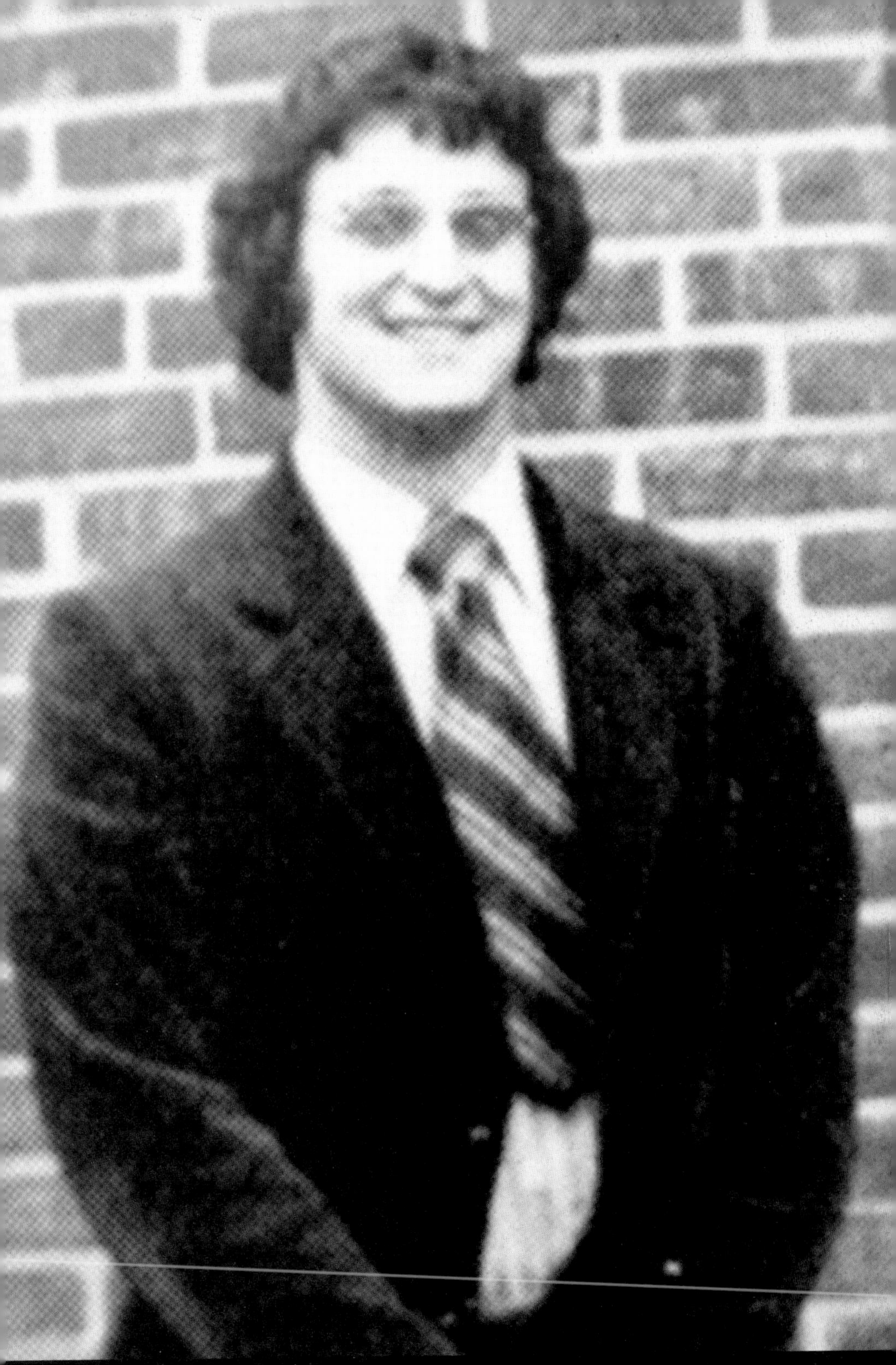

*[illegible] the day Martha was killed*

*The back of the Skakel home*

*The path Martha took on her way home the night of her murder*

*The Greenwich Police Department in 1978, including Frank Garr (bottom row, second from right), Steve Carroll (bottom row, third from right), Jim Lunney (top row, fourth from right), and Tom Keegan (top row, second from right)*

*A piece of the broken golf club, the murder weapon*

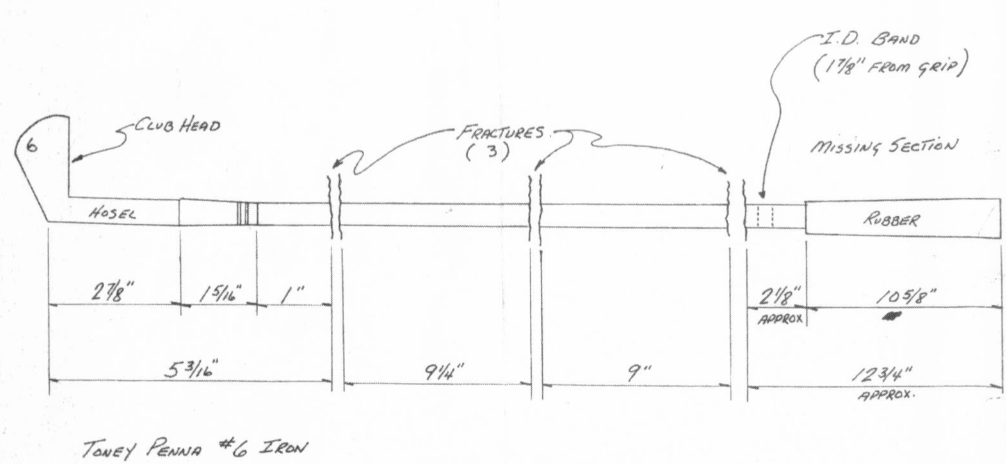


*From the Greenwich Police Department's case file: their diagram of the broken murder weapon, including the shaft portion missing from the crime scene that has never been recovered.*

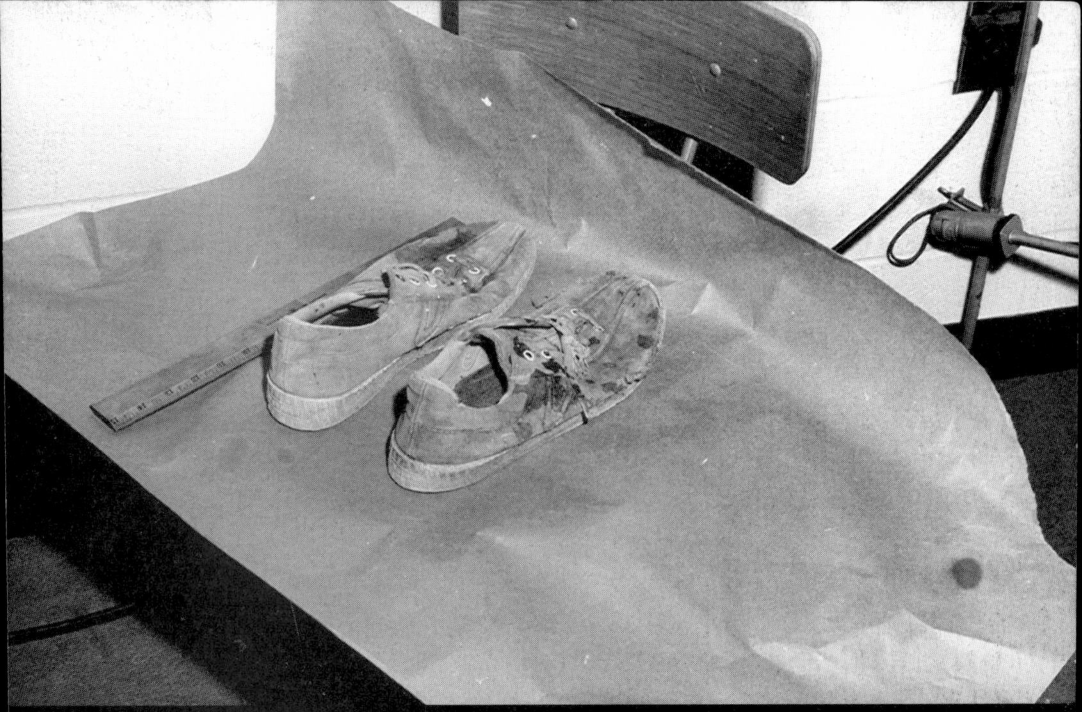

*A pair of tennis shoes found by Greenwich sanitation department workers in a garbage bag outside the Skakel home less than a week after Martha's murder. The stains were tested as potential evidence, but the tests came back inconclusive.*

*Michael Skakel's jeans were found in a discarded garbage bag with the stained tennis shoes pictured above. Michael denied that the jeans were his. When Frank confirmed this to be a lie, his gut reaction was that Michael was hiding something—maybe murder.*

*Frank Garr (center) at his swearing-in as an inspector on the case. With him are Donald Browne (left), Fairfield County state's attorney, and Jack Solomon, Browne's chief investigator, who would become Frank's superior and nemesis.*

*Frank and I bonded over the case—and more than occasionally argued over it. "Let's just leave it that we disagree," I would say. "Yeah, but you're the writer," Frank would reply. "You always get the last word."*

*Me and Frank in one of our sessions*

*At the Lakeside Din* [illegible] *e years as we worked on the case*

*Frank Garr (right) and Michael Skakel (center) on the day of Michael's arrest for the murder of Martha Moxley*

*Michael Skakel (right) with his bodyguard during the trial*

*Michael Skakel's booking photos*

*The prosecution team from the state's attorney's office, left to right: Chris Morano, John Benedict, Susan Gill, and Frank Garr*

*With Dorthy Moxley, celebrating justice at last*

Instead, Tom Sheridan called. It was the first time Frank had spoken to him. He explained that he'd been Michael's criminal attorney since 1978 when Michael was arrested for drunken driving in Windham. Writing of the incident years later to the private investigators the Skakels had hired, Sheridan described Michael as "obviously a disturbed person and hooked on either booze or pot. He showed little or no remorse for having nearly killed the companion in his car and when confronted with the potential problem of a subsequent conviction for drunken driving, his only comment was, 'Next time I won't get caught.' "

What Frank would later learn was that Michael's drunken-driving arrest had raised concerns among the Skakels about his possible involvement in Martha's murder.

Sheridan asked Frank not to contact Rushton or any of the Skakels about the test results until Margolis was notified. Frank knew then that he would never see them.

Now, six months later, in early 1992, Frank decided to call Sheridan about the jeans.

He told Sheridan of Rushton's statement in November 1975, that the dungarees were Michael's. Sheridan promised to find out. A few days later he called. Michael, Sheridan told Frank, didn't know why his father had said this. Michael said he had never gone to camp in New Hampshire or anywhere else.

"So I'm thinking, why would Michael say he had never been to camp when, back in 1975, the old man said he had?" Frank mused as he returned to the police file, searching now for the results of the testing of the long blonde hair, comparing it to Martha's.

In the file, he discovered a December 5, 1975, report from the FBI lab, indicating the tests had been completed. But there was no mention of the results. A notation on February 9, 1976, stated that all evidence sent to the FBI lab had been returned to the Greenwich police.

All the Moxley case evidence was kept inside a large carton in a safe in the basement of Greenwich police headquarters. Inside the carton were smaller boxes and envelopes with more evidence.

"I pull it all out. I am going through that box like a madman." Inside one of the envelopes, he located photographs of the jeans and the sneakers. But the items themselves were missing. He called Jim Lunney. Lunney remembered the jeans, although he had no idea where they were.

But the long blonde hair was there. It had been removed from the jeans and returned from the FBI lab. It was mounted on a slide inside one of the smaller evidence cartons. It had been sitting there all these years.

Frank called Henry Lee, the chief of Connecticut's Forensic Science Laboratory to compare the hair to Martha's. Frank was so excited he drove it up himself to Lee's office in Meriden. A few days later, Lee called him. The hair was Martha's.

Okay, Frank thought, what did he have? There is this pair of lost jeans that Rushton says belongs to Michael, which he could have worn the night of the murder. Martha's hair is found on it. But that's not proof of murder. The hair could have come off when she brushed against him, say when they were sitting in the Lincoln parked in the Skakel driveway. But why did Michael deny the jeans were his?

The key, he believed, was the name Matthai of the laundry mark. What could that be?

Not long afterward, Frank discovered a directory with phone numbers and addresses with every kind of name east and west of the Mississippi. From the directory, he obtained a list of ninety-nine Matthais. He started calling. Every night, he would take the list home with him and call.

"This is Frank Garr," he would begin. "I am calling from the Greenwich Police Department. Please bear with me." And he would explain what he was looking for.

And then two months after he had begun, he found a Betty Matthai of Baltimore. Betty Matthai said she had a thirty-four-year-old son, Dr. William [Bill] Matthai, a cardiologist at Cooper Hospital in Camden, New Jersey, and two nephews, Bruce and Chris Matthai. All had attended Camp Pasquaney in Bristol, New Hampshire. Bill, she said, probably wore size 36–30 jeans.

Frank called Dr. William Matthai. Yes, he told Frank, he had gone to

Camp Pasquaney in 1975, at age sixteen. Yes, he did own Wrangler dungarees, size 36–30.

"Crazy question," said Frank. "Did you ever hear of a kid named Michael Skakel?"

"Oh, that nut?" Matthai answered.

Frank's heart began pounding. He didn't want Matthai to think he was jumping for joy, but he had to fight to keep himself under control. Matthai remembered Michael. Michael hadn't wanted to come to camp and had been his usual disruptive self. Michael had gotten wet and Matthai had given Michael his jeans.

There it was. There was the lie. The jeans were Michael's. He had lied about it. Why?

Frank called the camp and reached its director, John Gemmill, who had been there in 1975. There had been eighty-five campers that year. Michael was among them. Gemmill even found Michael's picture in the 1975 camp yearbook.

So what did it all mean, linking the dungarees to Michael? As far as evidence, it meant nothing, as the jeans had been lost. The stains on them had been determined not to be blood. And Martha's blonde hair could have come off at another point earlier in the evening.

But to Frank, the key was Michael's lie.

"For me it was a gut thing. That's when I knew Michael was our guy."

# 11

PART TWO / CHAPTER ELEVEN

# In Love with the Poly

GREENWICH, CONNECTICUT
1991–1995

And yet the case against Michael went nowhere. The reason was Frank's partner from the state's attorney's office, Jack Solomon. Though in theory they were equal, Solomon was running the show.

Of medium height, stocky, and gray-haired, Solomon was a legend in Connecticut law enforcement. He had begun as a state trooper and was considered a "a detective's detective." But he became Frank's nemesis. Approaching sixty, he had worked under Fairfield County State's Attorney Donald Browne for twenty-five years and was so relied upon by Browne that he virtually ran the office.

He told anyone who would listen that Browne was his hero—"the man I admire more than any other in the world," the only prosecutor he knew who'd never lost a murder case.

Solomon talked nonstop and seemed in perpetual motion, which was why he later had the nickname "Richochet Rabbit." He had two speeds, Frank liked to say of him, fast and faster. "Yeah, yeah, yeah," was how he spoke. All jokes and chit-chat. When he walked, Frank had to run to keep pace with him.

Although the Greenwich Police Department had a no-smoking rule, Frank found himself bringing in ashtrays for Solomon, who tore through three and a half packs a day. When people became angry at this, Frank explained to them, "If I didn't let that man smoke he'd spiral right up through the ceiling."

Driving up to Ken Littleton's alma mater, Williams College, Solomon popped a button on his pants during one of his rants. They had to pull off the highway to get a needle and thread to sew the button back on because the pants were falling off him.

Solomon seemed to know everyone and was forever discussing his high-profile cases. He told a story about sitting down to Thanksgiving dinner with twenty people around the table when the phone rang. It was the state's attorney's office in Bridgeport.

"We have a murder," they told him. He had to go, he told his wife and guests. The job came first. He was away for two days. He had a twinkle in his eye as he related the story.

As Frank came to know him, he realized that Solomon viewed himself as better than the local cops. He could be unforgiving of them for the slightest perceived infraction. For Solomon, there were no extenuating circumstances. A local cop might go into the wrong restaurant or bar, say, one that New York City mob boss Joe Bonanno had visited thirty years before.

Solomon would then say of the cop, "The guy's mobbed up. He's dirty," and give his little laugh, "Heh, heh, heh," which meant he knew things no one else did.

"And he always had an angle," said Frank. "Even with me. He never considered me an equal. Not a boob but never an equal."

One year Solomon invited Frank to his house for a Christmas party. "Mr. Browne is coming," he said. "I'm a little nervous. He's never been to my house, and I've got an uncle who drinks."

Frank was surprised. No, shocked. Hell, if Browne had come to Frank's house and seen his uncles, they'd all be drunk. But so what? That was no reflection on him.

And this was the first time in twenty-five years Browne was coming to Solomon's house for dinner? The way Jack talked, it was as though they went to dinner three times a week. Frank began to wonder whether Solomon had been making up these stories about his closeness with Browne to impress him.

Unlike Frank, Solomon had been on the Moxley case from the beginning. Like Frank, he was consumed by it.

Unlike Frank, he discounted Tommy and Michael as suspects. Tommy had supposedly passed his polygraph. Michael had never taken one.

Littleton, however, had failed his. "In twenty years, I've never had a bad call from the poly," Solomon would say to Frank.

Solomon was intrigued by Littleton's phone call from Florida to David Moxley, in which he had referred to "our mutual tragedy."

"To me," said Frank, "that phrase meant that both their lives—Littleton's and David Moxley's—had been destroyed because of Martha's murder. Jack saw it as Littleton's confession."

Not only did Solomon believe Littleton had murdered Martha. He also considered Littleton a serial killer and tried to link him to the murders of teenage girls in Williamstown, Massachusetts; Saratoga Springs, New York; Newport, New Hampshire; and Stowe, White River, and Manchester, Vermont—all of which were towns Littleton had visited.

Solomon compiled a forty-three-page, single-spaced, typewritten profile, comparing Littleton's movements up and down the East Coast from 1976 through the fall of 1991 with the murders of those teenage victims. He put his report into a three-ring, black spiral notebook and carried it with him everywhere.

Early in the investigation, before Frank came on board, Solomon had accused Lunney and Carroll of "tunnel vision" when it came to Tommy. Solomon said they had locked in on him and refused to consider anyone else. But to Frank, Solomon had tunnel vision when it came to Littleton. Solomon downplayed all the calls they received about Michael. When Andrea Shakespeare told them Michael had not gone to the Terriens', Solomon's response was, "She's got her times mixed up. She's confused." When Frank discovered the dungarees, Solomon insisted that on the night of the murder Littleton, not Michael, had worn them. His theory was that because Littleton had been sleeping in Rushton's room, he had found the pants in the closet and worn them when he killed Martha.

"Jack," Frank said, "those pants are size 36–30. Littleton couldn't get a leg into those pants."

"Well, I wear my pants short and high," Solomon answered. Then, he'd tug at his pants to illustrate.

"Jack," Frank would say, "answer me one question and I'll go along with it. Why did Littleton kill her?"

"He was drinking. His horns came out," Jack replied. Then placing his hands by his ears, he imitated a bull in heat and pranced around the room, mimicking Littleton following Martha home.

Or he'd say, "The Skakel kids must have told Kenny something about Martha to make him think he could score with her."

Then, Frank said, "Solomon would start in again about Littleton's flunking the polygraph."

At one point, Littleton accused the police of being willing to plant his fingerprints on the golf club shaft and theorized that a hunter in the woods might trip over it. Hearing this, Solomon contacted the Skakels and arranged for tracking dogs to sniff out hundreds of acres of hunting area on their Windham estate. He selected Windham because Littleton had driven the Skakel kids there the day after the murder. "Although there was no evidence, Jack said he believed Littleton had carried the club and thrown it into the woods," Frank said.

"Jack hears mutual tragedy and sees a confession. He hears a hunter in the woods and runs to Windham. It sounds good until you realize he's got an ego the size of a house and is so obsessed, so devoured by this case you can't trust anything he says."

So certain was Solomon that Littleton had murdered Martha that he attempted a ruse. He persuaded the Skakels to allow him and Frank to photograph the interior and exterior of the Skakel house on Otter Rock Drive. Then, he and Frank—who knew nothing of Solomon's plan—drove over to Belle Haven.

As Frank began photographing, Solomon disappeared. "The next thing I see Jack is sitting out on the porch with the Skakels' attorneys,

Margolis and Sheridan. Now, I know Jack is a bullshitter. He talks to everyone. So I don't think anything of it. I continue doing what I thought we were down there to do."

Driving back to headquarters, Frank asked Solomon what he had been doing with Margolis and Sheridan. Solomon answered that he had shown them his folder on Littleton—his three-ring, black spiral book.

Frank thought Solomon was joking, as he often did. "C'mon, Jack," he said. "Knock it off."

"No, I'm serious," Solomon answered. "I told them we are after Littleton. I want them to know we are not looking at Tommy or Michael. See, I want a shot at talking to Tommy to see what he can tell us about Littleton."

" 'Jack,' I said, 'how can you tell them something like that?' Hell, I wasn't ready to close the book on anybody. And I'm increasingly worried about Michael. I said, 'Jack, let me tell you one other thing. Even if you get a confession from Littleton, on videotape, saying, "Yes, I killed Martha Moxley." And even if you played it when you brought Littleton to court, convicted him, and sent him to jail, Margolis will never let you talk to Tommy.' "

Solomon also began cultivating Littleton's recently divorced wife, Mary Baker.

"What can I say about Jack Solomon?" Mary wrote to me years later. "Jack was charismatic when I met him. I had to avoid my original characterization of him—that he reminded me of John Wayne. He had the gift of seeming strong, trustworthy and physically powerful, straightforward and blunt like JW, but wearing a brown polyester suit with a bad tie instead of cowboy duds.

"He entertained my children, then seven and four, like a grandfather would. Taking us out to dinner at Swiss Chalet and offering them hats with CT [Connecticut] Police on them. He then realized he couldn't give them the hats as their biological father might ask questions if he ever saw the hats.

"He treated me as one would a daughter. On our two road trips, he was very amusing, [told] anecdotes about being lost around the Statue of

Liberty, asking bums for directions in Boston when he got lost, stories of airplane flights with prisoners where the flights ended with crashes. . . . He offered me protection from Ken and did this in a paternal fashion. He offered to send me his wife's hand-me-downs when he realized I was not well-off. He appeared to be what his credentials said, an Inspector for the State of Connecticut Police and a very nice human being."

What Solomon wanted was Mary's help in trapping her ex-husband. And Mary agreed. She trusted cops. And she had her own history. When she was thirteen, she told him, her mother had disappeared. Six months later her body was discovered. She'd been murdered.

"Do you think Kenny did it?" was the first thing Solomon asked her.

I could only imagine what Mary must have thought of him at that moment. How could Littleton have killed her mother when he was just a boy himself, lived 1,000 miles away in Massachusetts, and didn't know her?

What about Martha Moxley's murder? Solomon asked her. What about his phone call to David Moxley?

Mary told him she had first heard Ken talk about Martha's murder in 1983 in Florida when he had been drinking. She said he had wanted to go under sodium Pentothal because he felt the police had tried to frame him. Ken had called David Moxley, she said, after fighting at a bar. At the time of the call, Ken had been hallucinating. He had taken to phoning the FBI and former U.S. Attorney General Edwin Meese.

By 1984, she and Ken were fighting about money and she refused him access to her bank account. The following year he suffered a breakdown and ended up in Charles River Hospital in Mt. Auburn, Massachusetts. Upon his discharge, the only job he found was with a landscaper, who turned out to be a drug dealer. Unknowingly, Ken had been transporting drugs in his boss's truck.

In 1989, he and Mary separated. A year later, they were divorced and he returned to Boston and entered the McClean's mental institution. Between his binges and bouts of depression, he talked of reconciling.

Hearing this, Solomon sprung his trap. His plan was to bring Mary to Boston under the guise of a reconciliation, then trick Littleton into a confession. He rented Mary a motel room and bugged it, then listened in from an adjoining room.

With Browne's backing, Solomon applied for a wiretap order. He had to ensure that the judge who signed the order kept it sealed so that the operation would not become public. Then, he obtained technical support from the Boston Police Department to plant the wire and connect it to the next room.

Though skeptical, Frank was impressed enough with Solomon's investigative skills that he went along. "If it turned out Jack was right and Littleton said something incriminating, great. We'd solved the case. But I knew it wouldn't happen."

By February 1992, all was ready. Solomon—with Frank in tow, powerless to stop the equivalent of a runaway locomotive—drove up to Boston to meet Mary, who had arrived from Ottawa. Solomon had rented her a room at a Howard Johnson motel. He and Frank moved in next door.

When Littleton arrived, Mary said that before she could consider reconciling with him, she had to know the truth about Martha Moxley. She said that in 1984 while driving from New York through Connecticut he had been hallucinating and confessed to murdering Martha. He had even admitted stabbing her through the neck with the golf club shaft, she told him.

"I never knew you were in a blackout before," she told him in remarks sculpted by Solomon. "That . . . you were there when Martha Moxley died. And I mean all the other things you've never told me, things that would solve the case. . . . Like uh, 'Oh God, she wouldn't die. I had to stab her through the neck.' . . . I mean you convinced me that you did it." It was all a lie. Littleton had never said any such thing.

Solomon and Frank listened from the next room, waiting for Littleton to utter the magic words—his confession that he had killed her. Instead, Littleton replied, "I said that? No. I didn't do it. I wasn't anywhere near the murder site."

At Michael's trial years later, Browne's successor, Fairfield County

State's Attorney Jonathan Benedict, described Solomon's plan as "the most bizarre piece of investigative work I have ever seen."

"It was nuts. The whole thing was nuts," said Frank. "But Jack wouldn't quit."

Ten months later, Solomon came up with another plan. On December 7, 1992, he called Frank at home. "He says he's watching television, one of those shows like *48 Hours*, and he sees this psychiatrist—a Dr. Kathy Morrall from Denver, who works in the prison system one-on-one with inmates.

" 'This woman, this Kathy,' Jack says, 'she sounds fantastic. I think we should look into something like this for Littleton.' "

So Frank called her. She sent him her curriculum vitae. He arranged for her to fly from Colorado to New York. "She said she would need two days with Littleton. I book her into a hotel in Manhattan and make arrangements for her to come to Greenwich."

At Solomon's direction, Frank also persuaded Littleton to return to Connecticut for further testing. "I had to schmooze him," he said.

Sounding like Keegan fifteen years before, he told Littleton that if wanted to clear himself, this was the only way. "I said I didn't know what went wrong with the early polygraph but let's clear it up now and you are out of it. If you want the truth, if you want to get the monkey off your back, this is the only way."

Still unsuspecting of Mary, Littleton asked if she could be there. "That won't be a problem," Frank told him.

Littleton was still afraid of the Connecticut State Police, who had conducted his first polygraph, so Frank assured him they would choose a private, neutral polygrapher.

Littleton asked whether he should have a lawyer. Sounding like a cop on *NYPD Blue*, Frank said, "You certainly have a right to one but if you want this over, you won't clear it up because he won't let you do it."

Did Frank have qualms about bringing him in again? I asked him. "No, I was simply doing my job. I didn't think Kenny did it, but if he did, I was open to it. Unlike Jack, I wasn't locked in. My ego wasn't on the line. If it turned out to be him, so be it. I didn't care who it was so long as we got him. And, no, I did not feel I was taking advantage of him by persuading him to be tested without a lawyer. I would do anything I had to do within the parameters of the law to get the job done. That's the business I'm in."

Frank arranged for Mary to fly in from Ontario. Littleton still did not realize the meeting in Boston had been a trick.

The first question was what testing method to use—sodium Pentothal, hypnotism, or a polygraph. "I don't have to tell you Jack wanted the polygraph," said Frank.

Morrall knew a psychiatrist in New York City, a Dr. Stanley Portnow, who practiced hypnotism. Portnow agreed to see them in his office after hours.

They drove down from Greenwich and waited for the doctor in a small, dark anteroom. Portnow appeared, saying he first wanted to see Littleton alone. Then, he called in Morrall.

A few minutes later, she returned. There was a problem. Littleton wasn't going through with the hypnosis. "Dr. Portnow," she said, "is a little uncomfortable. He feels Ken should not do this without legal representation."

Solomon took it calmly. Although Frank had regarded the hypnotism skeptically, he became furious at Portnow.

"I went nuts. He feels Ken should not do this without legal representation? Who is he to feel? I don't care what he feels. All I want him to do is his job. If Kenny wants to take the test, who is this Portnow to say no? Why did he bring us here then? I'm so angry, I tell Solomon I want to charge him with interfering with an investigation.

"A couple of weeks later, he has the nerve to send us a bill for $500. I tore it up. We never heard from him again."

But now Littleton was spooked. "We have gotten Kenny a little hincky," Frank remembered. "He's saying, 'Do I need an attorney?' "

Frank tried to soothe him. "I want to get him back to Greenwich and relax him. I'm saying, 'If you get an attorney, you'll never clear this up because he won't let you do it. We all know you didn't do it, but you can't clear this up if you have a lawyer. He won't let you take the polygraph."

That, Frank realized, was the reason Solomon had been so calm when Portnow refused to go through with the hypnotism. "Jack didn't care about it. He only cared about the polygraph. This Kathy was just the opening to soften Kenny up for the real deal."

By the next day, Littleton had calmed down enough to allow Morrall to interview him, without an attorney. The interview took place in the Greenwich police library. It lasted all day.

As he and Solomon listened from another office, Morrall told Littleton she was aware of the burden he was carrying. She wanted to help him recall things. She then took Littleton through his conversation with Mary in the Howard Johnson motel. Still not realizing Mary had lied to him and believing he had confessed to murdering Martha, Littleton repeated her lie to Morrall.

With that, plans were made to conduct the polygraph the following day. Here, however, things became tricky. Littleton had resisted coming to Connecticut because he distrusted the state police, who had polygraphed him fifteen years before. So Frank had found his own expert, Robert Brisentine, who had trained the state police.

"I wanted to be sure," said Frank. "I didn't want anyone saying Ken flunked the polygraph because he was nervous or afraid of the state police. No matter how it comes out, I don't want any doubt."

Brisentine arrived at Greenwich police headquarters late on the night of December 14, 1992. The following morning Littleton signed a release saying he was voluntarily taking the lie detector test.

Brisentine spent eight hours with Littleton in the police library preparing him for the polygraph, asking him about himself, relaxing him. At 12:42 the following afternoon, Brisentine felt Littleton was ready. Littleton was asked five questions.

"Did you have any quarrel with Martha Moxley on October 30, 1975?" was the first question.

Littleton answered, "No."

"Did you have a golf club in your possession on October 30, 1975?"

"No," Littleton answered again.

"Regarding that matter pertaining to Martha Moxley, do you intend to answer truthfully to each question about that?"

"Yes," Littleton answered.

"Did you cause those injuries to Martha Moxley on October 30, 1975?"

"No," he answered for a third time.

"Did you have a golf club in your hand on October 30, 1975?"

"No," Littleton repeated.

Brisentine emerged from the library and approached Frank.

"Frank," Brisentine said, "that guy killed that girl. I polygraphed three convicts in jail that confessed to crimes and their polygraphs were not as good as this guy's."

Frank couldn't believe it. "I just didn't think he did it. But I know I am stuck with it now. I know I can never turn Jack around on any other point after this. I am the one who found Brisentine. It was my guy who said he did it. Me, I just didn't believe Kenny did it. I see a sick, tortured individual who couldn't take a polygraph if his life depended on it. And it did. He had literally been trying to show he did not commit this crime. I mean, why is he here? He doesn't have to be. He is trying to show us he did not do it."

Two days later, it all came to a head. With Brisentine gone, a meeting was arranged in the police library with Littleton and Mary to discuss why Littleton had again failed the polygraph. What Solomon needed was Littleton's confession. Tortured as he was, Littleton wouldn't confess.

Before they entered the library, Solomon told Frank he was going in for the kill. "He did it," said Solomon. "I am going to hit him with it."

"He's not going to confess, Jack," Frank warned. "If you do this, you'll close the door on him. You may want to talk to him again."

They entered the library. Frank began chatting with Mary while eyeing Solomon. "We are standing there. I can see it coming."

Jack sat down next to Kenny, who at this point was calm, said Frank.

"The next thing I know Jack leans over him, confidential-like. Jack's father-figure routine."

"Listen, Ken," Solomon began.

He's going to do it, Frank thought to himself. And it's not going to work. He tried to interrupt, to stop him but he couldn't get a word in.

"Ken," Solomon began, "before you go, remember, if you did it—I am not saying you did but the polygraph says you're lying and I never had a bad call on a polygraph, Ken. Ken, you did it. I know you did it. Give it up. You have been living with this for seventeen years. It's time to be a man, Ken, do the right thing."

Littleton looked up at Solomon before he spoke.

"So this is what this is all about. This is why you brought me here. It was the same thing in 1976. To accuse me. To try and make me say I did something I didn't do."

As he spoke, he stood up. He was shouting. "This is all you wanted to get me here for. I knew this was all you wanted. I'm getting out of here."

The police report of December 17, 1992, reads as follows: "Upon Littleton's request, he was transported to the Stamford railroad station for his return to Boston, Massachusetts. Miss Baker was subsequently transported to John F. Kennedy Airport for her return to Canada."

As for Jack, said Frank, "That was the end of the line for him and Ken Littleton. It was also the end of Solomon in the Moxley investigation. When Littleton didn't crack, Jack lost all interest, even though his beloved polygraph suggested he did commit the crime. A few days later, Jack began taking his equipment back to the state's attorney's office in Bridgeport. His heart was out of it."

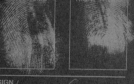

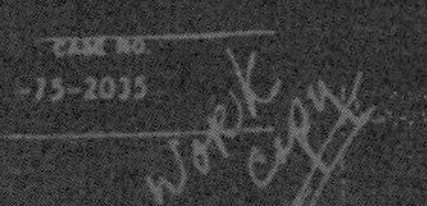

# PART III

ESIDE

# 12

PART THREE / CHAPTER TWELVE

# The Caller

1992–1995

Around this time, I received a visit at *New York Newsday* from two men. The first was stocky and dark-haired in his late forties. He introduced himself as Jim Murphy, a retired FBI agent who headed a Long Island–based private security firm, Sutton Associates. He explained that he had been hired by Rushton Skakel as a private investigator "to clear the family name."

The second was the Skakels' attorney Tom Sheridan. He was white-haired and heavyset, in his late sixties, I guessed. While he moved in the Skakels' social circles and had made a pot of money in real estate, he and his family were Al Smith Democrats, and he was comfortable among society's lower strata. His father had had a successful law practice in New York and one of his associates was Burton Turkis, who had prosecuted high-level Brooklyn mobsters known as Murder Incorporated. It was Sheridan who had hired Murphy for the Skakels.

Both said they had sought me out because the Skakels felt my article in the *Greenwich Time* and *Stamford Advocate* the year before had been

***With Frank at the Lakeside Diner, our favorite haunt.***

fair. They had been upset by statements from the Greenwich police and State's Attorney Browne that they had had refused to cooperate with the investigation. My article made clear that Rushton had cooperated—at least during the first few months of the investigation.

Murphy and Sheridan then explained what they wanted. They asked me to help them obtain the Greenwich police file. Although it was now a public document due to our Freedom of Information suit, the police were refusing to give them a copy.

"You can have mine," I said without hesitation. "Make a duplicate and return it to me."

They seemed surprised at how easily their mission had been accomplished. But I had no reason to keep the file from them. It was a public document. They were entitled to it, no matter whose side they were on.

Sheridan then explained that he had hired Murphy after he had met with Jack Solomon. Unlike Frank, I knew nothing then about Solomon's theory of Littleton as a serial killer or of Solomon's bizarre meeting with Sheridan and Margolis at the Skakel home to seek their help in pursuing him.

Nor was I aware of Solomon's disagreements with Frank, whom I barely knew. Frank and I weren't yet on the same track, though we were heading in the same direction.

"Solomon said he had a lot on Littleton," Sheridan said. "He said he had something going with Littleton's wife, that he thought Littleton had disposed of the golf club handle in Windham, and that they were close to indicting him."

I was stunned to hear this. Littleton had disposed of the golf club at the Skakel's home in Windham? He was close to being indicted? Sheridan had to be making this up, I thought, or at least exaggerating.

Murphy said that one of his employees—a six-foot-seven-inch former New York City police lieutenant named Willis Krebs—had recently interviewed Littleton's ex-wife and former girlfriends, seeking to link him to the murders of four teenage girls on the East Coast. That was precisely what Hale in Detroit had told me the Connecticut authorities needed to do to solve the Moxley murder—interview the suspects' wives and ex-girlfriends. Of course, Hale hadn't been referring to Littleton, but to Tommy. And Murphy and Sheridan weren't working for the state of Connecticut, but for the Skakels.

I remained skeptical. Littleton had no motive. And why would he hide the golf club handle with Anne Skakel's name on it? What Sheridan and Murphy were saying about him made no sense.

"Let me ask you something," I said to Murphy. "What if, after your investigation, you conclude Littleton did not kill Martha?"

This time it was Murphy who did not hesitate. "Before I agreed to take the case," he answered, "Rushton Skakel assured me I could pursue the investigation wherever it led."

"What if your investigation brings you back to the Skakels?" I persisted.

"I was assured," Murphy answered, "that if any Skakel committed this murder—and Rushton Skakel never for a moment believed any of his children did—the family would publicly acknowledge the crime and seek to provide him with medical help.

"I felt Rushton Skakel was an honorable man," Murphy continued. "I felt he was acting for the right reasons. I felt he was convinced that none of his children had anything to do with the murder and needed someone to demonstrate this to the public."

Murphy added that he would keep me abreast of his investigation and suggested that I might want to write something about it. I wondered whether this was the real reason he and Sheridan had sought me out.

"Let's see what you turn up," I said.

A year later, a story about his investigation appeared in the *Daily News* (by Joanna Malloy, July 7, 1993). "NEW EYE ON TEEN DEATHS," it was headlined, and under it, "Connecticut probers seek link in girls' unsolved killings."

The story began by saying that Connecticut law enforcement authorities were seeking to link Martha's death with at least five other unsolved homicides and disappearances. It added that Murphy and Krebs "have learned that the unsolved killings of four other girls, and the disappearance of a fifth, in Maine, Massachusetts, and Florida, occurred when Littleton was living in those areas."

It concluded with Murphy saying his mandate was to determine whether anyone in the Skakel family had knowledge of Martha's death. "We were told that wherever the chips may fall, they want to know the truth. The Skakel family recognizes Mrs. Moxley's pain and have instructed that any information that develops or contributes to the solution of the homicide is to be immediately shared with Connecticut authorities."

Short as the story was, I saw it as a Skakel public relations ploy. They had taken their own hypothesis about Littleton and put it onto Connecticut law enforcement authorities. Murphy's quote from the Skakel family about recognizing Mrs. Moxley's pain depicted, the Skakels as compassionate.

But Murphy's claim that the Skakels would share information he had developed with Connecticut authorities would return to haunt him.

•

Murphy and I met numerous times over the next two years. In all our meetings I never brought up the *Daily News* article, which I assumed he had given them. I viewed him as the quintessential FBI man—polite, polished, professional—and manipulative.

Over the years, however, I came to see another dimension to him. While acknowledging that the Skakels had compensated him well (the figure I heard was just south of $1 million), Murphy said he viewed this investigation, like all others, as involving more than money. I subsequently learned he had lost a son to cancer and was a lay deacon in the Roman Catholic church. As much as the Skakels had paid him, he understood money's limitations.

And then, two years after we met, I received a phone call. The caller said he had information about Murphy's investigation. He said that if I could be patient, it would prove worth my while.

I assured him I could be. What choice did I have? The reopened investigation had been under way for three years. Except for the story in the *Daily News* that I felt Murphy had planted, I had heard no more of Littleton, either as Martha's murderer or as a serial killer. No one had been arrested. As far as I could tell, the case was going nowhere.

Early in 1995, the caller contacted me again. He began by saying that Murphy had sought an analysis by two former FBI colleagues who had run the Bureau's Behavioral Science lab in Washington. The two, Kenneth Baker and Roger DePew, had studied hundreds of serial killers, including the sociopath of the film *The Silence of the Lambs*. Now retired, they had formed their own consulting company, known as the Academy Group of Manassas, Virginia.

The Academy Group, the caller said, had noted Martha's lack of defense wounds on her arms and hands and the fact that no screams were heard. This indicated, he said, that Martha did not expect the attack and knew her attacker.

Over the phone, I said, "You're saying Martha knew her killer."

"Martha didn't know Littleton," I heard myself saying out loud. Littleton had moved into the Skakel house the night of the murder. He had never spoken to her or even seen her before that night.

"That's what it would look like," replied the caller.

But he was not finished. As part of the investigation, he continued, Murphy's investigator Krebs had interviewed Tommy and Michael. Tommy's interview had occurred in Margolis's office. Margolis had been there with another Murphy employee and former FBI colleague, Richard McCarthy, who was a friend of Sheridan. It was through McCarthy that Sheridan had found Murphy.

Krebs, said the caller, had begun his questioning of Tommy with a warning: Henry Lee, the state's renowned forensic pathologist, was conducting tests to determine whether the killer had left DNA traces. With that, Tommy confided something he had never told the Greenwich police.

In 1975 at age seventeen, Tommy told the Greenwich police he had last seen Martha at 9:30 P.M. outside his house when he went inside to write a school report on Abraham Lincoln—a report no teacher had assigned. Now, on October 7, 1993, at age thirty-six and the father of two young children, Tommy told Krebs he had returned outside, where Martha waited for him. He said he and Martha had spent the next twenty minutes together before he returned home. As he had told the Greenwich police in 1975, Tommy maintained Martha was alive when they parted. The last he saw of her, he said, was walking across his lawn toward her house. Only now he said it was just before 10:00 P.M.

As Tommy told this story, he began to cry. The caller said that Krebs felt he was on the verge of a breakthrough, perhaps a confession. But McCarthy interrupted, asking if Tommy wanted to collect himself. Margolis used the break to halt the interview.

I could not believe what I was hearing. This was the break all of us connected to the case had been waiting for. Even without a confession, those twenty minutes placed him with Martha just minutes before the time the police believed she had been murdered.

But the caller was not finished. He said Krebs had also interviewed Michael. The interview had occurred at Sheridan's home in Windham on August 4, 1992. Krebs had given Michael the same warning that he had given Tommy about Henry Lee and the DNA. It was then that Michael told the most bizarre story Krebs had ever heard.

In 1975, at age fifteen, Michael told Greenwich police he had returned from his cousin Jimmy Terrien's at 11:00 P.M. and gone to straight to bed. Now in 1992 at age thirty-five, he told Krebs that around midnight he went to Martha's house and climbed a tree outside her window.

"Martha, Martha," he said he yelled, but there was no answer. He threw stones at the window but she did not appear. He then masturbated to orgasm in the tree.

When he climbed down, he stopped under a streetlight. He said he could feel someone's presence in the very place her body would be discovered the next day. He yelled into the darkness, threw something, then ran back to his house. Everyone was asleep. All doors were locked so he climbed in through a window and went to bed.

•

Stunning as all this was, I wasn't ready to publish the story. First, I needed corroboration. The word of a man on the phone, who refused to allow me to use his name, was not enough. I called Murphy, who for reasons I only later understood, refused to speak to me. Then, I called Sheridan.

He invited me to lunch at the New York Athletic Club overlooking Central Park, with its full-length gymnasium, basketball and squash courts, swimming pool, and upstairs bedrooms for men on the lam from their wives.

I began by saying I was aware of Tommy's and Michael's new stories. Seated across from me, Sheridan said nothing. His silence was my confirmation.

Michael's account did not seem to concern him. Bizarre as it was, he agreed that if Martha had been murdered at 10:00 P.M., whatever Michael had done in the tree by her window and whether or not he had passed the murder scene was irrelevant.

But Tommy's situation was different. "Why would he place himself with Martha at precisely the time she had been murdered?" I asked him.

"Oh," he said, "So you know about the mutual masturbation."

"The what?" I wanted to shout. The what? Poor Sheridan. He had just blurted out something I hadn't known. The caller had merely said Tommy and Martha spent another twenty minutes together. Did Sheridan mean that during those twenty minutes they had engaged in mutual masturbation?

Not wanting to reveal my ignorance, I said as nonchalantly as I could, "Okay, let's say Tommy is telling the truth—that Martha was alive when he left her. Why didn't he tell this to the police? Why did he make up the story about the Abraham Lincoln report?"

"He was afraid of his father," Sheridan answered. "Old man Skakel was a nut about sex," he said, describing how Rushton had thrashed Michael after catching him reading *Playboy* magazines.

"He would have come down on his children very hard if they had anything to do with sex. And that's why Michael didn't tell the police about what he had done in the tree."

I didn't buy it. Fear of their father about sex was the reason both Tommy and Michael had lied to the police about their whereabouts on the night of a murder? If that were true, why couldn't each have told the truth and just omitted the masturbation? Why couldn't Tommy have told the police he last saw Martha shortly before 10:00 without revealing the sex? Why did he make up the Abraham Lincoln report?

Why couldn't Michael have said that after arriving home from the Terriens', he had gone outside around midnight, climbed the tree, and thrown stones at Martha's window, leaving it at that?

And why had Tommy broken down before Krebs? That couldn't have been because of his concerns about sex. He was a man then. He was thirty-six years old.

No, a more likely reason, I felt, was that both Tommy and Michael were using their masturbation stories to explain away their DNA. That could only mean that one or both was involved in Martha's murder or in moving her body.

My caller had also promised to show me documents supporting all he had told me but said I'd have to wait a little longer. It had been thirteen years since I had started on the Moxley case. It had taken me two years to write the story, and seven years for the *Stamford Advocate* and *Greenwich Time* to run it. As far as I knew, the four subsequent years had produced nothing—no arrest, no indictment, and no new evidence.

I could wait a little longer. Because with what I had, I knew everything was going to change.

•

In July 1995, the caller came to my house. I remember it was a Saturday. Susan was out with the children. Jennifer, that three-and-a-half-pound baby, was now twelve and playing in a fast-pitch softball tournament. Mike, now ten, was playing Little League. Ordinarily, I would have been at their games. I was a baseball nut as a kid; now I was a baseball nut as a parent. But ever since the caller had approached me, the Moxley case had taken on a new urgency.

We sat in my living room. The caller opened a briefcase. The first document he showed me was the Academy Group report.

It began with a description of Belle Haven—"a small community comprised of large expensive estates owned by the very wealthy."

It described David Moxley as "a hard charger—very intense, ambitious and upwardly mobile in the world of business, a man destined to achieve success at the highest levels of New York City business circles."

Dorthy was "an unpretentious 'homebody' who loved to sew and cook"; Martha "very pretty with a well-developed body who wore bikini bathing suits" that were "somewhat more revealing than those worn by her female friends."

Then, the report got down to business. It noted the savagery of the murder and concluded that the killer had acted out of a "personal rage," perhaps because Martha had rejected him sexually.

Again, I found myself thinking that if this were true, it ruled out Littleton. He had moved into the Skakel house the night of the murder and didn't know Martha. Baker and DePew were all but exonerating him.

"The fact that the offender chose to confront the victim outside, on her driveway, provides several useful clues in understanding his approach, method and mindset," the report continued.

"It is apparent that he (1) knew the victim, (2) knew she would be coming home at around that time-frame and (3) knew she habitually walked up her driveway then across her lawn toward her front door. . . .

"The fact that the offender chose this outside location to make his initial contact with the victim indicates he was comfortable functioning in the neighborhood."

The report then described how Martha had run from the gravel driveway across her lawn after the first attack and how the attacker had overtaken her and knocked her to the ground, then struck her repeatedly with the golf club.

"The initial blows to the head were struck with the entire club and were done with full powerful swings. These repeated blows to the victim's head provide a clear indication of personalized rage again, indicating an acquaintance with the victim. Due to inexperience . . . his attack resulted in 'overkill' in that he struck the victim on the head 14 or 15 times."

Reading those lines, I had to put the report down. I took a deep breath. Perhaps because I now had a daughter nearly Martha's age, the force of the words hit me in a way they never had before. Yes, I knew Martha had been savagely beaten. But I had never before visualized what had actually occurred to her. Those full, powerful swings . . . repeated to Martha's head fourteen or fifteen times. That poor, poor girl. And Dorthy, who couldn't allow herself to ever think of this. Was it any wonder that she lived in torment?

Baker and DePew then described the personal traits of the murderer: "an explosive temper; a history of fighting; strong sibling rivalry tendencies; behavioral problems at school and at home; under the influence of alcohol and/or drugs.

"He may well have been viewed as the 'problem child' or 'black sheep' of the family. In all probability, he regularly fantasized about having sexual relations with the victim, and on the day of this crime may have consumed both alcohol and drugs as a means of building up his courage to seek a sexual encounter.

"His sexual fantasies regarding the victim were probably accompanied by viewing pornographic magazines and masturbation," it continued. "We believe he also would have practiced window-peeping in the immediate neighborhood. . . . Any window-peeping activities by this offender would have been in conjunction with his nocturnal tendencies in that he was very comfortable being out late at night and functioned well under the cover of darkness. He was an emotional 'loner' and would have spent solitary periods while out at night either pursuing his fantasies, window-peeping or brooding. . . ."

Experts though they were, I wondered how Baker and DePew could describe such specific character traits unless they had been told of them. Whether or not they realized it, they were describing not Tommy but Michael.

•

The caller said I could keep the Academy Group's report for the weekend to study but that I would have to return it. That meant he knew I would make a copy. He was in effect giving me permission to do so.

The caller then handed me two other documents. They were Murphy's Sutton Associates reports. I could take notes on them, he said, but I could not keep them. The first, in boldface captial letters, was headed TOMMY SKAKEL.

It began with Dr. Stanley Lesse's evaluation of him, based on testing in 1976 at New York City's Presbyterian Hospital's Division of Psychology. The Skakels had used the alias Thomas Butler to hide his identity. This secret exam appeared to belie Murphy's statement to me that Rushton had never for a moment believed any of his children had murdered Martha. Did that mean that Murphy lied? I didn't think so. Rather, he had probably given Rushton the benefit of the doubt.

Tommy claimed to Lesse that he had spoken with Martha for less than five minutes outside his house before she left him at 9:30. "Maybe it was two minutes, maybe more," Lesse quoted him as saying. "She asked whether I wanted to meet later . . . I told her I couldn't because I didn't have time and I had homework to do."

Tommy then described the homework to Lesse as consisting of "something about log cabins."

"We were studying the Puritans," Tommy told him. "I studied for about five minutes. Then I needed a book that was in the guest room. It was a book on Lincoln. . . . I was in the guest room for about five or ten minutes and I brought the book back to my room. After another five minutes I went down to Dad's room to watch television with Ken [Littleton] and then I went back up to sleep."

Murphy's report all but called Tommy a liar. "He has no recollection of what was said between him and Martha at the side of the house," it read, "but recites in specifically contrived detail right down to the log cabins, exactly what he was doing after she left—carefully accounting for his all his time in five-minute blocks.

"The one detail of his conversation with Martha Moxley which Tommy could recall is a blatant lie. There was no homework assignment and Tommy wasn't sending Martha away at that point anyway."

The report suggested Tommy also lied to his sister Julie after Dorthy had called the Skakels, looking for Martha. At 1:15 A.M., Julie had answered her call, then awakened Tommy.

"A very troubling point of conflict is when exactly Julie and Tommy were first made aware that Martha Moxley was missing," the document stated.

"I went upstairs and asked Tommy where she [Martha] was, when was the last time he had seen her," Julie was quoted as saying. Tommy answered that he'd seen Martha at 9:30 by the back door when he went to write his Abraham Lincoln report.

Years later, however, he admitted he had seen Martha after that. The fact that in 1975 he had told Julie 9:30 meant Tommy had lied even before Martha's body was discovered. Did he know then that Martha was dead? Or had he merely sought to hide his sexual involvement with her? But if Tommy didn't know she was dead, why wouldn't he have mentioned those extra twenty minutes to Julie when she came to his room at 1:15 A.M., omitting the mutual masturbation if he was so afraid of his father or embarrassed for Martha's mother?

Murphy's report agreed. "The first omissions can be written off as knee-jerk insecurity from a frightened teenager," it read. "However as the weeks, months and the years go by, his continued deception—even presumably under lie detecting tests—can no longer be viewed by any standard as the misjudgment of an innocent. . . . On at least two occasions he was able to fool the polygraph. He has fooled or fabricated the polygraph, the police, analysts and his own investigators."

If Tommy knew Martha was dead at 1:15, the report concluded, "It could mean only one thing. He was involved in her murder."

•

The caller wasn't finished. As I returned Tommy's report to him, he handed me another one. In boldface capital letters were the words MICHAEL SKAKEL.

"Some feel Michael and other suspects were not thoroughly examined at the time due to a somewhat premature conviction on the part of local authorities that Tommy Skakel was the murderer," it began.

"It was only later that the spotlight of serious scrutiny was placed directly on Michael. His arrest on drunk driving charges in 1978 probably did as much as anything to renew the police's interest."

I was brought up short by those last two sentences. Right away, I knew something wasn't right. The Greenwich police had never considered Michael a suspect. I knew that because I had read every page of its report on the case.

As late as 1991 when I had written my article, the Greenwich police had never placed Michael under "serious" or any other kind of scrutiny. Yes, the police file had noted his drunken-driving arrest in 1978. But no one—least of all Keegan, Lunney, Browne, or Solomon—had ever considered him a murder suspect. If the murder had occurred at 10:00 P.M., Keegan had told me in his office years before, Michael could not have returned from the Terriens' in time to have done it.

So how had Murphy's group come up with the information that Michael's 1978 arrest had "renewed" the police's interest in him? Sheridan had represented Michael in his drunken-driving arrest. He had also hired Murphy and Krebs. Who else but Sheridan would have suggested to them that Michael had been a suspect? I was beginning to suspect that Sheridan knew more about the Moxley murder than anyone realized.

My suspicions were confirmed a few pages later. Murphy's Sutton Associates report cited a memo, written on June 6, 1978, after Michael had been sent to Elan, following the drunken-driving incident.

"A Tom Sheridan memo of 6/6/78 stated that it was possible Michael could have committed the murder and doesn't know it and possibly someone else, i.e. Tommy, could have hidden the body and taken Michael to the Terrien's [sic] to provide him with an alibi."

How had Sheridan devised that scenario? Was he merely speculating? Or was there a basis in fact? Whatever the truth, Sheridan's memo indicated to me that he trusted neither Michael nor Tommy. Years later, when I asked Sheridan about the memo, he said he had no recollection of it.

The report then turned to motive.

"Coupled with our extensive knowledge of just how vehemently Michael and Tommy fought with each other, we at least believe Michael had more than ample reason to be extremely upset when Tommy was carrying on with Martha by the side of the house just before 9:30 P.M.

"She turned down an offer to hang out with Michael that night, in order to be with his older brother. It is hard to imagine how such a spectacle would not have made him both increasingly depressed and overtly hostile. . . ."

This puzzled me. How could Michael have seen Martha carrying on with Tommy at 9:30 if by then he had gone with his brothers to the Terriens'? As far as I knew, no one—least of all the police—had doubted that Michael had made this trip. I knew nothing then about Andrea Shakespeare's claim to Frank that Michael had never gone there.

Murphy's report, however, raised questions about whether or not Michael had gone to the Terriens'. "There is curious evidence suggesting this is not exactly what happened," the report said.

Rush Jr. initially stated to Lesse that Michael had never gone to the Terriens', it continued. Michael's brother John, who had gone, appeared to confirm this. In an interview under hypnosis on May 4, 1993, he could not place Michael in the car during the ride there.

"The interviewer on repeated occasions tried to get John to place Michael in the car and then at the Terriens'. John could not. He could only recall that someone else was in the car and that someone else was at the house. As much as the interviewer persisted, John could not identify that person as Michael."

But before I could begin to digest this, the report raised another possibility—that Michael had murdered Martha not at 10:00 P.M. but after he returned from the Terriens'.

"Many investigators believe the only way Michael could have committed or participated in the murder of Martha Moxley is if she was killed later than the 9:50/10:00 estimate," the report stated.

"There is a possibility that Martha may have actually gone home for an indefinite period of time after being with Tommy and then sneaked back out."

When we'd first met in 1992, I had asked Murphy what would happen if the investigation led back to the Skakels. Murphy said Rushton had assured him he would "back the search for the truth wherever it led and share the information with Connecticut authorities."

Now as the caller packed up his briefcase, I asked him what Rushton's reaction had been when Murphy presented him with these findings. Recalling Rushton's promise to Murphy, I asked what the Skakel family was now prepared to do.

The caller stopped what he was doing and stared at me. For a moment, our eyes met.

"You don't know?" he said. "After Murphy showed his report to Sheridan, Sheridan fired him."

13

PART THREE / CHAPTER THIRTEEN

# Sitting on a Bombshell

July–November 1995

I knew I had a bombshell.

Now I could write that Tommy and Michael both admitted lying to the police about their whereabouts the night of the murder.

The Sutton Associates report had returned the case to the Skakels' doorstep. Contrary to Rushton's promise to take responsibility and share whatever information Murphy had developed with Connecticut authorities, Rushton had fired him.

I didn't know who murdered Martha. I didn't know the truth about both Tommy's and Michael's activities the night of the murder. But I knew that once again, my story would change the direction of the case.

The question was where to publish it. Although Ken and I had mended our relationship, I did not want to deal with him again. Instead, I decided to write it for *New York Newsday*. Although the paper was losing money, it had grown to a circulation of 225,000 and had established itself in the city.

The year before, I had begun a new assignment. With Rudy Giuliani as mayor, vowing to get crime under control, I moved back downtown to police headquarters and began writing a column about the department, called One Police Plaza. Some of my columns had been picked up by the wire services and the other city papers. By running my Moxley story in *New York Newsday*, I felt the story would be picked up nationally, forcing Ken to run it in the *Stamford Advocate* and *Greenwich Time*. Then, the Connecticut authorities would follow up on my leads.

But here fate intervened. On July 20, 1995, *New York Newsday* folded. Despite its journalistic excellence, Times-Mirror's board in California viewed it as a financial drain. After the closing was announced, the company's stock price soared.

People at *Newsday* on Long Island had also disparaged *New York Newsday*. The rivalry between Tony and Don had become institutionalized.

*Newsday*'s plan was to maintain a scaled-back version of the New York paper by reducing circulation to 50,000, with Long Island's editors taking full control. But when I presented my Moxley story to them, they showed no interest. Even the fact that Murphy's company, Sutton Associates, was based in Jericho, Long Island, made no difference. Whether they were merely provincial or retaliating against *New York Newsday*, I didn't know.

For the second time, I was sitting atop a story that would break open the Moxley case, with nowhere to publish it.

In desperation, I called Joe Pisani, the editor under Ken at the *Greenwich Time*. Joe had urged Ken to publish my original Moxley story four years before. Now with his intercession, Ken agreed, albeit reluctantly, to consider publishing this one.

I broke it out into four parts, the first detailing Tommy's changed story, a later one detailing Michael's. But as Ken and I put it together, the same pattern emerged as a decade before. Ken would raise a question. I would answer it. A week later he asked the same thing. Only this time he couldn't offer Isenberg as his excuse.

The summer passed. I continued to meet with the caller as I refined the story. He never mentioned *New York Newsday*'s closing. Nor did I. I never let on to him that the story was in trouble.

But the frustration was getting to me. I found myself waking up in the middle of the night, plotting what to do next. I considered writing it for a magazine. Maybe *Esquire* or *New York* magazine. Who did I know there? An editor at *Newsday* gave me the name of someone at *The New Yorker*. I wrote him, offering a synopsis.

I could write the story as speculation, he said, though he advised against it. He wrote back, "I'm sorry I can't offer you much hope."

Of course, I couldn't tell Dorthy of my difficulties. I had told her I was on to something major, though I couldn't say what, other than to assure her it would alter the investigation. I didn't want to put her through any more than she had already suffered. Now I was suffering for her.

By the fall, relations between Ken and me had so deteriorated that in a memo to Pisani, he referred to me not by name but as "the reporter." That was when I decided to take the story back from him. I was convinced Ken would never run it. Joe pleaded with me, saying he could get it through. But I had had enough. It was now November. Ken had held the story three months. I wasn't prepared to wait another three years.

In the midst of this, Dorthy decided to throw a party. With absolutely nothing having been accomplished in twenty years, she announced that its purpose was to thank everyone who had worked on solving Martha's murder.

The place she selected was none other than the Belle Haven Club, where the Skakels had dined the night of the murder and where she had retained her membership.

Some fifty people attended. Keegan had long since departed for South Carolina but Lunney and Carroll came from the Greenwich Police Department. Browne and Solomon represented the state's attorney's office. Both were about to retire. Browne, however, had agreed to remain on solely to supervise the Moxley case.

Frank accompanied them. I barely knew him then, though that was about to change. He had recently left the Greenwich Police Department and joined Browne's office, replacing Solomon as the lead investigator on the Moxley case.

Dorthy gave a short speech. Knowing I was on to something, she glanced at me and asked if I would reveal my story. From the table where

Susan and I were sitting, I smiled back at her and shook my head. Not only couldn't I tell her what I had; I couldn't let on that I was growing desperate about where, or even if, the story would be published.

"Len knows something," she told the dinner guests and smiled at me. "He won't say what it is but I think he's going to solve the case."

•

I had one last call to make. I had one last chance. I called Don Forst. He had remained as editor of the scaled-back *New York Newsday*, although he was to leave shortly. Like Tony Insolia, he was familiar with the Moxley case. I had regaled him about it for years.

I explained my predicament—my problem with Ken and with the editors at Long Island *Newsday*.

"Okay," he said, "here's what we can do. We'll run it as a local story in what's left of *New York Newsday*."

The remnant of *New York Newsday* with its limited circulation was the last place I wanted to see the Moxley story. I worried that if it appeared in the back of the paper, neither the wire services nor the other city papers would pick it up and it would simply die. And furthermore, given the paper's reduced exposure, there was no guarantee the story would be picked up even if it were splashed across page one. But I had no choice.

The first of the four parts ran Sunday, November 26, 1995. Don played it on page three. "Suspicions of Murder Won't Die. A key figure changes his story in unsolved 1975 case," it was headlined.

"Twenty years ago this Halloween eve, the teenage daughter of a Manhattan executive was murdered as she left the Greenwich, Connecticut home of her neighbor, a 17-year-old nephew of Ethel Kennedy," it began.

"Martha Moxley, 15, was found the next day at the edge of her property, a few hundred yards away, beaten to death with a golf club, hit so hard that the club broke into three pieces. Her dungarees and underpants were pulled down around her knees, although there was no evidence of sexual assault.

"Thomas Skakel, Ethel Kennedy's nephew, was the last person known to see Martha alive and became the prime suspect after police found a golf club in the Skakel house they believed was the murder weapon."

I'd had to waste these three first paragraphs on background material because four years had passed since my last story and the public had forgotten the Moxley case. It was not until a few paragraphs later that I wrote the words that were to alter the direction of the investigation, returning it to the Skakels.

"Now Thomas has admitted to private investigators that he lied to Greenwich police in 1975 about his whereabouts the night of the murder.

"Then, he told police he last saw Martha outside his house at 9:30 P.M., then went inside to write a school report. Witnesses told police the two had been 'making out,' which witnesses described as including pushing each other playfully and flirtatiously.

"In 1993, married and the father of two, Thomas told the private investigators that shortly after 9:30 P.M., he returned outside to meet Martha, who he says waited for him. They remained together, he says, for an additional 20 minutes in a sexual encounter."

I was on edge all morning the Sunday the story appeared. Around noon Don called me at home. "Good news," he said. "The AP just moved the story on their national wire."

Then, Joe Pisani called from Greenwich to say that Ken wanted to run the story in the *Stamford Advocate* and *Greenwich Time* the following day. Because it had already appeared elsewhere, he was no longer afraid.

Michael's story ran on December 4, a week later. It was headlined "Brothers' Tales/Second Kennedy kin admits lying in murder case."

In this article I didn't have to waste time in starting the story with background material.

"A second relative of Ethel Kennedy now admits he lied to Greenwich police about his whereabouts the night a teenage neighbor was murdered as she left his Greenwich, Connecticut home," it began.

"In 1975, a few days after the murder of Martha Moxley on Halloween eve, Michael Skakel, then 15, told Greenwich police he had left the victim with his older brother, Thomas, in the Skakel driveway at about 9:15 P.M.

"Michael said he then drove with two of his other brothers and his cousin James Terrien, to Terrien's house a few miles away. Michael told police he returned home about 11 P.M. and went to sleep."

Then came the paragraph that would attract the attention of Detective Frank Garr.

"Now Michael has admitted to private investigators that he went to the Moxley house around 11:30 P.M. and, apparently believing Martha was alive, threw stones at a window to awaken her, sources said. He then passed what was later found to be the murder site, where he says he heard noises but saw nothing."

The story continued with this: "Greenwich police believed Martha was killed at approximately 9:50 to 10 P.M., based on the fact that two neighborhood dogs began barking uncontrollably at that time. If Martha's death occurred then, Michael's admission that he lied would have no significance."

*Newsday*'s editors had omitted Michael's masturbating in the tree, maintaining that it was not necessary to the story. As they put it in newspaper jargon: "It doesn't add anything to the story." I disagreed, to say the least, but at that point I had to live with it.

Besides, the stories were having their intended effect. Their publication in Greenwich meant that the Connecticut authorities would be forced to take notice.

As I said to Dorthy when I telephoned her, "Well, Mrs. Moxley, it looks like we're back in business."

# 14

PART THREE / CHAPTER FOURTEEN

# The Lion and the Crocodile

GREENWICH, CONNECTICUT
1995

Frank Garr picked up a copy of my story about Michael, took it with him as he drove to Bridgeport, walked into his office, and began reading.

"Holy shit," he said to himself.

He had never seen Murphy's report or even heard of it. What Tommy had said about spending an additional twenty minutes with Martha was surprising enough. But here was Michael throwing stones at Martha's window and then placing himself at the murder scene. The fucking murder scene.

Article in hand, Frank rushed into Donald Browne's office. This showed, he said, that he had been right all along about Michael. And, Frank said to himself, because he couldn't say it to Browne, Jack Solomon had as usual had his head up his butt chasing Littleton.

Not that Frank fully accepted Michael's new story. He didn't think Michael was telling the full truth. Michael threw stones at Martha's window? He just happened to be passing the murder scene? He heard noises, got scared, and ran home? No, there had to be more to it.

No, part of what Michael had told Murphy and Krebs was bullshit,

Frank believed. But which part? There was simply no reason to place himself at the murder scene. Michael had to have been afraid of something. Krebs, the six-foot-seven-inch ex–New York City police lieutenant, had probably said something that had scared the shit out of him.

Frank knew Krebs. At the beginning of their investigation, Murphy and Krebs had come up to Bridgeport, supposedly to share information about Littleton. Solomon had arranged the meeting and prodded Frank into it. Anything that had to do with Littleton had excited Jack.

"They're not going to share," Frank had warned him. "They just want to know what we have." And Frank had been right. Nothing had come of it.

"Interesting," Browne said as he looked over the article Frank had handed him. Interesting? Nothing more? Frank was surprised. No, he was stunned.

Granted, Browne was not a demonstrative man. He barely acknowledged attorneys who had worked for him for years. Still, Frank felt this was the break they had been waiting for. It was, in effect, Michael's unspoken confession. He was placing himself at the murder scene and all Browne said was "Interesting"?

It was then that Frank decided to call me. It's unusual for a detective to contact a reporter about a homicide investigation. Sure, detectives use the media when they want to release a description or a picture of a suspect. In the Moxley case four years before, Frank and Solomon had called a news conference to announce a reward and the establishment of a tip line. That was accepted procedure.

But a detective making a personal call to a reporter on a murder case is like handling dynamite. No formal rules or codes exist, but detectives know to avoid reporters. Should a detective become chummy with a reporter and his name be mentioned, even inadvertently, in a newspaper article or on television without his superior's approval, or should a detective divulge a word too many about a case and the indiscretion appear in the media, said detective could face holy hell or worse.

Still, Frank had no fear that approaching me was wrong or that anything untoward would result from it. He was calling to get information, not to give.

This wasn't the Greenwich Police Department where he had worked for twenty-seven years. This was the state's attorney's office where, with Solomon's having retired and Browne's lack of interest, Frank was the case's lone detective. It wasn't that Browne was a stupid man. Rather, Frank was the new kid on the block, saying things about the case that contradicted what Browne's confidant Jack Solomon had been telling him over the years. Browne's faith in Jack had caused him to ignore all else. Because no one thought the case was going anywhere, no one was following Frank's time. He had free reign. What he wanted to know from me was only one thing: Did I know more about Michael than I had written?

"Hey, Len, this is Frank Garr," he said when he reached me at my office at One Police Plaza in New York. "I saw your stories. How's about we get together?"

I love it when detectives you barely know address you familiarly. In Frank's case, we'd merely made small talk at Dorthy's party. That was the extent of our relationship. Unlike Solomon, who wanted nothing to do with me, Frank had at least been friendly.

He never came out and said on the phone what in the articles he wanted to discuss. He didn't have to. I was ahead of him on the case, or at least I thought I was. I was only too happy to bring him up to speed. This would give me the opportunity to get to know the case's chief source.

There was another reason Frank's call caused my heart to race. His call was vindication. Years before, Keegan and Lunney had given me a very hard time. Now here was their buddy Frank seeking my help.

And there was something else I realized. For Frank to call me meant his case was in trouble. How much trouble, I had no idea.

We agreed to meet for breakfast one Saturday morning at a place I selected, the Lakeside Diner in Stamford. It was just off the Meritt Parkway and convenient for both of us. As Frank drove over, he formulated a plan: to have no plan, to let our conversation move along and see how it developed. Either I would tell him what he wanted to know or I wouldn't, he thought. What did he have to lose?

The Lakeside was a tiny spot with a formica counter and tables overlooking a stream. We took a place by the window so we could look out and wouldn't be overheard. It was a gray day in December. Winter was approaching and parts of the water were beginning to freeze. Across the table, we sized each other up. Frank was around fifty, average height, stocky, thinning gray-white hair. He looked like he'd been around the block.

Keegan I had regarded as a showman. Lunney I viewed as his strong-arm guy who never lightened up. Solomon made everyone nervous because he never shut up. But Frank leaned back in his seat, expressionless. He seemed relaxed. He made me feel relaxed.

"So I saw your stories," he began. He wasn't indulging me with chit-chat about the cold weather. No "Nice place, the Lakeside, what do you recommend?" Beneath his easygoing façade, he was all business. As was I. The Moxley case had become my obsession. I didn't realize it was also his.

"So what do Murphy and Krebs think?" Frank said. He spoke in a shorthand I understood. He meant which Skakel brother did they believe had murdered Martha. My articles hadn't suggested a favorite. I had merely described Tommy's and Michael's lies to the Greenwich police. Let the reader choose.

"Tommy, I would say." Neither Murphy nor Krebs had ever come out and said that to me. It had been Tommy they were hired to clear. Until Solomon came along with his "Littleton failed the lie detector so he must be the murderer" theory—which the Academy Group had debunked—Tommy had been everyone's prime suspect. Although Michael fit the Academy Group's profile of the killer, his passing the murder scene, and his admission that he'd whacked off at Martha's window (a fact my article had prudishly not revealed), Tommy had admitted having a sexual encounter with Martha just minutes before the police believed she was killed. His mutual fondling-to-orgasm story, Murphy and Krebs believed, had been concocted to protect himself, should his DNA be discovered at the crime scene.

"What about you?" Frank asked. "Who do you think did it?" Later, he would tell me he knew what I would say. Or, rather, that he hoped I would say what he thought I would. For him, it was a test question. A test for me. To see if I would hedge. He felt he knew from my articles who I thought had murdered Martha and wanted to see if I would tell him the truth. That, he decided, would determine how our relationship would go.

"Tommy," I answered. That was the truth. I had no reason to tell him anything else, just as I had no reason to withhold the Greenwich police report from Murphy and Sheridan when they'd asked me. Tommy was who I thought then.

Echoing Murphy's report and what I had written in my article, I said, "Tommy places himself in a sexual situation with Martha just minutes before she is killed."

"You don't think Tommy could be telling the truth?" Frank said. "That when he left her, she was alive?" There was no tension in his voice, no excitement. I had no inkling of what he suspected about Michael or how far ahead of me he was.

"What do you think?" I answered. "Do you think Tommy was telling the truth?"

"Yes, I do."

"You don't think he murdered Martha then."

"That's right."

"You don't think he had any connection to it?"

"I didn't say that."

There was a pause. Okay, so Frank was being cute. Well, I could wait him out. He had called me. He obviously wanted something from me, though I wasn't sure what it was.

"Look," Frank said, breaking the silence, "what seventeen-year-old boy would volunteer to adults he'd just engaged in mutual masturbation with a girl? Especially if, just after she'd left him, that girl was murdered?

"Say the murder occurs around the time the dogs are barking, I don't believe Tommy could have killed her, moved her body, discarded the murder weapon, cleaned himself up, and then sat watching television with his tutor a few minutes later. No seventeen-year-old kid could have pulled that off."

Frank sounded as though he had thought this through. Maybe many times. I didn't realize he had analyzed it for years and fought about it ad nauseam with Jack Solomon.

"And you know the strongest indication that Tommy is innocent?" he asked. "It's Littleton's statement that he had noticed nothing unusual when Tommy entered his room after ten o'clock to watch television."

"But is Littleton telling the truth?" I asked. Keegan and Lunney hadn't believed him. They'd suspected he was covering up for Tommy. Murphy and Krebs sounded as though they suspected the same thing.

Frank nodded his head. "The strongest indication of Littleton's innocence is that Tommy says the same thing about him. Without intending to, each alibis the other. Believe me, if Tommy or any other Skakel knew Littleton had done this, they'd have given him up in a heartbeat."

Well, Frank had a point there, I supposed. How had I missed that? Murphy and Krebs had apparently missed it too. Forget about Solomon.

Years later, before the trial, I asked Krebs about Frank's theory that no seventeen-year-old kid could have pulled off a murder and minutes later have so collected himself that his tutor saw nothing wrong.

"He has a point," Krebs said.

"If you accept that, how can you say that Tommy did it?" I asked.

"I can't," Krebs answered.

Now, at the Lakeside, Frank turned to Michael. For the first time, I sensed this was the reason he had called me.

"Why would Michael, never a suspect, inject himself into the middle of the crime? Why would he place himself at the murder scene, perhaps while the murder was occurring?"

"What about the time of death?" I said. That seemed key in determining whether he had murdered Martha. Keegan and Lunney had set the time around 10:00 P.M., based on the dogs' barking. Murphy and Krebs appeared to have accepted that. They'd felt Michael's story about whacking off in the tree and passing the murder scene was intriguing but irrelevant to Martha's murder because it happened around midnight, two hours after she was killed.

But Frank had another explanation. "I was never as certain as everyone else about the time of death," he said. "Back in the '80s, I would say to Lunney, 'Jim, are you sure about those dogs? Aren't you hanging a lot on them? What if they were barking at a squirrel?' "

Then, Frank told me something Billy Krebs had said to him at their meeting years before, something that had confirmed his doubts. "Hey, Frankie," Krebs had asked him, "what do you think about those dogs?"

"The minute Billy said that, I knew what he was thinking," Frank said. "And we were thinking the same thing. Dogs bark every Halloween eve in neighborhoods with kids. If they didn't, there'd be something wrong with them. I stood alone on that for years until that meeting. Krebs's words said to me he wasn't so sure about the time of death either."

But Frank didn't say any of that to Krebs, just as he didn't say what specifically he was looking for from me. Instead, he flung what I came to learn was a typical Frank one-liner.

"Yeah, Billy," he said, "I sure wish I could interview them."

"But what about Tommy's breaking into tears as Krebs questioned him?" I pressed. "It sounded as though Tommy was about to confess."

"How do you know that?" Frank answered. "After all these years as the case's prime suspect, having been under pressure not just by the police but by the media—so much so that strangers in Greenwich whispered or pointed at him as he passed—maybe Tommy was ready to reveal what he'd kept inside him all these years. That someone else killed Martha."

I know detectives are intuitive. The best of them have a sixth sense ordinary people don't, even police reporters like myself who have been around cops for years. But how could Frank concoct this scenario about Tommy with such certainty? No, this wasn't mere intuition.

"You think Michael did it," I said. "You know something, don't you, that you're not saying."

"Let's just say I've heard some things."

This seemed like a good time to drop something on him—what my article about Michael had left out, what my editors at *Newsday* felt didn't "add anything to the story."

"What if I told you that while Michael was throwing stones at

Martha's window, he was up in a tree jerking off?" I said. I stared at him, awaiting his reaction.

But Frank gave away nothing. "Interesting," he said.

•

Our meeting had gone well enough, I thought. Or at least it hadn't gone badly. We'd established a rapport, however limited. Like Lunney and Keegan, there seemed no question that Frank sincerely wanted to solve this case. Unlike Lunney and Keegan, he sounded as though he knew what he was doing.

And he seemed to have formed a favorable impression of me. Or at least not an unfavorable one. "A lot of reporters are full of themselves," he would say years later. "They think they are smarter than everyone else. But you came across as a regular guy. I remember you were wearing a Mets hat. And I like the Mets."

"How about we get together again?" I said a couple of weeks later.

"Sure," Frank said. He explained he was glad to keep the door open. "Jack and I used the media in the past. I think we owe something to reporters like yourself who pushed the case along."

That was, of course, bullshit. If Frank felt he could have solved the case without me, I would only have seen his back, and maybe not even that. No, there had to be another reason why he was willing to see me again, one I would come to understand a year later.

This time Frank picked the time and the place—breakfast at the Putnam Coffee Shop at the bottom of Greenwich Avenue. This time, we began by discussing the case's participants.

"We're off the record here, right?" Frank began. That was fine with me. We weren't exactly breaking any news here. We merely wanted to get each other's take on people. What Frank said about them would also give me an insight into him.

"Are you taping this?" he asked.

"No," I said.

"How do I know you don't have a hidden tape recorder?"

"Frank, we're only having breakfast."

"How do I know I can believe you?"

Was he kidding? The way I worked, the way McCulloch had taught me a reporter should work, trust was everything. That was why I'd opposed Ken's idea years before of secretly taping Keegan.

Cops, detectives, federal officers, and whoever else in law enforcement can lie to suspects to obtain their confessions. But reporters can't lie to anyone, least of all a source like Frank. Were I to get caught in a lie or print something he had told me in confidence, I would be out of business with him, and with every other law enforcement official in Connecticut.

Hell, how did Frank think I'd gotten a look at Hale's report? "I felt I could trust you," McCreight had told me. Of course, as I would learn, Frank had no use for McCreight. To say nothing of Hale.

"How do you think I got a look at Murphy's Sutton Associates report?" I said to him. Someone had trusted me to keep my mouth shut about where my information came from.

"Yeah, okay," Frank said. He seemed satisfied, although his face remained expressionless. Frank, I was beginning to learn, was pretty good at hiding his thoughts and feelings, when he wanted to.

"So what do you think of Murphy and Krebs?" he said.

"I respect them," I replied. Murphy still hadn't spoken to me since the Skakels fired him. I would see him six years later at the funeral of his cousin, Vincent Danz, one of the twenty-three New York City police officers killed at the World Trade Center attack on 9/11. Murphy delivered the eulogy, followed by Rudy Giuliani. Giuliani spoke of war and acting accordingly toward our attackers. Murphy said our response should be based "not on vengeance but on justice."

Frank said he'd never warmed up to Murphy but felt a rapport with Krebs. I understood that. Murphy was FBI formal. Frank and Krebs were both detectives. They both seemed street-savvy and easygoing, at least on the surface.

"I have great respect for Billy," Frank said, referring to Krebs. "I just don't understand how he could work for the Skakels."

"What about Tom Sheridan?" I asked. Sheridan, I believed, had played a larger role in the Moxley case than anyone realized. Rushton's oldest friend, he had become Michael's criminal attorney after the drunken-driving accident at Windham. He had hired Murphy and Krebs "to clear the Skakel name," as he had put it. It was Sheridan who, at Solomon's behest, had pointed Murphy and Krebs toward Littleton—a red herring if there ever was one.

"I wouldn't trust him." said Frank. "His only concern is his friendship with Rushton. 'Rucky,'" he said sarcastically. "He'd do anything to protect his friend Rucky. Including framing Littleton." Yes, Frank was good at hiding his thoughts and feelings—when he wanted to.

"I have no problem in being candid when it comes to the Skakels," he continued. "I never hid the fact that these people were despicable."

"You don't like the Skakels, I take it? I never would have figured that out."

"Liars. Liars and drunks. They refuse to take responsibility for anything they do. They actually see themselves as victims."

"Margolis?" I asked, referring to their longtime attorney.

"Manny's had this case for twenty-six years. He's used the Skakel family as a golden goose. He's made a small fortune stonewalling the police."

Yet the person Frank harbored the most ill will toward was one of his own—Solomon. Frank never raised his voice when he spoke of him. His hand never shook in anger. But get him started and he could rant. "You know Jack's problem? He thinks he's smarter than everyone else. He thinks everyone else is stupid. He's in love with the polygraph and with his image and can't admit when he is wrong."

What Frank didn't say was that he felt Solomon had poisoned Browne against him.

•

We seemed to enjoy ourselves so much that we arranged a lunch at a pub in Greenwich. Another evening we met for dinner at an Italian restaurant in Stamford. Here we were, two grown men with wives and children, now spending an increasing amount of time together. At each meeting, we'd talk for hours.

Our coming together—a reporter and a detective—seemed so unnatural I said to Frank, "Jesus, if anyone noticed what was going on between us, they might think we're gay."

"Who gives a fuck?" he answered. "We've developed a friendship. It's the truth."

In fact, we discovered we had plenty in common. We discussed our bosses, mine at *Newsday*, his at the state's attorney's office. Neither of us had any use for them.

We compared restaurants we liked. Frank's favorite was Dominick's on Arthur Avenue, an Italian section of the Bronx.

"I know Dominick's," I said, and regaled him with stories about my old friend Judge Fusco. "Friday afternoons he held court at Mario's, a restaurant right across the street."

"That's where we'll go if this case is ever solved," Frank said. "That's where we'll celebrate."

One area where we disagreed was politics. Frank loved Rudy Giuliani and said he would campaign for him if he ran for president. I told Frank I wasn't sure whether Giuliani's final destination was the White House or a lunatic asylum.

Then there was golf. Frank had recently taken it up. He played every weekend at the public course in Greenwich. "Why don't we play sometime?" he said. I begged off. "C'mon," he said. "I'll teach you. Don't worry, I'm no good myself."

"Frank," I said, "what happens when I bring up Solomon and you start to rant and we get thrown off the course?"

Once I called him on his cell phone in Rhode Island to ask about a rumor that Browne was retiring. I caught him on the third hole. "You're killing me," he said. "I can't even get a shot off."

Lastly, there were our families. Both of us agreed they came first, before work. At least in theory. Like Susan, Frank's wife Mariann had spent months in bed, pregnant with their daughter Angela. Frank said her difficulties stemmed from a motorcycle accident before they were married. I pictured the two of them tooling around Greenwich. Frank's hair hadn't turned gray then. Mariann was sitting behind him, arms wrapped around his shoulders.

"We were broad-sided on the Post Road in Old Greenwich," he said. "Mariann spent three months in the hospital. Her injuries were so serious doctors warned us she might never have a child."

Mercifully, it had turned out well for them, as it had for Susan and me. Their two children were a few years older than ours. Frank's son Dave, who was six inches taller than Frank, had been a star pitcher at Greenwich High. Our son Mike, who was six inches taller than me, was struggling to make his high school team.

Our daughter Jennifer was shy. "Angela was too," Frank said. "Don't worry. It all works out. It all just happens. Now she's getting married. She didn't even start dating until she was in her twenties."

One night we were at his home in the Glenville section of Greenwich. Friendly as we were becoming, I remained a reporter and was probing why he thought Michael, not Tommy, had murdered Martha. Frank was resisting telling me. Mariann was working a late shift at the hospital. Dave was out with his friends. Angela was with her fiance, and we were alone in his kitchen, watching the Mets. That was something else we had in common. We both agreed they stank.

Another time, Frank said he had been prepared to dislike me. "Keegan and Lunney had told me about you," he said. I could imagine what they had said.

"Your first article hadn't come out yet but Lunney knew something was wrong. He was complaining you kept harping on the search warrant and were just trying to make the department look bad. You were always a thorn in his side. Whenever your name came up, he'd say you're not a cop. 'He doesn't know what's going on and is writing about things he doesn't know about.'

"But I saw something else," he continued. "I saw a reporter who was motivated and tenacious, who just didn't want to do a story and go home but who wanted to see this thing get solved, the way I did."

Frank also mentioned that years before he had seen me going into the police library to interview Keegan and Lunney. I asked him if Lunney told him how he'd grabbed my shirt.

"Lunney denies it," Frank said the next time we met. "He says it never happened." I tried to determine if Frank was smiling. I decided that he wasn't.

"Why don't you ask Keegan?" I said.

"I did. He denies it, too."

"You think I'm making this up?" I said.

"Hey, Len, they tell me it never happened. What do you want me to say? Maybe you're mixing them up with someone else." He sounded like my former publisher at *Newsday*, Isenberg, who told me he'd poisoned the well, then claimed I was confused. As for Frank, he seemed torn between his loyalty to his department and his common sense.

Another time, Frank said, "You know when I started to trust you? A lot of media people had been around this case, from Dominick Dunne to Tim Dumas." At Dominick's urging, Dorthy had entreated Frank to talk to him and the two had spent an afternoon together. Dumas, a young writer from Greenwich, was a good resource, Frank said, because he knew the kids. He was their age and had grown up with a lot of them.

"But you were the one who seemed the most consistent," he said. "I felt there were times when I would say things to you about the case, about what I thought about Tommy and Michael, then wait to see if they ever came back to me. I waited to hear if they would be repeated and they never were. I knew you talked to Dominick and to Dumas. But nothing I told you ever came back. So a trust developed. And from trust came friendship. And here we are."

Years before, when I'd begun this case, I promised myself to make no alliances with sources. Frank said he felt the same. "I always thought through the years never to develop any personal relationship or feelings towards people in an investigation," he said. "That it had to be strictly business. Otherwise, it can be dangerous. It can dog your thinking."

But we both agreed the Moxley case was different. Frank felt the difference was Dorthy. "I think it was because of my own personal relationship with her," he said. "I felt so bad for her. And I knew you felt that way, too. I felt you truly cared about her, that you weren't there just as a reporter, not just as someone who came after a story. I felt you truly wanted to see this solved. That you truly wanted to see Dorthy get some relief. That you felt she was a person. I felt you saw this case as beyond a job. That you went home with it. That you slept it and lived it like I did. That's why I could talk to you the way I do."

That was all true, of course, but for me Dorthy was only part of it. Oh yes, she and I were close, closer perhaps than she was to Frank. I knew her family and she knew mine. There was never a time we spoke that she didn't ask about Susan, Jennifer, or Mike.

She invited me to bring Susan and the kids to stay with her at her ski house in Vermont. I never did. For reasons I couldn't quite explain to myself, I felt I shouldn't be in the position of accepting a gift or favor like that from her. But one winter when I was near there with Mike and two of his friends, we stopped by. Her grandchildren were with her—her son John and Kara's children, a little blonde boy and a little blonde girl. They had sheets over their heads and were running around the house as ghosts. I saw what joy they gave her, and refused to allow myself to think of the obvious—they were filling the void left by Martha's death.

And then there was an incident with Jennifer. At age 13, she played on a fast-pitch softball team that traveled to Missouri and won a national championship. They had a great pitcher who later starred in high school and college. Jennifer played left field. As a reward they were invited to Yankee Stadium and, dressed in their uniforms, ran out to their positions with the Yankees. Jennifer trotted out to left with Tim Raines.

Standing behind third base watching her, tears of pride running down my cheeks, I happened to turn around. Who was sitting there but Dorthy's son John and his wife Kara? They happened to have tickets for the game.

This had to be more than coincidence, I later told Dorthy. "Let's take it as a sign that our lives will be forever intertwined."

And yet Martha's murder had become more to me than my relationship with her. It had to do with what I believed about journalism—what I believed the role of a reporter should be. As much money as Dorthy may have had, she was a victim, unable to help herself. Corny as it may sound, I still believed in the magic of what I had seen as a boy on *The Big Story*: that the job of a reporter and a newspaper is to help those who cannot help themselves—in this case, someone whom every other institution has failed.

My articles had not solved the Moxley case but they had started a chain reaction. If McCreight hadn't given me Hale's report, I would not have known about the police's discovery of the golf club inside the Skakel house or the disagreements between the Greenwich police and the state's attorney's office. Without knowing that, I would not have sought the Greenwich police file. Without that file, I could not have written my first story that helped restart the investigation. Without the reinvestigation, Solomon would not have met with Margolis and Sheridan to push his cockamamie theory of Littleton as a serial killer. That meeting led Sheridan to hire Murphy and Krebs "to clear the Skakel name." Instead, their Sutton Associates report revealed that Tommy and Michael had lied about their whereabouts. That, in turn, would lead Frank to new witnesses.

Yet as close as Frank and I were to become, neither of us forgot that he was a detective and I was a reporter and that a gulf of values and experiences separated us. It wasn't merely that Frank's job was to obtain information and withhold it from the public to make his case, while mine was to report it. It also involved Frank's loyalty to his fellow detectives and the Greenwich Police Department. Whereas I respected that, I saw such loyalty as cutting two ways. Loyalty to the institution that I felt had screwed up the Moxley murder had led not to corruption—because so far as I could tell there was no corruption—but to the cover-up of its mistakes.

Throughout our relationship, there were barriers we never crossed. Frank never asked who had given me Murphy's Sutton report. He knew I could never divulge it. I never pressed him for copies of the Greenwich Police Department's initial interviews with Tommy and Michael, which were not included in the police file we obtained from the Freedom of Information lawsuit. I understood Frank's reluctance to provide them. He was shielding his partner Lunney, Lunney's partner Carroll, and other Greenwich detectives who obviously had been less than thorough.

That was one of two subjects we could never discuss—how the Greenwich police had screwed up the case. Frank refused to hear it. Never blame Keegan or Lunney unless you wanted another Frank rant.

"They did the best they could with what they had," he would say.

"Frank, they screwed it up. Accept it."

"What do you think they should have done that they didn't?"

"Well, for one thing, they didn't get a warrant to search the Skakel house. They found the matching golf club the day the body was found. They didn't immediately get a search warrant."

"You weren't there. Unless you are there, you don't know the circumstances. They already had access. Maybe they thought they could get more with sugar than with vinegar. They felt they had an open door and maybe could develop things. Maybe they were concerned that if they shut that door, it would remain shut.

"Sure, they might do things differently," he'd allow. "There's no investigation I ever did, I wouldn't do things differently.

"And let me tell you something else. Lunney and Carroll were senior detectives with upwards of twenty years' experience. They worked around the wealthiest people in the world. Nobody was intimidated by the Skakels' wealth."

"Carroll told me he was intimidated, Frank. He went on television and said he was intimidated."

"That was after the fact. Who knows what was going on with him then?"

"Carroll said it himself. They eliminated, rather than zeroed in on the Skakels."

"There is nothing wrong with eliminating. You do both."

"Frank, the whole mindset was wrong. Chief Baran's first words to the media were that kids always leave golf clubs lying around outside and someone might have come in and picked it up to murder Martha." I didn't bother mentioning the hundreds of wasted manpower hours they'd spent investigating the neighbor, Hammond.

"What about their refusal to expand the time of death beyond 10:00 P.M.? They locked themselves in to that 10:00 P.M. because of the dogs.

You yourself said that back in the '80s, you'd say to Lunney, 'Are you sure about those dogs?' Because of that, they refused to consider Michael because they felt that at 10:00 P.M., he was at the Terriens'."

"Okay, maybe people made bad decisions. But that's not screwing it up."

The second subject was my 1991 article. Bring that up and Frank turned testy. "That article you wrote in 1991 that you always refer to as restarting the investigation," he would begin. "It didn't restart anything. I was already looking into the case. That April, some guy called the Palm Beach, Florida, police. It was during the William Kennedy Smith rape trial. The guy mentioned he and Michael had been together in a drug rehabilitation place called Elan."

"You don't think my article helped restart the investigation?"

"It had no impact at all."

"Frank, the article came out in May. Two months later, the Greenwich police and state's attorney hold a news conference saying they're reopening the case."

"You think that was because of your article? We restarted the investigation because of William Kennedy Smith. Someone started a rumor that he had been at the Skakels the night of Martha's murder. The timing of your article was coincidental."

These arguments got us nowhere. I decided they were pointless.

"Let's not discuss it anymore," I said to Frank.

"But you're the writer," he said. "You get the last word."

The question I continued to ask myself was not why I had chosen to befriend Frank. That was obvious. Whether or not I liked him—and I did—he was the case's primary source. No, the question was why Frank had chosen to befriend me. His closest friends and longtime colleagues, Keegan and Lunney, had warned him off me. Lunney had told him I only wanted to hurt him. Yet here was Frank opening up to me about the case, albeit not fully, never sharing key details as much as dropping hints.

One night as I left his house, he said to me, "Thanks for listening. Thanks for keeping an open mind." It would be another year before I understood what he meant.

15

PART THREE / CHAPTER FIFTEEN

# The Confession

STAMFORD, CONNECTICUT
1995–1996

What Frank had to do was to find an eyewitness. Not necessarily to the murder, since that would prove next to impossible, but an eyewitness to an admission, a confession. In early 1996, three months after we met, Frank would use my articles on the Sutton report for that. He didn't tell me about it, though. As much as we were coming to trust each other, he didn't share with me with what he knew about Michael—at least not then.

The year before, Frank had approached some nationally syndicated television shows, urging them to feature the Moxley murder. He felt there were kids in the neighborhood who might have seen or heard something they hadn't told the police. God knows who Michael or Tommy might have confided in. At the time, those kids were teenagers and wouldn't talk to the cops. Teenagers like Andy Pugh.

At age fifteen, Pugh, like all teenagers, was not about to volunteer information to the police unless specifically asked—and maybe not even then. But now, twenty years later, many of those kids' attitudes and outlooks might have changed. Many of them had families of their own. They might feel differently about cooperating.

But every TV program turned Frank down. The Moxley case may have been news when it was reopened in 1991. But by 1995, the networks had lost interest.

In December, a month after my Sutton articles appeared, Frank again contacted *Unsolved Mysteries*. "Now you have something," they said. They sent a film crew to his office in Bridgeport.

Two months later, they called him from Burbank, California. They wanted to air a segment on the Moxley murder and needed someone from the investigation in the studio, in case viewers phoned in with tips.

"I think I should go out there," Frank told Browne.

But while on the plane, he panicked. "I got everyone believing this program is the icebreaker. But what if no one calls? Or what if people call and say it's Tommy or Littleton and I am thinking Michael?"

•

Inside the Burbank studio, he was ushered into a huge room with operators seated at telephone screens. After the show aired he was to walk around the room, waiting for calls. The operators would hold up different-colored cards. A white card meant "Come over when you have a chance." A green card was more urgent. A red meant "hot tip."

As the show aired, Frank saw hands go up holding red cards. The operators were typing the information out on screens. Frank scurried around the room with a pencil and pad, speaking briefly to callers. He had only time to get their name, phone number, address, and a quick recap of their stories before moving on.

There were no calls about Tommy or Littleton. Virtually every tip concerned Michael. Most came from former residents of Elan. "This is so and so. I just want you to know I watched the show. Michael Skakel was nuts," someone said. Or "I was up at Elan with Michael and he said he killed a girl with a golf club."

Frank scribbled all this down. He was afraid others would hang up before he reached them. A Phil Lawrence called from Florida, saying he had attended a group therapy session at Elan where Michael confessed to killing Martha. "I was there. Michael admitted he was under the influence of alcohol and killed her with a golf club."

Elan's owner, Joe Ricci, must have heard Michael admit to killing Martha, Lawrence added. "Michael had these private meetings with Joe that most people didn't get the luxury of having," said Lawrence. "Ricci was my legal guardian. I had maybe one."

And Ricci tape-recorded everything, Lawrence added. "I guarantee you he has a recording of Michael's confession. I'd bet the moon on it. I bet you anything he taped any conversations he had with Mike 'cause he's not dumb."

"Who is this Ricci?" Frank asked. "Is he a psychiatrist? A psychologist?"

"Are you kidding? He's an ex-junkie from New York." As it turned out Ricci was from Port Chester. He'd lived in the same housing project as a cousin of Frank's.

Frank returned to Bridgeport with leads and prayers that these people were telling the truth. He began with former Elan resident Diane Hozman, who was now, of all things, a clinical psychologist in Palm Springs, California, telling people how to run their lives. Hozman remembered talking to Michael in Elan's dining room, where he had been confined after one of his escapes. Michael told her he thought he'd killed a girl but was unable to remember details. Michael recalled getting out of bed late at night after a party at his house. He said he'd walked a girl home and that something had happened under a tree. Michael told her he had kissed the girl and made out with her under the tree. Then he returned home, climbing in through his window.

Another Elan alum, Anna Goodman, saw Ricci confront Michael about the murder at a therapy session, and forced him to wear a sign around his neck that read: "Ask me why I killed my friend, Martha Moxley." Frank had heard this before. Dorothy Rogers, the Greenwich girl he'd traced to Graham, North Carolina, had said something similar. As part of their therapy at Elan, she said a staff member had asked Michael, "Why did you crush Moxley's chest with a golf club?"

Why would Ricci confront Michael about the murder, Frank asked himself again. When Michael was sent to Elan in 1978, he hadn't been a suspect. How would people at Elan have had suspicions about him unless someone in or close to the family had told them?

These stories sounded true and dovetailed with what others had told him. He recalled Phil Lawrence's read on Michael. "He was very nice, very friendly but the things he used to talk about didn't seem to fit with him. He'd talk about weird things. The big thing he used to talk about was he'd go out and get drunk and wake up in women's clothes the next morning." That information, Frank knew, Lawrence hadn't made up.

By now Frank was convinced the crime was sexually motivated. Had Michael been spurned? Had he been unable to perform? Had Martha taunted him? Frank knew Michael hadn't gone out that night intending to kill her. But something had gone terribly wrong. He was drinking, smoking pot. He had lost control.

Yet again, Frank thought how Michael was like a pressure cooker, how he needed to talk about the murder to let off steam. From the first day, he couldn't shut up about it. He was the only Skakel who couldn't. When the body was discovered he was rushing around outside telling people, "They found the body." He was telling people he and Tommy were the last two people to see Martha alive.

He talked about it at school. He brought in newspaper articles. Later, he spoke about it at AA meetings. On the Triborough Bridge he said he had done something so bad, he had to kill himself. He couldn't shut up about it at Elan. He said he was drunk and may have killed her but he couldn't remember.

But each time he told his version of innocence, his story changed because it was a lie. Regardless of the details, each version revealed Michael's involvement.

•

Frank was so close but he wasn't yet there. He knew in his gut Michael had done it, but he remained just beyond Frank's reach. What he needed was someone who had actually heard Michael's confession. A lot of people had heard things to suggest Michael killed Martha. But Frank needed a credible witness to go on the witness stand and testify to that.

Frank felt strangely confident he would find one. "I knew there was someone out there who knew. I had no doubt that this person was out there because Michael talked about the murder to anyone he spoke to. Even after I had left L.A. and flown back to Greenwich, calls were coming into the station from people who knew him. My only question was would that person who knew come forward."

In his obsession to talk about the murder with anyone he encountered, even with people he had barely met, Michael was almost like Littleton, Frank thought.

"People thought Littleton had done it," said Frank. "He was easily manipulated and he couldn't stop talking about it because he wanted to clear himself. Michael was the same way. Only he couldn't shut up because I think it was eating away at him."

The call Frank was waiting for came on Halloween, eight months after he appeared on *Unsolved Mysteries*. It came to the Greenwich Police Department. A Chicago man, Chuck Seigan, said he had been at Elan with someone named John Higgins. Higgins had heard Michael say he beat Martha to death with a golf club.

Seigan had been admitted to Elan in February 1977 at the age of twenty, and Michael arrived in 1978. Everyone at Elan, he said, believed the Skakel family had committed Michael, fearing he'd killed Martha. Michael said his father had put him there, believing he was too weak to withstand questioning from the police or the press.

Often, Michael broke down in tears, claiming he didn't know whether or not he committed the murder, Seigan said. At group sessions, Michael would shake his head and cry, "I don't know if I did or didn't, I don't know."

"Cry about what?" Frank asked.

"The fact that he just didn't know whether he did or didn't."

He didn't know if he did or didn't? Who wonders whether or not they killed somebody? thought Frank. Who was so drunk that they couldn't remember the next morning whether or not they had killed someone?

Seigan said he felt uncomfortable with Michael because he was a Kennedy nephew, but his friend Higgins seemed at ease around him. The pair roomed together for four months. During that time, Seigan said, Higgins confronted Michael about the murder.

"Well, did you or didn't you do it?" Higgins had asked.

"Yes, I did it," Michael replied.

Seigan told Frank he learned this only a few months ago—after *Unsolved Mysteries* aired. Higgins telephoned Seigan, saying he had information about a murder. Higgins said he felt "shitty" that Michael had confessed to him. He said he was "pissed" at Michael. "Why did he have to tell me?" Higgins had said to Seigan.

Frank knew his call to Higgins could break open the case. As he dialed, he found himself panicking. It wasn't the panic he'd felt on the plane to Burbank. Rather, it was that he didn't know what to expect. From Seigan's description, he couldn't read Higgins. He decided to tape the call. If Higgins changed his story, Frank could lock him into his statement.

"You obviously are familiar with the murder of Martha Moxley," he began when Higgins answered. It was an open-ended sentence, allowing him to begin sizing up Higgins by his response. Years later, as Frank told this to me, it reminded me of how meticulous he was, how he tried to peer into someone's character before he'd met him and set him up to reveal his true nature. I had visions of him planning his first interview with me at the Lakeside.

"Well, it's interesting that anyone else would know that I know, other than a few select people," Higgins answered. "I've almost called the state's attorney's office to say what I know because this family is, as far as I'm concerned, getting away with murder and there's a problem because they're an extremely powerful family and the last thing I want is any kind of problem."

"We are certainly the last people on earth that are going to cause you any problem," Frank answered. That was certainly true.

"Well, I was at a place called Elan," Higgins continued. "And I was there at the time Michael Skakel was there, which was shortly after the murder. I'm thirty-four now so it was when I was sixteen or seventeen, and we ended up being on the same security staff and we would sit out at night on the back porch and keep an eye out for people running away from the place. It was a pretty bad place. They probably should have run away."

Frank found himself liking Higgins for that remark. From the little he'd learned about Elan, Higgins was on the money.

"I'd been there a year already and he never really said why he was there," Higgins went on. "And we got into a conversation about the fact that he didn't know whether he murdered somebody or not. Now, obviously, I knew nothing about Moxley or anything else at this time. He told me he remembers being in his garage, having a golf club, being in tall pine trees, and waking up back in his house, and his big dilemma at the time was he doesn't know if he did it or not. . . .

"He said they sent him and they left his brother because he's the cool, calm collected guy to deal with whatever might come to the family on the case, and obviously Tom was good at dealing with this and Michael apparently wasn't."

Oh, this is good, Frank thought. This is real good. He knows the family. He knows the Skakels. He's got it exactly right.

"He described a party. I think it was near Halloween," Higgins continued. "Yeah, I can remember him telling me about walking through the woods, being in the pine trees."

Only Michael could have known about the pine trees, Frank thought. No way Higgins could have known that on his own. He has to have heard that from Michael.

"He was like crying when he was telling me this," Higgins continued. "The nut of the conversation was he had no idea what had happened but he knew that he was sent away after this whole thing occurred because he thinks his parents thought he did it or he doesn't know if he did it and that they were trying to protect him."

"Did he mention he blacked out?" Frank asked.

"Yeah, he did mention a blackout." Higgins paused. "This is tough." Uh oh. Frank sensed resistance. Higgins was hesitating.

"My feeling is that this has been bothering you," Frank said. He wanted Higgins to keep going.

"Let me ask you something," Higgins interrupted. "Is my talking to you right now, is there any way that I can be subpoenaed to give this information?"

"Uh, no," Frank lied. Higgins, of course, had no idea Frank was taping him, that he could in fact be subpoenaed. Reporters must never lie but detectives do all the time.

Then quickly, seamlessly, so that Higgins would not dwell on it, Frank shifted direction. "You have to think in terms of the victim's family."

"Let them put it to rest," Higgins answered. Yes, that was the type of response Frank wanted.

"He remembers being in his garage, going through a golf bag," Higgins continued. "The first part of the conversation was that somebody got murdered. He remembers running through the pine trees. He doesn't remember where he ended up but he ended up back in his house, and everything after that was a blackout, and then the next day he heard that this girl was killed with a golf club and that's why he thinks that he may have done it but he doesn't know that he did it. I asked him how can he not know if he did it or not?"

"And what did he say?" Frank knew he shouldn't have interrupted but he couldn't resist. That was exactly his question. How can you not know you killed someone?

"Well, that was his blackout. He just blacked out and he doesn't remember any of it. He was just sitting there, crying. In my opinion, it's best when people are doing that just to let 'em go and that's pretty much what we do at Elan. It was kind of a standing rule. He said he just remembers looking up and seeing pine trees and he's running through pine trees."

Higgins was almost there. But he hadn't quite given it up. He still hadn't uttered the magic words: Michael told me he did it. But that was as far as Higgins would go today. He announced that he needed to take a break. "I want to think about this," he said.

Frank didn't want to let him think about it. This was Friday, November 1, 1996. It was a year after Frank and I had first met. Not that I knew anything about this then. It would be years before Frank would tell me about Seigan and Higgins.

Higgins told Frank to call him back on Monday. But Frank couldn't leave it at that. "Let me ask you this and then I'll let you go and I'll talk to you on Monday," he said. "Now be honest with me, it's a yes or no answer. There is more you have to tell me, right?"

"Yeah," Higgins said.

•

It was the longest weekend of his life. Frank passed the days thinking how he would approach Higgins. He had to try not to seem too anxious. He wanted Higgins to see that he understood him and what he was going through.

"The fact is," Higgins began on Monday, "that the Skakel family, whether you say so or not, is an extremely well-connected family. I mean, I don't know how well you know the Skakels."

"I know them fairly well," said Frank. So that was it. Higgins was afraid.

"John," he said. It was the first time Frank had called Higgins by his first name. "I don't want to use the word 'afraid' but maybe that's an accurate term."

"Nothing wrong with fear," said Higgins.

"Like I told you last week when we talked, my intentions here are not to harm you or to cause you problems," Frank replied. "My intentions here are to work with you and together get to the bottom of this. We are on the same side. You and I are teammates."

Of course, Higgins didn't know that his teammate was tape-recording this call, as he had the first one.

Until now, Frank had been circling Higgins. Now he was ready to go for it. "You said at the end of our conversation, we'll start with that, what exactly did he say?"

"Well, Michael was just obviously destroyed and he was just sitting there crying, and he was probably crying for five minutes or so. I then asked him quietly, "'Did you do it or didn't you?' He said, 'I did it. I killed her.'"

I got it, thought Frank. There it is. I got it: "I did it. I killed her."

"What did you say to him?" Frank asked. He had it but he wanted more.

"I don't think I said anything to him. He just, I mean that was the only words he said about it. He said, 'I killed her,' and you know, I probably gave the guy a hug."

Oh, sweet Jesus, this guy is telling the truth, Frank thought, exhilarated. I probably gave the guy a hug! You don't make up a detail like that. I've got a guy, a credible witness who is going to get on the witness stand and say Michael Skakel told me he killed Martha Moxley!

•

Frank told me nothing then about Higgins, although when we met three weeks later, for the first time he named Michael as Martha's killer to me. Not that it took me by surprise. He had been leading me in his direction without ever saying so.

We were at the Lakeside on a Friday morning at our table by the water. The breakfast crowd had come and gone and the place was emptying. Frank began by saying he had spent the past eight months traveling around the country interviewing witnesses. I knew that. I knew he had used my articles to get on *Unsolved Mysteries* and had been contacted by people. But until the day at the Lakeside, he never told me more than that.

"I've come up with three or four key witnesses," he said.

"You can't tell me who they are?"

"Nope."

"Or where you found them?"

"I can't tell you any more than what I told you."

I knew better than to push him. Frank may have viewed Michael as a pressure cooker, but he was one himself. He, too, I felt, had a need to talk about the case. Except that unlike Michael he released only tiny bubbles.

Then, when I least expected it, Frank said to me, "Michael did it. I found witnesses. I've got proof. But I can't tell you any more than that."

I didn't know what to say. This was a breakthrough. This was major. This was a major fucking breakthrough. Twenty years after the murder, five years after he'd begun investigating, Frank had found his witness. And it had been in part because of my articles.

And yet instead of celebrating, he was telling this to me as calmly as if he were discussing the weather. I didn't get it. Not knowing what Frank had and still uncertain about Tommy's role, I wondered if Frank was as certain about Michael's guilt as he claimed to be.

What Frank didn't tell me was that he felt he had enough to arrest Michael for Martha's murder, that Higgins's statement matched accounts Michael had given to others at Elan.

What he didn't tell me was that on November 12, 1996, he had completed a memo to Donald Browne, describing how the *Unsolved Mysteries* television program had led to several people confined to Elan with Michael in the late 1970s.

"These individuals speak of a common belief among the residents at Elan that Michael Skakel had committed a murder," Frank wrote.

"On Thursday, October 31, 1996, an individual identifying himself as Chuck Seigan contacted this office claiming that six to eight months before, he was informed by a fellow resident of Elan, John Higgins, that Michael Skakel had confessed to the murder. This fellow resident, John Higgins, was contacted and as a result of this telephone conversation along with a second conversation on November 4, 1996, confirmed that Michael Skakel did in fact admit to him that he had murdered Martha Moxley."

What he also didn't tell me was that when he presented his memo, Browne took no action.

# 16

PART THREE / CHAPTER SIXTEEN

# "The Truth Remains the Same but a Lie Always Changes"

CONNECTICUT
1997–2000

For the next eighteen months until he left the case, Browne did nothing. With long-unsolved cases, the state of Connecticut has a kind of court of last resort—a special one-man grand jury. It is appointed by a panel of judges at the request of the state's attorney to determine if an arrest is warranted. But Browne refused to seek it in the Moxley case.

The reason, said Frank, was Jack Solomon. Although retired, he still had Browne's ear.

Only after the arrest and indictment would Frank tell me this and divulge the details he had discovered about Michael. Only then could I fill in what had happened to Frank during that time and understand why he had sought me out. Only then did it fall into place.

"I just couldn't understand why Browne wouldn't call the grand jury," Frank said. "I suppose he lacked confidence in me. Maybe if the tables were turned and it was coming from Jack, he might have."

Frank couldn't stop talking about Solomon. "Jack would call me to have lunch and ask about the case. He'd been my partner for four years so I felt I could tell him things. I also thought Jack wanted to see the case solved and was happy that information I had developed could lead to an arrest. How naïve could I have been?

"When I told him about Higgins, Solomon's reaction was: 'Maybe he's looking for something. Maybe he wants to be a big man.'

"When I pointed out Higgins's testimony complemented that of other Elan witnesses, Jack would say, 'Sounds kind of weak. Those kids are as bad as Michael. Where have they been all these years?'

"Whatever I would say, Jack would pooh-pooh it. He would never concede that maybe Littleton didn't do it and Michael did. He couldn't accept it. So I just stopped talking to him. But I knew he was talking to Browne. There may have been no evidence to link Littleton to Martha's murder but as far as Jack was concerned, that didn't mean Littleton hadn't murdered Martha Moxley."

Nearing retirement after twenty-five years as Fairfield County state's attorney, Browne prided himself on never having lost a murder case. "One morning," said Frank, "he enters my office, sits down in a chair by my desk and says to me, 'Do you have everything?'

" 'I got a lot more than anyone else,' I say. 'He did it and we can get him.'

" 'Are you sure?' Browne asks. 'Do you have it all?'

" 'I have a lot more than Murphy and Krebs. We can move on this. I have enough to arrest this guy.'

" 'I just don't want to go out a loser,' Browne answers.

" 'Mr. Browne,' I say, 'if you don't call the grand jury, you at least owe an explanation to Dorthy Moxley. If you call the grand jury and the panel turns you down, no one can fault you. If the panel calls the grand jury and they don't indict, you're still a hero because you did the right thing. If you call the grand jury and they do indict, you're an even bigger hero. Even if we lose at trial, you took your best shot.

'Mr. Browne, the only way you go out a loser is if you do nothing.' "

•

Frank wouldn't quit. But Browne's resistance was wearing him down. At his lowest point, Frank called and asked if I would come up to Bridgeport and see him. "We'll talk," he said.

Bridgeport, on an inlet on Long Island Sound, is a decaying city. From New York City, you take the Connecticut Turnpike northeast, exit on the left, go down a hill to the light, turn right, and hit Main Street. The downtown is a two-block strip of run-down buildings. The state's attorney's office is in the seven-story Superior Court building. You pop a right turn just past it and drive down into its underground garage. Two uniformed guards escort you to a parking space. Then they call upstairs for someone to come get you.

Frank met me at the elevator. As I turned to follow him into his office, I noticed he was wearing his hair in a ponytail. It was tied with a rubber band and made him look like an aging hippie or an undercover cop. He wasn't either. His ponytail was a sign of rebellion, not fashion.

More than two years had passed since our first meeting at the Lakeside Diner, more than a year since Frank had found Higgins. At the time I still knew nothing about Higgins or Frank's other Elan witnesses. Frank said only that the case was going nowhere. Browne was refusing to move.

He led me down a hallway to the small, windowless cubicle where he was sequestered. He had a bookshelf that was empty, save for three books that indicated his resolve—some would say his obsession—with the Moxley case. They were Jerry Oppenheimer's *The Other Mrs. Kennedy*, the biography of Ethel Kennedy; *The Senator*, a nonfiction book about Ted Kennedy; and *A Season in Purgatory*, Dominick Dunne's novel based on the Moxley case.

The stillness of the office was unnerving. The phone didn't ring. No clerks or secretaries bustled in or out. Frank was out of the flow of the office's daily activity, estranged from his law enforcement colleagues.

"No one comes in here to speak to me," he said. "I walk down the hall, people see me coming and make the sign of the cross, as though to ward me off. I'm the office joke. A royal pain in the ass to everyone."

As he spoke, he paced his cubicle like a prisoner. "Am I crazy?" he asked. "Am I paranoid? Why am I the only one in this office who sees the case the way I do? Why am I the only person pushing this? Why didn't Krebs see it this way? Why didn't Lunney and Keegan? Why don't you see it? The whole world is wrong and I am right? Is something wrong with me?"

I'd never seen Frank this way. He'd always been mellow, his sense of humor just below the surface. I wasn't sure now what to say to him.

"It's probably because you know more about the case than anyone else," I ventured. "And more than you are telling me."

Even Connecticut's forensic science laboratory chief Henry Lee had been dropping hints, warning him off the case, he said. "At one point, I am driving him to a lab in Stamford. Out of the blue he says to me, 'Frank, are you sure you want to do this?'

"I say to him, 'What do you mean?' Lee says, 'The next thing you know, there will be cameras, press, media. Not only you but your family will suffer.' By now he knows I am looking at the Skakels, in particular at Michael. I am saying to myself, 'What the fuck is he talking about?'

"I often alert detectives that they have to know how to handle the pressure," Lee explained years later. "I tell them to mentally prepare, that you have to be aware for your family. I didn't pressure Frank to drop the case."

I think it was that day in Bridgeport that I began to view Frank as I had myself a decade before, the lone anguished figure battling Ken Brief and Steve Isenberg at the *Stamford Advocate* and *Greenwich Time* for seven years. But Frank's position was more precarious than mine had been. I could rail at Ken, privately and in public, knowing he could not retaliate. I had another job. I worked for *Newsday*, covering the New York City Police Department. I could even annoy Isenberg, up to a point.

But Bridgeport was where Frank came to work every day. These were people he saw each time he entered the building. And Frank was a cop. If he opened his mouth, not only would the case be taken from him, but he risked being fired. And unlike me with my education, he could not walk out into another job.

"You know the worst thing?" he said. "The loneliness. Most investigations, especially ones of this magnitude, you work with a partner. You have someone to discuss them with, to trade ideas, to knock off and go have a drink with. In my narcotics investigations in Greenwich, I had Lunney. Here in Bridgeport I have no one."

That was another difference in our roles, I realized. Even at my lowest points, there were people I could talk to, commiserate with, people who had supported me. For years I had grumbled about Ken to Don Forst. I had complained about Isenberg to my friend Cotter at the *Post*. Cotter had finally come through, printing the interview in which I had lambasted Ken. A month later Ken had published my story.

So had Don. After the editors in Long Island had refused to publish my story on the Sutton report, it had been Don who had shepherded it through in what remained of *New York Newsday*.

I think it was at that moment in Frank's cubicle that I understood why he and I had developed a friendship. Or rather why he had sought me out. For me, the reason had been simple and straightforward. I had gravitated toward Frank because he was the case's prime source. And unlike Keegan, Lunney, Solomon, and Browne, I believed he knew what he was doing.

But not until that moment did I understand why I had become his friend. When we first met, he told me he felt I cared about the case as he did, that I lived it and slept and took it home like him, that it was more than just a job.

That was all true. But there was something more, which he had never articulated. It was not until that day in Bridgeport that I realized why I had become so important to him.

Now I understood why Frank had told me that night when I left his house in Greenwich, "Thank you for keeping an open mind. Thank you for listening to me." Frank needed me. All those years, he had been out there alone. All those years, he had been fighting Solomon. Even after Solomon retired, whenever Frank spoke to Browne, he was fighting Jack's shadow.

Here in Bridgeport, I realized I was the only one he could talk to. I was the only one he had to listen to, to hear him vent, to bounce ideas off, even if he could not share with me the details he had discovered about Michael.

I was the closest thing to his partner.

•

Frank knew he had no smoking gun. The golf club handle from the murder weapon with Anne Skakel's name had never been recovered. The Greenwich police had lost the dungarees Frank was certain Michael had worn the night of the murder. He wasn't even sure about the time Martha had been killed, whether at 10:00 P.M. when the dogs started barking or at midnight after Michael had returned from the Terriens'—if he went at all.

Yet everything in his thirty years as a cop, every pore and fiber in his body pointed to Michael. He could not share his reasons with me. He could not tell me about Dorothy Rogers, who'd heard Michael admit he'd been drunk, blacked out, and might have killed Martha. He couldn't discuss Larry Zicarelli, the family chauffeur, who said Michael had tried to jump off the Triborough Bridge because he'd done something so bad he would either have to kill himself or leave the country. He couldn't tell me of Higgins, who'd actually heard Michael's confession.

Finally, there were Michael's own words from the Sutton report, which I obviously did know about—his bizarre story of masturbating in the tree outside Martha's window, then placing himself at the crime scene, perhaps as the murder was occurring. Michael had volunteered this information when he was not a suspect. Why? Was he afraid someone had seen him? Had he left semen behind? Or was he so consumed by guilt he had to say something that implicated him? Frank didn't care what his reasons were. All he knew was what Michael had said.

And where was I in all this? Like the Sutton Associates report, I'd ruled out Littleton early on. No motive. Never met Martha. No knowledge of the neighborhood. End of story.

Unlike Frank, I couldn't exculpate Tommy or explain away those extra twenty minutes he said he'd spent with Martha. If she were killed at 10:00 P.M., he'd placed himself with her at precisely that time. Nor did I accept Frank's theory about why Tommy had lied to the police. As the Sutton report had noted, he was a consummate liar who'd fooled not only the police but the polygraph and his own doctors. I even questioned whether his mutual masturbation scenario had even occurred. Could Tommy have made up the masturbating scenario because, like Michael, he was afraid he had left semen behind?

Finally, I didn't accept Frank's theory about why Tommy had broken into tears as Krebs questioned him. Frank believed Tommy had taken the heat all these years and was about to finger Michael. I felt Tommy feared Krebs was closing in on him.

And knowing nothing of Frank's witnesses, I was not as certain as he was about Michael. Watching Frank in emotional disarray, I didn't dare press him on it.

•

Then, Cissy Ix revealed something to Frank she'd never said before. Over the years, he had remained in touch with her and her husband Bob. He'd been surprised at how cooperative they seemed, considering how close they were to the Skakels. Periodically, Frank would telephone, then drive out to visit them in Belle Haven.

"I kept going back because I knew she wasn't giving me everything. She was too intimate with the Skakels not to know more than what she was telling me. This time, I had told them I was coming and I assumed they must have been talking about the case."

"You know about the change of stories," he began, referring to my articles. "I can understand why Tommy would lie but why would Michael humiliate himself and say something like that, placing himself at the murder scene?

"I know you felt he was more capable of this than the police had thought," Frank said to Cissy. "And that's when she spilled it."

This time, Cissy told Frank that sometime after Martha's murder,

Rushton had visited Michael's bedroom and told her he'd found him dressed in women's clothing. Rushton discussed having tests performed on Michael and Cissy agreed.

"I don't know if I should tell you this, Frank, . . ." she said.

"Tell him, Cissy," commanded Bob Ix, seated beside her. "Tell him."

Sometime after the murder—Cissy was not sure of the date—Rushton came to their house and said Michael had confided that he may have murdered Martha.

"According to Mrs. Ix," Frank's report of November 20, 1997, read, "Michael told his father he had been drinking on the night in question, had blacked out, and may have murdered Martha. Mrs. Ix claims that due to a confidence she believed she owed Mr. Skakel, she has never revealed this information to anyone."

Frank sat there, wearing his best poker face, not letting on that this was another breakthrough. Now he felt he had someone on the inside, someone as close to the Skakel family as he could find.

"You can't do much better than that," he thought, "short of the old man himself telling this to me. And that wasn't going to happen."

•

Three months later, Father Mark Connolly, the Skakel family priest, told Frank of another admission Michael had made. It had occurred nearly twenty years before at Elan.

Frank had interviewed Connolly early in the investigation. He and Solomon had driven out to the rectory at St. Michael's on North Street, where he was the monsignor. Connolly had been forthcoming but afraid.

Just days before the murder, he said, "the boys," Tommy and Michael, had put up a ladder against Martha's house to peep in her window, he told Frank. Connolly then asked Frank to protect him by not even filing a written report of their interview.

"Why is that, Father?" Frank asked.

"Well," said Connolly, "Michael could be hard to control." Connolly said he was careful in what he said to Michael because he knew of Michael's temper and that he was capable of destroying the rectory.

Connolly was also a psychologist and had advised the family on schools for Michael. He had been consulted about sending Michael to Elan. Shortly after Michael was admitted, Connolly now told Frank, he visited him with Rushton Skakel and Tom Sheridan. A counselor advised them that Michael had described being covered in blood the night of the murder.

"He said Michael told him there was blood all over the place," Connolly remembered.

Later, Connolly told Frank, Michael visited him at his home and denied that the talk with his counselor had ever taken place. "Michael said it was all a lie," Connolly said.

•

Frank had also stayed in touch with Andy Pugh, Michael's best friend as a teenager. Frank knew how valuable Pugh could be as a witness. In one conversation he told Frank how, after the murder, everything about the Skakels changed. Before the murder, their house was wide open. The day after the murder, it was locked down.

"You couldn't get in; it was like a fortress," Pugh said. When a few days after the murder Pugh came over to see Michael, a suit—someone hired by the Skakels—had stopped him at the door, then went and fetched Michael for him. Why the change? Frank wondered. Were the Skakels afraid that the hitchhiker off the turnpike might return and harm their children? Unlikely, Frank thought.

Now, early in 1998, Pugh told Frank something he'd never revealed before. As teenagers, Pugh said, he and Michael had played together every day after school, climbing trees. Their favorite was a pine at the edge of the adjoining Moxley property that was surrounded by smaller, thinner pines. Unlike the smaller ones, their pine tree had branches like a ladder. Six feet off the ground, the branches swept down and covered the ground, resembling a tee-pee where they could go in the rain. He and Michael referred to the pine as "The Tree."

"In the early 1990s," Pugh said to Frank, "Michael contacted me. He suggested we restart our friendship. He said that because the golf club had come from his house, he could understand why I thought he might have killed Martha. He denied he had, but he told me that by a strange coincidence he had been outside on the night of the murder and had climbed a tree and masturbated in it."

"You mean the tree outside Martha's window?" said Frank.

"No," said Pugh, "It was 'The Tree'—the pine at the edge of the Moxley property."

That was the tree where Martha's body was discovered.

•

Then Frank's former employer, Frank Gifford, told him about Michael Meredith, the troubled son of former Dallas Cowboys football star Don Meredith, Gifford's television partner on ABC's original *Monday Night Football.* Gifford also had a Kennedy connection. His daughter Vicki had been married to Ethel's son, Michael Kennedy. In a horrible scandal, Michael Kennedy was caught cheating on his wife with the family's teenage baby-sitter and later that year died in a freak ski accident.

A few years younger than Michael Skakel, Meredith had also been at Elan. In 1986, after both had graduated, Meredith spent the summer at the Skakel house in Greenwich as he and Michael prepared a lawsuit against the school and its owner, Joe Ricci.

One evening, Michael Skakel told Meredith that on the night of Martha's murder he had been in a tree on the Moxley property where he jerked off while watching Martha through her window after she'd come out of the shower. While in the tree, he said, he saw Tommy walk through Moxley's property toward their house. He then climbed down from the tree and went home without his brother seeing him.

The truth remains the same but a lie always changes, Frank thought. Here was yet another variation. This time, Michael claimed to have seen Martha in the shower, and implicated his brother Tommy. In addition, this masturbation-in-the-tree story predated the one Michael had told to Krebs of Sutton Associates, who had heard it in 1992. Jesus Christ, Frank thought, Michael had been telling a version of that story for years.

•

Frank felt that Elan was the key. He obtained a warrant for Michael's medical records and on a crisp fall day drove up to Poland Springs, Maine. Leaving the main road, with red and gold leaves covering the ground, he passed fields of tall grass that opened into a campsite with wooden dormitories and quonset huts. Frank found himself thinking that Elan resembled a summer camp. He half-expected to see kids running around in their sailing gear, except that there was no water.

Instead, the first thing he heard were screams. Although he was to learn they were part of what was known at Elan as "primal scream therapy," he wasn't prepared for them.

Frank's warrant also sought notes and recordings by Ricci and other staff about Martha's murder. Detective Mike Pulire of Maine's attorney general's office, who accompanied him, had briefed Frank on Ricci, a self-made, wheeler-dealer millionaire in his forties from New York, who roamed the grounds at Elan like a commandant with a Doberman.

Ricci also owned Maine's Scarborough Downs race track and had made an unsuccessful run for governor. When he applied for a loan with Key Bank in Maine, they somehow connected him with organized crime and rejected it. Ricci filed suit and won a judgment of $16 million.

So far as anyone knew, he was not married but had two children. Female residents supposedly came over to "baby-sit" for him. One of them reported finding him drunk in his trailer with a half-inch stack of $100 bills.

John Higgins, Chuck Seigan, Dorothy Rogers, and Michael Meredith had all told Frank horror stories about Ricci and Elan. Residents, known as "gorillas on duty," walked around with baseball bats, making sure no one escaped. One resident had been forced to stay up thirty-six hours. When he nodded off, they put him in the shower to wake him up. He was denied food for another thirty-six hours.

Another punishment was the boxing ring, where, one at a time, the "gorillas" took turns beating up the more fractious residents. Then, there was the story of Kim Freehill. She had been paddled so hard because of her bad attitude that she collapsed and had to be airlifted to a hospital.

As he and Pulire walked around, they happened to see a father and his teenage daughter. She was a beautiful, blonde, angelic-looking girl, Frank thought. He didn't know anything about her. She could have been the devil. But he had this urge to run over to the father and say to him, "Whatever you do, don't send her here."

Instead, he and Pulire went searching for Ricci. He was not there. Through his attorney in Portland, he stated that he did not believe any files concerning Michael existed but directed staff members to cooperate.

Frank walked up an old wooden staircase to a stuffy, dormer-like attic, lined with old metal filing cabinets that supposedly contained the records of all Elan's past residents. Each file, Frank noted, was two to three inches thick. Except Michael's. It contained only a few pages.

As Frank glanced through them, he saw they contained only Michael's education and employment history. There were no tapes of interviews, no notes of meetings, nothing about the group sessions in which Michael was supposedly questioned about his involvement in Martha's murder. Frank believed the file had been purged.

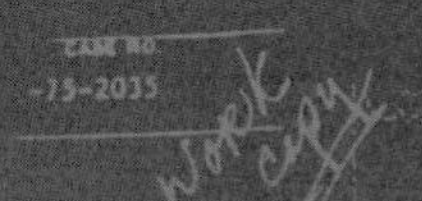

# PART IV

22
12

# 17

PART FOUR / CHAPTER SEVENTEEN

# The Stars and the Hacks

CONNECTICUT
1997–2000

I wanted to throttle Dominick Dunne.

The cherubic-looking, seventy-something celebrity writer, supposedly a source of comfort to families of murder victims, had just sent Dorthy into hysterics.

In early 1997, she called me in tears after a phone conversation with him. Dominick had told her that in all the years the police investigated Martha's killer, they'd focused on the wrong person.

"Who is the right person?" Dorthy asked him.

"I can't tell you that now," he answered, then hung up.

Amidst her tears, she told me that one of Jim Murphy's employees had given Dominick a copy of Murphy's Sutton Associates report, which Dominick claimed contained shocking revelations. She asked if I would call him to learn what he meant.

I, too, wanted to know. Had he discovered something I'd overlooked when writing about the report two years before? Dominick and I were acquainted. One might even say we were friends. We'd met at the Greenwich police news conference in 1991, where the reopening of the

***A 1975 yearbook picture of Michael Skakel (top center).***

case was announced. With his shock of gray hair and wearing a suit and tie, Dominick had arrived with Dorthy to begin researching his novel about Martha's murder. When she introduced us, he offered that he might be able to help the police solve the case through what he termed his "upper-class connections."

I nearly burst out laughing. Did Dominick think he could waltz into a fifteen-year-old murder case and help the police solve it like Hercule Poirot? Maybe that happened in Agatha Christie mysteries, but this was real life.

Little did I suspect that after his novel about the murder appeared, people would flock to him with all sorts of tips.

After meeting him that day in Greenwich, I bought his first best-seller, *The Two Mrs. Grenvilles* (New York: Random House, 1985). Coincidentally, it was based on something I knew about—the murder of Long Island horseman and socialite William Woodward.

That was the murder detective Frank Steiner had supposedly solved. When I interviewed Steiner at *Newsday* twenty years after the case, he explained to me that shortly before Woodward's death, he had arrested a German immigrant, Paul Wirths, for a series of burglaries on the north shore of Long Island. Wirths had come to the United States to live with his aunt and uncle and train as a bricklayer's apprentice. A scaffold had fallen on him and he had broken his arm. Unable to work, he began to steal.

The day after Woodward's shooting, Wirths was arrested just over the county line for another burglary. When Steiner questioned him in jail, Wirths denied knowing about the Woodward shooting.

"Paul," Steiner said to him, "Ann Woodward has two young children. Is there anything you can say that will help her?"

At four o'clock the next morning, Steiner said Wirths telephoned him at home and confessed to being the prowler on the Woodward estate. He was swiftly deported and Ann Woodward was never charged. The Woodward estate was rumored to have paid Steiner $50,000 for Wirth's false confession.

In *The Two Mrs. Grenvilles*, Dominick captured all of this. Although

Dominick had never met him, he even captured Steiner's legal shenanigans. He had melded the mores of upper-class society with the factual details of the Woodward murder into a larger fictional truth.

He would do something similar in the Moxley case. With his novelist's eye, he would turn the Sutton report into the murder's Rosetta stone, providing him with the psychological underpinnings to make Michael—with his history of bed-wetting, cross-dressing, window-peeping, alcoholism, drug abuse, and violence—the obvious murderer.

Of course, Dominick knew even less about Frank's investigation of Michael than I did. But when Michael was arrested years later, Dominick took credit. As he wrote in the introduction to *Justice* (New York: Crown Publishing Group, 2001), a collection of his *Vanity Fair* articles, "A young man appeared out of nowhere to hand me a secret report by a private detective agency hired by the father of Michael Skakel that led directly to the indictment and trial of Skakel for the murder of fifteen-year-old Martha Moxley twenty-five years earlier."

I subsequently began reading Dominick's books and articles to discover all I could about him. He had grown up in Hartford, Connecticut, the son of a heart surgeon. His younger brother was the novelist John Gregory Dunne (married to the writer Joan Didion) and the author of *True Confessions*, based on the Black Dahlia murder in Los Angeles, one of the grittiest crime novels I've ever read.

Dominick had attended the same boarding school as Rushton Skakel and been a guest at Robert and Ethel Kennedy's wedding. Despite his family's wealth, the Dunnes had remained outsiders to Hartford's Protestant society, which dismissed them as Irish Catholic and nouveau riche. George Skakel Sr.'s family had suffered similarly when they'd moved to Greenwich in the 1930s.

Dominick also shared common ground with Michael. Like Michael, he had been tormented by his father, who wanted his son to be an athlete—"more manly," as Dominick put it. Once, his father became so enraged, he beat Dominick with a wooden coat hanger, striking his left ear so severely it turned purple and swelled to three times its size. To this day, Dominick says he remains partially deaf in that ear.

"I'm surprised you never made the connection to Michael when you wrote about the case," I said to him.

"You're right," he answered. "I never thought of it," adding that his father died before they ever made peace. "We never had that talk," he said, as though a conversation can heal a childhood of wounds.

For reasons I never understood, Dominick never wrote about the one thing he had done that pleased his father. At age eighteen, during World War II, he was drafted and fought in the Battle of the Bulge, and received a bronze star for saving a soldier's life.

As he related this to me over lunch years later, his eyes filled with tears. "I was so scared. There were two wounded men and the lieutenant said we had to leave them. I don't understand what happened next but another soldier and I—another rich kid; he had gone to Choate; the two of us were known as "The Gold Dust Twins"—ran back to them. I don't know how but I had this surge of adrenaline and carried one of them to a passing ambulance. He squeezed my hand in thanks. I never knew his name."

The story made the Hartford newspapers, but his father never acknowledged his son's bravery. One night, his family went to dinner at their country club. "It was a Thursday night—maid's night out," Dominick said. "A woman, a friend of the family, approached me and said how proud everyone was of me, especially my father. I don't know why but I started to cry."

After the war, Dominick moved to Los Angeles, where he became a movie and television producer. Thirty years later, his career flamed out and he sank into alcoholism and drugs. He was, he wrote, "as my agent told me, all washed up, which I already knew."

By force of will, he spent six months in a cabin in the Cascade Mountains of Oregon, drying out. At age fifty, he began his second career as a writer. His catalyst was David Begelman, a Hollywood executive who'd forged a $10,000 check in the name of actor Cliff Robertson. When two reporters from the *Washington Post* came around, Dominick provided them with information he says broke open the story.

"It was thrilling for me to know I played a part in it," he wrote in an article titled "Justice" in *Vanity Fair*. "I felt a kind of excitement within myself . . . *I could do what these guys are doing. . . .*"

Then, in 1982, Dominick suffered the personal tragedy that was to launch his writing career. His daughter Dominique, an actress, was murdered by her boyfriend. Dominick's first *Vanity Fair* article, "A Father's Account of the Trial of His Daughter's Killer," in March 1984, described how the boyfriend pleaded temporary insanity, then walked virtually scot-free from a Los Angeles courtroom.

Since then, he'd covered trials of the rich and powerful and become a celebrity himself. My friend Cotter at the *Post* had met him in Newport, Rhode Island, at the trial of Claus Von Bulow, who was accused of poisoning his comatose wife Sunny. Cotter told me how helpful Dominick was to reporters with daily deadlines. Cotter referred to him as "Nick."

Since that news conference at Greenwich police headquarters, he and I had become friendly. He professed to admire my work and, after my first article, called from time to time. When his novel about Martha's murder, *A Season in Purgatory*, was published in 1993, I tagged along to his book signing in Greenwich, hoping to meet some of his upper-class connections who might help solve the case. Alas, none materialized.

I assumed that Dominick's friendliness stemmed from this: While all investigative reporters I know want to become best-selling novelists, Dominick was the only best-selling novelist I knew who wanted to become an investigative reporter.

But as events revealed, my career as an investigative reporter and his as a novelist would prove mutually exclusive. An investigative reporter is concerned first with accuracy. If a fact is incorrect, his entire work is diminished. If he does his job properly, he remains faceless and invisible.

A novelist paints on a wider canvas. He can omit, alter, or even make up facts. Sometimes, as Dominick did in the Moxley case, he can write himself into the story.

Perhaps because he had been rendered powerless in the murder of his daughter, I think Dominick came to see himself as a Lone Ranger–like figure, an avenger righting wrongs, helping victims like Dorthy, who were unable to help themselves. In fact, I thought he seemed like me.

Before I called him, as Dorthy had asked me to do to follow up on the Sutton report hint that he had dropped, I telephoned Jim Murphy to learn how Dominick had obtained his report. Murphy blamed a twenty-one-year-old employee, Jamie Bryan, the son of a family friend Murphy had hired to write it. Then, I called Dominick.

But as I described to him Dorthy's call to me and mine to Murphy, Dominick dispelled any inkling that we were kindred investigative spirits. He cut short our conversation. He did not speak to me again for two years.

Some months later, he responded to a phone message I'd left for him by sending me a fax at my office at Police Plaza in New York, mistakenly accusing me of unmasking Bryan as his source: "After you heard from Dorthy Moxley that I had a copy of the Sutton Report, you called your friend at Sutton Associates to tell him that a young man working for him had given a copy of the report to me. The young man had performed a decent act and your call to his boss put him into a state of abject fear for which I felt a responsibility. I knew then I would never give the report to you."

Dominick did provide a copy of the Sutton report to Frank. But when Frank showed no interest in it, having been apprised of much of its contents by me, Dominick was no kinder to him. As his fax to me continued, "In time I gave a copy to Frank Garr. . . . That was a total waste of time. I really regretted having given the report to Frank."

Dominick also claimed, incorrectly as far as I knew, that Frank was planning to write a book. "Only my innate good manners," Dominick's fax continued, "kept me from saying. 'On what? On how you couldn't solve the case for over twenty years?' Or maybe he was planning on using the Sutton report as his plot. Over and out with Frank."

I was stunned. I was so angry with Dominick, I called Frank in Bridgeport. "You've got to see this," I said.

"Read it to me," he said.

"No, you've got to see it to get the full flavor."

That night I drove over to Frank's house. "Here," I said, throwing it on his kitchen table. "Read it and weep."

Frank said nothing for a few moments as he scanned the fax. Then he shook his head and looked up. "Writers," he said, staring at me an extra second, I thought. "They're all the same."

For a moment I was taken aback. Frank was being his wise-ass self but I wasn't amused. Perhaps because I was so pissed at Dominick, I didn't feel like being included as the butt of one of his flippant remarks.

"Where did he get the idea you were writing a book?" I asked. "I didn't know you were a writer, too." I, also, could be a wise-ass.

"I have no idea," Frank replied. I think he realized how upset I was, although I wasn't sure he knew whether it was more at him or at Dominick. At that moment, I wasn't so sure myself.

"I remember telling Dominick," Frank continued, "that Dorthy suggested I write a book. But I told her my job is solving this case."

Then Frank told me how years before, at Dorthy's urging, he had met with Dominick. "I didn't want to but she claimed he had information he wanted to share. 'Promise me one thing,' she said after I agreed to do it. 'Promise me you'll be nice.' "

Frank and Solomon drove up to Dominick's house in Hadlyme on the Connecticut shore. "And what a place it was," said Frank. "It overlooked a river, with marshes and tributaries. I didn't want to leave. And Dominick and I hit it off. By the time we finished, he was showing me all around the place. He had a picture of Elizabeth Taylor in the living room. And he and I, a one-time actor, just got to talking."

As Dominick had with me, he began passing tips to Frank. One involved Paul Terrien, whose brother George was Jimmy Terrien's stepfather. Paul Terrien had appeared at one of Dominick's book signings and told Dominick there had been a conspiracy to kill Martha and that two boys were involved. Dominick hadn't been able to speak to him then in more detail. When Dominick visited him at his home in nearby Essex, Paul Terrien refused to say more. Nor would he say more to Frank when he called him.

A second tip concerned Dr. Kathy Morrall, the Colorado forensic pathologist Solomon had brought to Greenwich years before to examine

Littleton. She, too, had appeared at one of Dominick's book signings, in Denver, and showed Dominick Martha's autopsy pictures that Jack Solomon had given her.

"I thought I was serving as an intermediary between Frank and Dominick because of the breakdown in communications between them," she told me years later.

Frank didn't see it that way.

Frank also called Morrall, and threatened her with arrest. "I told her, 'I know what you did. I am going to tell you right now, I want you to put all that material that we gave you in an envelope. You send it to me and I better have it and all copies of it.' She knew what she had done. I also told her that if I didn't receive those items immediately I would contact the Denver police."

"Now let me tell you about this Sutton report," Frank said to me. "I first heard about it from Dorthy. She calls me at home on a Saturday and tells me Dominick has it and Len Levitt knows about it. It was one of the few times I was upset with her. No, I was furious. I mean, what good does Dominick Dunne or Len Levitt having the report do? Are they going to make an arrest? Why hasn't anyone told me? So I called Dominick and he gave it to me. But there was nothing in it. It was all theories and speculation."

There was more in Dominick's fax that foreshadowed our troubles with him.

"Then along came Mark Fuhrman," the fax continued. "His literary agent was Lucianne Goldberg, who used to be a friend of mine. She told me Mark was looking for an unsolved murder to write about for his next book. . . .

"To give this report to Mark was a calculated decision and a brilliant one if I say so myself. It has nothing to do with the fact that I knew him from the O. J. Simpson case. It had everything to do with the fact that he is both famous and infamous, and I knew that he would get on every television show on network and cable and tell the story of Martha Moxley over and over and over, until it finally began to sink in. . . . Whatever you think of Mark, he's a star. . . .

"By the way, his publisher would only make the deal on the condition that I write the introduction . . . I was paid nothing and I'm a very high-priced author. . . ."

Reading the fax with Frank at his kitchen table, I felt as though a giant wave had knocked us down, then rolled over us. For the past fifteen years, he and I had done the case's grunt work. I had kept it alive in the media. My articles on the Sutton report had redirected the investigation back to the Skakels. Without Frank, the case would have died years before.

Now, a new team had arrived: a celebrity writer and a disgraced detective. They would ride that wave to stardom.

I had laughed at Dominick when I first met him and he said he could help solve the case through his upper-class connections. Now he had turned the tables on me. I was furious—less at Fuhrman, whom I'd never met, than at Dominick by whom I felt betrayed. Well, perhaps betrayed was too strong a word. You had to know someone well to feel betrayed. I only thought I knew Dominick.

"Writers," Frank had said, "they're all the same." When he'd said that, I'd become angry at him. Now I could understand what he meant.

I tried to dispel Dominick's claims but I found I was powerless to correct them. He and Fuhrman were names. Frank and I were the grunts. An article in the *New York Observer* called them the stars. It called Frank and me the "hacks."

I was also furious at myself for feeling the way I did. All these years I'd been telling myself and anyone else who asked that my sole concern was helping to solve Martha Moxley's murder. So why should it matter that Dominick and Fuhrman got the credit? For all my high-minded talk about a journalist's proper role, my jealousy made me feel like a smaller person.

# 18

PART FOUR / CHAPTER EIGHTEEN

# "Nobody Will Believe You"

CONNECTICUT
1997–1998

In the fall of 1997, Fuhrman arrived in Connecticut. His ghostwriter Steve Weeks asked if I would meet with them and I invited them to my house for lunch. We ate sandwiches on my back porch and sized each other up.

Like everyone in America, I know Fuhrman as the detective in the O.J. Simpson case, charged with perjury for denying he used the slur "nigger." There seemed something bizarre about someone who was trashed in the O.J. case as a liar, then wrote a best-selling book about it. His decision to come to Connecticut to pursue a murder he knew nothing about seemed foolhardy but bold.

Realizing the difficulties I knew he would face, chiefly a short deadline for his manuscript, I offered to help. But our meeting did not go well.

I told him I wanted to write an article for *Newsday* about Dominick's giving him the Sutton report.

"I don't want you to do that," Fuhrman said.

"Why not?" I asked.

"It won't be helpful."

"What does that mean?"

Fuhrman did not answer.

I wrote the article the following week.

I never heard from him again.

•

Through Dominick, Fuhrman sought to meet with Frank.

Frank and I were having breakfast at the Lakeside. Fuhrman and Weeks were holed up at the three-star Homestead Inn in Greenwich.

"Dominick says to me, 'Did you ever hear of this guy Mark Fuhrman?'" Frank began. "What does he think, I live in a cave?

"'I think he got a bad rap,' Dominick says. 'I want to help him. I want to bring you two together. I want you and Mark to come into the city. I want you to work with him.'"

"'I can't tell him anything more than he could get at the local library, from the Freedom of Information report, or from old newspaper reports,' I say. There is a silence—dead air on Dominick's side of the telephone.

"That ended my relationship with Dominick. From that point on, I was no good. Any time Dominick had a shot, he took it. It was all because I refused to meet with Fuhrman."

Writing in "Trail of Guilt" (*Vanity Fair*, October 2000), Dominick put it this way: "I gave a cocktail party for [Fuhrman]. I've always admired cops and I hate to see the way they are treated on the stand by defense attorneys at murder trials. I invited several local cops and their wives, as well as some O.J. junkies among the weekenders who wanted to meet the famous—or infamous—Mark Fuhrman. I also called to invite Frank Garr, thinking he would be thrilled that another book on the case was in the works. He wasn't thrilled at all. . . ."

"Next," Frank continued, "Fuhrman calls me. 'How about we get together?' he says. 'I am writing this book. I can use some help. I know you have a lot of stuff.'

"'I do, Mark,' I say, 'but I can't share it with you. All I can tell you is, go to the Greenwich library and get the Freedom of Information report that Len Levitt wrote about in the newspaper. That is the best I can do.'

"Then he asks me to have lunch with him. He says, 'I never heard of a cop who turned down a free meal.' Well, I took that as an insult. That was the end of that conversation."

•

Next, Dorthy telephoned him.

"She says, 'Frank, would you do me a favor?'

" 'What is it?' I say. She knows I could never refuse her anything. Remember how I told you she got me to agree to see Dominick?

" 'Mark is here,' she says. 'Would you please speak to him?'

" 'Okay,' I say. 'Put him on.'

" 'Frank, I know you said you wouldn't but I need some help. Frank, I want to work with you.'

" 'Mark, I told you I can't share anything with you.'

" 'You'll be sorry,' Fuhrman says. 'If you don't cooperate with me, I'll make you look like shit in my book.'

"Well, I'm furious at him now. I'm furious at Dorthy Moxley for putting me in this position. Fuhrman knows better than anyone that detectives can't talk about ongoing cases. If someone came to him when he was a homicide detective in L.A. and asked him to share information, Fuhrman would have thrown him out of his office. And he would have been right.

" 'Who the fuck do you think you're talking to?' I say to him. 'Put Mrs. Moxley back on the phone.'

"When she comes on the line, I say to her, 'Mrs. Moxley, don't ever do that to me again.' "

•

Frank's situation with Fuhrman only grew worse. In the spring of 1998, there were rumors about Fuhrman's book. Dominick was saying Fuhrman would name Michael as Martha's killer.

Again, Frank went to state's attorney Donald Browne. "We have to move on this," he said. "If Fuhrman's book comes out before we act, no one will believe we had the information first. We will never convince people. They will all say, 'Mark Fuhrman solved the case.' "

"What's he got?" Browne answered.

"Nothing I don't already have."

It was then that Browne broached the possibility of withdrawing from the case. Jonathan Benedict—his successor as Fairfield County's state's attorney—had begun familiarizing himself with it.

"Maybe it is better if Benedict picks up on this," Browne said.

"It's your call," Frank answered. He felt Browne was not aggressive enough but Browne knew the case. Benedict didn't. To get up to speed, Benedict would need time, which they didn't have.

"You have been on it since it happened," Frank said. "It will take Benedict two, three months to review the case. But you have to make a decision one way or the other."

Meanwhile, early in 1998, another book on the Moxley case was published, *Greentown* (New York: Arcade Books, 1998) by Tim Dumas, the young Greenwich writer.

"Some journalists on this story have wondered," Dumas wrote, "whether Browne has been 'paid off.' They note that, strategically, he'd be the right man to pay off since he holds the power to keep the case in abeyance."

After supervising the Moxley case for twenty-three years, Browne cited those two sentences to bail out of the case. Frank called me to tip me off.

"You're not going to believe this," he said. "Browne is out. And you know the reason he gives? He says that because of Dumas's book, he has a conflict of interest. The real reason he's withdrawing is because he's afraid to make a decision whether or not to go forward with the case. He used that line as an excuse to bail out."

I called the *Stamford Advocate* and told them I had a story for them. I told Frank I wanted to use his line.

"Use it," he said. "Just attribute it to a law enforcement source."

Then I called Browne at home. I told him I heard he had resigned.

"There's a perception of conflict now," he said. "If I proceeded to indict, I am leaving myself exposed as having done it to avoid the perception I have been paid off. If I don't, then the perception is I have already been paid off."

I then read him Frank's quote.

"Where did you hear that?" he said.

"Is it true?"

"I can figure out where it came from."

Those were Browne's final words on the case. No one heard from him again.

•

And so Benedict, another career prosecutor, took over the investigation. Lanky and white-haired, married with three grown children, he looked like a shorter version of Jimmy Stewart. The son of a lawyer, he had graduated from Lafayette College and St. John's Law School in New York and served three years in the army, including one in Vietnam. He had worked in private practice with his father for two years, then in 1976 joined the state's attorney's office, where he'd remained ever since.

Frank went after him with the same argument he'd made to Browne: If Fuhrman's book appeared before Benedict sought the grand jury, the world would believe it was Fuhrman who'd caused them to call it. If the grand jury indicted Michael, everyone would think Fuhrman had solved the case.

But Benedict refused to be pushed. He was waiting for some lab work that later proved inconsequential. "Even if we move now," he said, "Fuhrman and Dominick will say we rushed it just to beat his book."

Frank saw another problem. Benedict wanted a "second chair," an experienced criminal lawyer working under him, someone from the chief state's attorney's office. Frank protested. He distrusted the motives of the chief state's attorney, John Bailey Jr. Bailey's father had been Connecticut's Democratic state chairman in the 1960s and supported John F.

Kennedy for President. In return, Kennedy had appointed him national Democratic chair. While John Bailey Jr. reveled in the spotlight, seeking out newspaper and television reporters, he had avoided the media in the Moxley case, perhaps the most publicized murder in the state's history.

"You never saw him at any press conference," Frank said to me one night that spring, just a month after Browne had resigned. We were alone at his house. His children were out. Mariann was working the late shift at the hospital. Again, we were sitting in his kitchen, assessing the case, discussing how far it had come. Benedict was about to call the grand jury. It seemed like a miracle.

"When we announced a reward, Bailey didn't appear," Frank continued. "He never wanted any part of it. So I am thinking, 'Why does the chief state's attorney's office want to be involved now?' "

At Benedict's request, Bailey sent two assistants—Chris Morano and Dominick Galluzo. "I'm asking myself, are they here to help or to watch what is going on? I didn't trust either of them. I had no use for them and they knew it."

Frank felt his suspicions proved justified when he discovered both of them meeting with Fuhrman. At least twice, he said, he discovered they'd been together in New York. Their intermediary was Dominick Dunne, who was Morano's neighbor on the eastern Connecticut shore.

"I am telling Benedict that Fuhrman is the most notorious liar in America. I am hearing that Fuhrman is pushing to get himself called as a witness before the grand jury and that Morano and Galluzo are helping him. I'm telling myself it will be over my dead body," Frank said.

"Frank," I said, "you're making too much of this. Benedict is going to call the grand jury. That's what's important. That's what you've been waiting for."

It was nearly midnight when I left his house. As I drove home, I couldn't decide if what he was telling me were true or whether he had been out there so alone for so long he had lost his sense of proportion. He seemed oblivious that his moment of triumph was about to arrive.

That night I had a dream. The two of us were, of all places, at the north pole. We were standing just a few feet apart. I was on the shore but

Frank was on an ice floe, moving past me, beyond my reach, heading out to sea. As Frank passed by, he was waving his arms, shouting his warnings about Fuhrman.

As it turned out, Fuhrman never testified before the grand jury. As much as he tried, Benedict refused to let him.

He had apparently picked up Frank's SOS.

•

Then, just before the grand jury was called, Fuhrman's book appeared, naming Michael as Martha's probable killer. For years, Frank had complained to me that no one saw the case as he did. Finally, someone had: Of all people, it was Mark Fuhrman.

Not only that, but Fuhrman's theory about the time of death matched Frank's. Like Frank, Fuhrman believed the murder had occurred not at 10:00 P.M. while Michael was at the Terriens' but around midnight, after he returned.

On the book's cover was a color photo of Martha with long blonde hair to her shoulders. "Using his detective skills to analyze the case and uncover explosive new information—including top secret documents compiled by the Skakels' own investigators," the book jacket stated, "Mark Fuhrman will reveal how the local police mishandled the case from the beginning; how wealth and influence interfered with the investigation . . . and how authorities tried to stop Fuhrman's investigation."

Beating the drum for Fuhrman was Dominick. In his article "Trail of Guilt," he wrote, "I firmly believe that his book, *Murder in Greenwich*, for which I wrote the introduction, is what caused a grand jury to be called after twenty-five years."

I had to give Fuhrman credit. He knew little about the case—far less than Frank—but his instincts were right. He'd pieced together the general terms of it. I remembered hearing Alan Dershowitz, one of Simpson's lawyers from the O.J. case, say of Fuhrman that he was smarter than anyone else on the prosecution team including all the lawyers. But, said

Dershowitz, "If his own credibility is involved, the defense will make mincement of him."

Fuhrman was generous to me. He cited my articles and listed me in his acknowledgments although I had done nothing to help him. But he was brutal to Frank. To Fuhrman, Frank was one of the so-called "authorities" who had tried to stop his investigation.

"I tried at least to convince Frank to have lunch with me—I've never known a cop to turn down a free meal—but my efforts were fruitless," he wrote. "Frank wouldn't cooperate with me, wouldn't meet with me, wouldn't have lunch with me, nothing. He said he was too busy now, and in the future.

"As I hung up the phone," Fuhrman continued, "I could only assume that Frank was afraid of something. . . . I sensed that something else was behind Frank's refusal to work with me. Something was starting to smell, but I didn't know what it was."

I was also starting to smell something. It was only then that I realized what Fuhrman was about. Just as Dominick's forte—or schtick—was celebrity murders, Fuhrman's was murders the police had bungled. And the person Fuhrman claimed had bungled the Moxley case was the man who had figured it out six years before.

"Dominick Dunne gave Frank Garr a copy of the Sutton Associates files in the winter of 1997," Fuhrman wrote. "Yet apparently Frank had talked to hardly any of the people I interviewed whose names I got from the files. And none of the leads I followed showed any of Garr's tracks."

In the afterword to his paperback edition, he took another tack. "I did have evidence to give to the authorities but I had no intention of giving it to Frank Garr," he wrote. "Instead, I went over his head, contacting Connecticut state officials and offering my total cooperation with their investigation . . . as well as information I was not able to include in the book."

Frank was so upset he called me. I drove over to his house. While I sat at his kitchen table, Frank paced the room. "He is such a liar. He, better than anyone, knows I couldn't talk to him about the case, even if I wanted to."

With that he flicked on the television. There on CNN or Fox or one of the network talk shows was Fuhrman. He was crowing over how he'd solved the Moxley murder.

Frank and I turned and looked at each other. I didn't know whether to laugh or scream. Frank opened his mouth but no words came. If ever I saw a man crushed, this was it.

He'd fought with his superiors for nearly a decade over Michael. He'd been ostracized by his colleagues and ridiculed by his bosses yet had virtually single-handedly gotten a grand jury impaneled. And here was Fuhrman, with barely a connection to the case, taking the credit.

And I, with my Ivy League education, a graduate of the Columbia School of Journalism with thirty years of newspaper experience, was powerless to help him. I wanted to reach over and hug him, or at least touch his arm in commiseration. I didn't, though. Instead, all I could think to say was, "Frank, I'm so very sorry."

But I made a promise to myself, and to him. When the case was over, I promised that no matter which way it went, no matter how the grand jury ruled, I would tell the story, his and mine.

Frank shook his head. "I pray that you do," he said. "And I'll try to help you. But you're only jerking yourself off. Nobody will listen. Nobody will believe you."

# 19

PART FOUR / CHAPTER NINETEEN

# The Face of the Killer

CONNECTICUT
1998–2000

It was a Thursday night in December 1998. Late. Mariann and the kids were asleep. But Frank was just getting started. He sat in his study on the second floor. It had been Dave's room before he moved downstairs and took over the basement. Frank was seated on the couch, his tape recorder on, seven audiotapes spread out before him.

Just a few hours before, he had returned from Cambridge, Massachusetts, with Michael's audiotaped memoir and manuscript. He had obtained an out-of-state subpoena and driven up to the Cambridge home of Michael's ghostwriter, Richard Hoffman.

"Do I have to give you everything?" Hoffman asked when Frank presented him with the subpoena.

"Yes, you do," Frank answered.

Hoffman went upstairs and returned with a cardboard box. In it were Michael's manuscript and the seven audiotapes.

Late that Thursday night, Frank sat in his study, reading Michael's thirty-seven-page proposal: "The first account by an insider of the avarice, perversion and gangsterism of 'America's Royal Family.'" In it

Michael promised to unmask "the truth about the . . . cover-up and my betrayal at the hands of the ruthless Kennedy machine when I would no longer lie to hide the truth about my cousin's behavior." The cousin was his aunt Ethel's son, Michael Kennedy.

The memoir described how after Elan, Michael had found sobriety and become a mentor to his troubled Kennedy cousins, his aunt Ethel's children. When Bobby Jr. was arrested for heroin possession in 1983 after passing out in the bathroom of a Republic Airlines plane with a needle in his arm, Michael helped him begin treatment.

He also tried to get David Kennedy into a program. Ethel, however, refused to allow her son to register under his Kennedy name. A few weeks later, David was found dead in a Palm Beach hotel room of a drug overdose.

Michael also tried to help another cousin—Frank Gifford's son-in-law, Michael Kennedy, who was having an affair with his family's fifteen-year-old baby-sitter. The two Michaels had become close. Michael Kennedy managed the gubernatorial campaign of his older brother, Joe Kennedy II, and obtained a job there for Michael Skakel as a driver.

Michael Skakel wrote that he tried to help his cousin enter treatment for alcoholism and sexual addiction. Skakel said he asked Bobby Jr. and Joe for help but they refused. A grand jury was called to investigate Michael Kennedy for statutory rape of the baby-sitter, and Michael Skakel testified. Six months later, Michael Kennedy died in a skiing accident in Aspen, Colorado. The Kennedys blamed Michael Skakel.

"The timeless Kennedy strategy of circling the wagons and looking for a scapegoat began," he wrote. "I was blind-sided by a series of betrayals that were designed to assassinate my character and sacrifice me to the media in order to hide the sordid truth about my cousin's addiction and its many secret consequences. All the idealistic talk was conceived as a useful mythology to hide reality, not only about Michael but about his brother Joe and even about my aunt Ethel. . . ."

Specifically, Michael wrote, the Kennedys told a reporter for the *Boston Herald* that Michael Skakel was "a suspect in an old unsolved murder and was trying to extort $250,000 from them by fabricating a story about Michael Kennedy and the family baby-sitter."

One tape described the 1978 car accident in Windham that got Skakel sent to Elan. Michael described how Tom Sheridan brought in two goons, who literally kidnapped him from his Windham skihouse. Michael said he tried to escape by jumping out a second-story window into the snow.

"'I want a different lawyer!' I screamed. 'Sheridan! You're fired! You hear me? You work for my family, you bastard. You can't do this! You're fired! Now, I'm firing you! You hear me?'"

He then described how Sheridan had flown with him on the Skakels' plane to Poland Springs, Maine, where a van met them at the airport and drove them to Elan. Like Frank, the first thing Michael had heard were people screaming.

"They threw me into a horrible barracks. People were screaming. They had signs around their necks. I was strip-searched, given a cold shower, placed in a room with plastic covers over the windows."

In two years, Michael said he received only two letters from his father. One said Tommy was on a yacht in South America. The second said Rushton was in Vail skiing.

At monthly meetings, he said, the Elan counselors stood him up in front of a group of residents and asked him, "'Did you get any mail this month?' . . . just like to make sure everyone knew Skakel is a piece of shit.'" On the tape, his voice broke and he began to sob.

"They beat me up for failing school," Frank heard him saying. "I just couldn't do the work and they just humiliated me."

At one point, he was forced to wear a four-foot-high dunce cap and a sign around his neck with his name and the words, "Please confront me about why I murdered my friend."

He spoke of how another resident told him, "Just admit you did this, just admit you killed the girl and this will all end."

He escaped three times. After one attempt, his punishment was to clean toilets. After a second, he was placed in a boxing ring, where people took turns beating him up. One fall, he escaped a third time, hid in the freezing cold, then caught a ride with a trucker and ended up at the Terriens', where he stayed through Christmas.

At 2:00 A.M., Frank made himself a pot of coffee. He put on his earphones so as not to disturb anyone in the house. His tape recorder was at his side, his computer on his desk, in case he needed to transcribe, and the manuscript was open beside him.

For the next two days and nights, Frank listened. After seven hours, he fell asleep on the couch with the tapes going. He keyed his mind for the words "Martha Moxley," and "Halloween." Whenever those subjects were mentioned, he stopped the machine and transcribed them on his computer, giving each a heading and counter number to catalog them.

Then Frank came to the tape of that Halloween Eve, a tape that would be played at the trial. Here it was. Frank held his breath as he listened.

"I guess the best way to start," said Michael, "is to say that for us, for the Skakel home, Halloween was the best holiday of the year, better than Christmas, better than New Year's, better than the Fourth of July, because we got to go out.

"It was like our day. We got to go out and do mischiefness [sic]. I mean, actually, Mischief Night was better than Halloween. . . ."

Michael went into intricate detail on how they prepared for the big night. "We saved up fireworks, smoke bombs; we made funnelators, which are slingshots that you take twenty feet of surgical tubing, cut it in half so you have ten feet on each side."

Then he described how "you take a regular household funnel and you make two holes on the bottom of it, and you wire it through and you thread the surgical tubing through it and then you drop a rope with a knot in it and then it's a human slingshot.

"And you can take an egg or an apple and shoot the thing 200 yards. You could hit a parked car or anybody driving by from 200 yards away and safely be able to run away without getting caught. I mean you could hit houses. I mean it was like, hit other kids. I mean it was war time."

Listening to him, Frank had to remind himself this was a grown man talking. Michael was nearly forty, but he sounded like a teenager.

"And that particular Halloween," he continued, "my dad was on a hunting trip, which he usually was, up at this guy Gil Wayman's house up in Cambridge, New York. . . . And so it was great. It was like actually a weekend where we'd be away from him."

Michael then described how he'd come home early from school to get his "arsenal" ready for the following night. "Getting eggs together and shaving cream like taking a pin sticking it in a shaving cream can and then lighting a butane lighter so that it would make the hole really small so if you shot it the shaving cream went really far."

Then, there were the "snakes"—"the little cylinders you light and it makes a snake and tons of smoke. I got tons of those and crushed them up and put them in like canisters to make big smoke bombs." Michael was nuts, Frank decided.

Then, to make Halloween perfect, Michael's cousin Jimmy Terrien appeared. "Jimmy was great," Michael said. "Jimmy was like the Captain of Mayhem." Another nut, thought Frank. Two nuts.

Next, Michael described Ken Littleton, who was spending his first night at the Skakels'. The adult nominally in charge, Littleton, had taken them all to the Belle Haven Club for dinner, along with Terrien and Julie's friend Andrea Shakespeare. Littleton had allowed Michael to order rum and tonics and planter's punch.

"I thought, 'this is great,'" Michael said. "'He's gonna come live at our house and we can drink together and he won't give me such a hard time at school.' . . . Ken was like the football coach at school and we were eating at this great place and ordering drinks and he's not saying anything. I'm ordering planter's punches and rum and tonics and I just turned fifteen and the guy's not saying a peep."

Strangely, however, Michael had also said, "Littleton scared the shit out of me 'cause he just seemed like one of those people that wouldn't hesitate to pummel you. He was a big guy like a football coach and just seemed like he had absolutely no sense of humor. He just had that weird quietness about him."

That made Frank uneasy. Something was wrong. Michael had just said how great it was to be with Littleton and how they might become drinking buddies. But now, there was this "weird quietness." Frank wondered whether Michael could be setting Littleton up. He turned to the manuscript to see if it said anything more about Littleton.

Instead he read, "After dinner we went back to the house. We were all drinking my father's booze . . . trying to act like grown-ups. This turned out to be pretty boring, though, so after a while we began to chase each other around, whooping and giving out 'noogies' to each other and knocking things over." Typical Skakel behavior, thought Frank. What a family. What a bunch of lunatics.

"Then my cousin Jimmy suggested we go over to his house to watch a new show, *Monty Python's Flying Circus*, that was supposed to be really funny and was going on the air for the first time that night. He also said he had some great pot over at his place."

This was around nine o'clock. Martha had just arrived at the Skakels' with Helen Ix and Geoff Byrne. Michael threw in Littleton. "I remember standing in the kitchen drinking with Littleton and telling him that I thought Martha was really pretty.

" 'Yeah, she's hot!' he [Littleton] said.

"You should meet this girl," Michael replied. "She's a schmoke" (a term for someone who is loose).

Yes, that's what Michael was doing, Frank was certain. He was setting Littleton up. Michael was suggesting Littleton had lost control of himself and killed her. That had been another of Jack Solomon's insane theories. "What had the Skakel kids told Littleton about Martha?" Jack often said. "What had they said to make Kenny think he could score with her?"

When Solomon wanted Sheridan's help in pursuing Littleton, he had no doubt passed that thought along to the lawyer, who had probably repeated it to his client, Michael.

But Littleton wasn't the only one Michael tried to implicate. He also threw in the family handyman, Franz Wittine, who lived in a guest room in the basement. "We were in the kitchen and I remember going, 'Oh, where's Franz?' We called him Frank. It was only like eight o'clock at night and I remember walking down to the basement going, 'Frank, Frank,' and all the lights were off. So I went back upstairs and I was like, 'Where's Frank? You guys seen Frank? I can't find Frank.'" Again, a lie. If Franz Wittine were lying on the kitchen floor choking, Michael would have stepped over him without stopping, Frank thought. That was how much concern Michael had for Franz Wittine. And here was Michael saying he was interested in Wittine's whereabouts. Frank almost laughed out loud.

Michael's thoughts drifted back to Martha. He saw her from the window, standing apart from the others. "I think I said let's get in the car and smoke cigarettes," Frank heard him say on the tape. Here it comes, Frank thought. He wondered if Michael was going to discuss his feelings about Martha. He prayed Michael would.

"She and I were in the front seat of my father's Lincoln," Frank heard him say. "We were in the front seat talking. I was telling her that she should come over to the Terriens', Terriens' is great, it's so much fun, we go watch the show, *Monty Python*. She said, 'I can't. My mom said that I have to be in by nine. She gave me a curfew and she'll be mad.' I said like 'Screw your mom, come on,' and she said, 'Okay, great.' I said, 'Yeah, we'll trash the town, tomorrow night. We'll go egg the cop booth.'"

As Frank listened, he read along in the manuscript, hoping, praying that Michael would divulge more of his feelings toward Martha. "I really liked her," Michael said. "I wanted her to be my girlfriend but I was going slow, being careful. The truth is that with Martha I felt a little shy. I thought that maybe if we spent the evening together at my cousin's, something romantic might develop."

"Then she touched me on the shoulder. 'Tomorrow night, though, okay?'

"'Tomorrow night,' she'd said. She'd touched me. It was a promise. I nearly swooned with joy.

" 'We'll go nuts and trash this town,' she said and smiled.

" 'Great!' To try and get a kiss then would have ruined everything," Michael said. "Tomorrow night, I thought. Tomorrow night I'll kiss her." But Frank didn't believe it. He wondered whether Michael was telling another lie. If she had made the promise at all, could it have been for later that night? Yes, that was Mischief Night, Doorbell Night. That was when you rang doorbells and threw eggs. That was the night you trashed the town. Not, as Michael was saying, the next night, Halloween. The thought crossed Frank's mind: Could Martha have gone home, then come back out?

Martha got out of the Lincoln. Rush and Jimmy got in and sat in the front seat, Michael and Johnny in the back. "I said good-bye to Martha," Michael said on the tape. "It was like my brother Tommy, Helen Ix, I think Jackie Wetenhall and Marjorie Walker and Geoffrey Byrne at the back door of our house. I said good-bye to those guys, we'll see you tomorrow." Okay, Frank thought, so Michael was leaving Martha and Tommy.

"We spinned off to Terrien's, which was like fifteen, twenty miles away. Jimmy was driving the car, 'cause he always liked to race. He always liked to time himself how fast he could get to my house. He was driving through all the lights, driving like a maniac." That, Frank told himself, was probably the truth.

"At Terrien's," Michael continued, "you never had to worry about anything because his stepfather [George Terrien] was a drunk. And he was always away in New York, living at the New York Athletic Club or shacking up with his latest mistress. My aunt Georgeann was also drunk all the time and pretty much kept to her own wing of the house. They had a huge, castle-like place. You could do anything. We never got bothered. I felt at home there. Like my father couldn't get me. My brothers couldn't get me. And my brother Tommy couldn't give me a hard time there." Again, Frank thought, that was probably the truth.

"We smoked a lot of pot," Michael continued, "and drank some more and laughed through the whole Python show. Afterward, I wandered off to my older cousin Johnny's room." Another nut, thought Frank: Johnny had beaten up George Terrien, his alcoholic stepfather. God, what a family.

Michael continued that Johnny Terrien "was away somewhere. His room was a kid's fantasy. It was the like the biggest single person's bedroom you'd ever seen, so big it had a balcony and oval section with about twenty windows that looked out over a meadow and an orchard. He had a king-size bed with two life-size statues of palace guards, the Beefeaters, on either side, from what's that big palace in London? With the big hats on their head?"

Buckingham Palace, you moron, Frank thought. Frank heard Hoffman, the ghostwriter, in the background on the tape answering the same thing, "From Buckingham Palace."

Frank returned to the manuscript. "I lay on the bed, flanked by the stalwart Beefeaters, thinking of Martha," Michael went on. "I loved this room. I was sleepy with booze and pot. I wanted to fall asleep. I wanted to stay the night but how would I get back the next day? And the next day would become tomorrow night and I would see Martha. I roused myself."

So he wanted to go back and see Martha. Again, Frank wondered whether that promise Michael said she had made to meet him tomorrow night wasn't actually for later that night.

"My brother Rush decided to drive us home," the tape continued. "He was really hammered. Johnny, David, and I all rode in the back seat 'cause he was so drunk. We got out of the Terriens' driveway and on up to the end of Cliffdale Road, about half a mile. Then we turned into Riversville Road but after about 300 yards, Rush pulled over, put the car in park, and fell asleep. Johnny took the wheel even though he didn't have a license. He managed to get us home." What a family of drunks, Frank thought.

"No one was around. All the lights, most of the lights, were out. And I went walking around the house. Nobody was on the porch. I went upstairs to my sister's (Julie's) room. Her door was closed and I remembered Andrea had gone home." Yet another lie, Frank thought. He goes to Julie's room? Why would he do that? Julie is scared to death of him. He's thinking about Andrea? Hell, he's just making that up.

"I wandered into the master bedroom. There was nobody there. The TV was on but nobody was there." Ah, so that was it. Littleton had slept in the master bedroom the night he moved in because Rushton Sr. was away on his hunting trip. Michael was supposedly wandering around the house and happened to notice Littleton was not where he was supposed to be sleeping? No, Michael was trying to implicate him.

"I walked around and nobody was around and I went to the kitchen and got something to eat," Michael continued. "Then I went upstairs to bed."

But he couldn't settle down and go to sleep. "I know part of me wanted to go to sleep and then another part of me was—got horny. And I kept thinking about this lady on Walsh Lane." Yet another lie, thought Frank. He wasn't looking for a mom on Walsh Lane. Frank was certain Michael was thinking of Martha.

In the manuscript, Michael had written: "I was so ashamed. The thing I never told the police is that I did used to go and look in women's windows. And a lot was at my friend's mom. It wasn't sexual. I just wanted to be loved. I just wanted somebody to hold me. I was just looking for a mom." Frank didn't believe any of it.

"I decided, 'Fuck it. I'm going back out.' And I snuck out the back door." Well, that was probably one of the few things Michael said that was true, Frank decided. Here we go.

"But it was dark outside, and I'm scared of the dark." Another lie. Michael was used to being out at night. The Sutton report had concluded the killer was a night-crawler, someone familiar with the dark and also maybe a neighbor. Someone whom Martha knew because there were no defense wounds. She had not been afraid of him.

All this went through Frank's mind as he listened. He felt that for the first time he was seeing the face of the killer he'd always imagined. For years he had thought of this poor girl lying out there in the darkness. He could visualize her, see her running with her long blonde hair, trying to escape, being hit with the golf club, stumbling, trying to get up, falling. And he could see this figure, with his back to him, beating her, stabbing her through the neck with the golf club, pulling her pants down. Always, he saw the back of the killer. He had never been able to see his face. Until now.

As he listened to the tape, it was as though the killer had stopped, then turned around and stared at him. For the first time, Frank could see that person was Michael.

"I remember running past the pool, up Walsh Lane, stopping at the Ixes' house. Usually, their dog would chase you. And I remember getting into a full run, running past their house. And it was dark on Walsh Lane. And the dog didn't bark. And I just ran to that lady's house and it was like spying in her window and hoping to see her naked."

Sure, thought Frank. He was just looking for a mom. Which psychiatrist had used that line to explain Michael's craziness, his wildness, his drunkenness, his violence, his waking up in women's clothing, and God only knows what else? Michael wanted to see this woman naked? He was just looking for a mom? Who was he kidding?

"And I was kind of drunk and I couldn't get it up." Another lie, Frank thought, since a few minutes ago he'd said he was horny. "Why should I do this?" Michael continued, referring to the lady on Walsh Lane. "Martha likes me. I'll go get a kiss from Martha. I'll be bold tonight. You know, the booze gave me courage again." Okay, Frank thought, now we probably are getting a little closer to the truth.

"So I went over to their [the Moxleys'] house. I ran up the front [porch] stairs. They have huge front stairs. And I remember climbing up, seeing the light was on like the second or third floor. They had these huge cedar trees, pine trees, right at the front door and I remember climbing up 'em, like way up there."

A lie again. Those trees couldn't hold a cat. After my articles on the Sutton report, Frank had stopped by the Moxley house to see the tree Michael said he'd climbed. He was surprised to find there was only one tree by Martha's window and it wasn't large enough to hold a person at that level.

Frank had checked with Dorthy. Perhaps, he thought, there had been another tree at the time of Martha's murder that was later cut down. Dorthy sent him a photograph of the house in 1975. There was only that one tree. Dorthy said only a monkey could climb it. Michael may well have climbed a tree and masturbated in it but it wasn't the tree outside Martha's window.

"And I think I threw rocks or sticks at the window and I was yelling her name and I find out later on that wasn't her window, that was her brother's window." Except, Frank thought, that was not the story he had told Michael Meredith. He had told Meredith he had seen Martha through the window in the shower. And the tree outside John Moxley's window was so thin it couldn't have been climbed either.

"I'm a little out of my mind because I am drunk or high," Michael went on. "I pulled my pants down. I masturbated for thirty seconds in the tree and I said, 'This is crazy. If they catch me, they're going to think I'm nuts.' "

Except that Michael had told Krebs he had masturbated to orgasm. This was just another inconsistency in his lie. The masturbating story has to go in here because of whatever DNA Michael thought he may have left behind.

"A moment of clarity came into my head and I climbed down the tree. They had a half-oval driveway and I started—it would be a direct route from their front door to our house." My God, Frank thought to himself: He is describing the site of the first attack.

"I started to cut through the oval but it's really dark and when I started walking through, something in me said 'Don't go in the dark over there.' But I went under the streetlight and I remember yelling, 'Who's in there?' and chucking rocks, saying, 'Come on motherfucker, I'll kick your ass.' "

So, thought Frank, he is yet again placing himself at the crime scene—presumably while the murder is occurring. He is challenging the killer and throwing rocks with the same motion as he would swing the golf club. He has put himself under a streetlight just in case anyone sees so he can explain away his actions and his movements.

"And I remember thinking, 'Oh my God. I hope to God nobody saw me jerking off. And then I remember running home and thinking I was gonna tell Andy Pugh that I thought I saw somebody there that night." The same Andy Pugh who had told Frank that the tree in which Michael claimed to have masturbated was "The Tree," where Martha's body was found.

"And then I went to sleep. Then I woke up to Mrs. Moxley saying 'Michael, have you seen Martha?' And I'm like, 'What?' And I was still high from the night before, a little drunk, then I was like, 'What, oh my God, did they see me last night?' "

What Michael meant, Frank was convinced, was "Did they see what I did to Martha last night?"

"And I remember just having a feeling of panic like my worry of what I went to bed with. Like, I don't know. I just had a feeling of panic." Was that, too, a clue? Frank wondered. Could Michael be referring to the missing golf club shaft?

"Police cars were going down Walsh Lane and they found Martha. And like the second place where I was yelling in, that's where they said she was hit and dragged all the way back there. And I'm thinking, 'My God, if I tell anybody that I was out that night they're gonna say I did it.' "

You're goddamn right, Mike, Frank said to himself. You're goddamn right they will.

•

Before dawn that Sunday morning, my phone rang. I staggered to answer it. It was Frank. "I'm sorry to call you so late but there is something I want you to know."

"Are you okay?" I asked, looking frantically around and discovering it was 3:00 A.M.

"I'm fine," he said. "Don't worry about that. I just wanted you to know that I can't give you any details now, but you are going to love it when I tell you what I just found out."

"This is why you woke me up at 3:00 A.M., to tell me something you're not going to tell me?"

"Just trust me, Len, you're not going to be disappointed."

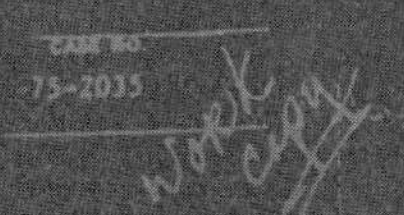

# PART V

D-20262
HOMICIDE
OCTOBER 31, 1975
12:30 P.M.

NAME, LAST
Skakel
NAME, FIRST
Michael
M.I.
D.O.B
01/12/59
NATIONALITY
American
ADDRESS
759 Rosewood Dr.
CITY
Greenwich
STATE
CT
ZIP
20234
CASE
Michael Skakel vs.
The State of Connecticut
FORM 5-6789-9870B
ROLL FROM LEFT TO RIGHT
LEFT THUMB
RIGHT THUMB
SIGN
ARRESTING OFFICER SIGN
DATE
DEPT.
11/05/02 Greenwich

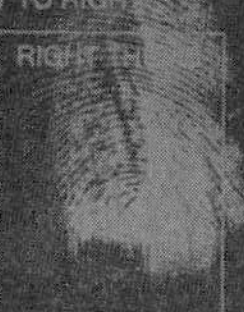

# 20

PART FIVE / CHAPTER TWENTY

# Moment of Triumph

CONNECTICUT
May 1998–January 2002

The grand jury sat for eighteen months before Superior Court Judge George Thim. Over fifty witnesses were called. They included John Higgins, Chuck Seigan, and dozens of others from Elan as well as Richard Hoffman, Andy Pugh, Cissy Ix, Andrea Shakespeare, and Father Connolly.

I drove up to Brideport to see Frank during that time. He was a different person from the one I'd visited the year before. He was smiling. Colleagues were talking to him. And he was no longer hiding out in his office. He led me down the corridors to show me the complex. He even introduced me to Jonathan Benedict.

"I had no doubt that with the information I presented in my affidavit there was enough for an arrest warrant," Frank said to me years later. "I had no doubt the grand jury would find probable cause to indict."

But at the time the grand jury sat, he was more circumspect. Since the hearings were secret, he couldn't tell me much about it. He couldn't even tell me who appeared before it.

Except for one person he had no hesitation in talking about. His

***The prosecution team on the Skakel case (left to right): Frank Garr, lead investigator; Chris Morano and Susan Gill, assistant state's attorneys; and Jonathan Benedict, chief state's attorney.***

name was Tad Baldwin. In the midst of the grand jury he had called Frank, claiming to have information about Martha's murder. Baldwin told Frank he was in Belle Haven that Halloween eve with the brother of a girl he was seeing.

Baldwin said the brother had been on acid that night. Baldwin had lost sight of him and when he caught up with him later on Walsh Lane, Baldwin said he admitted killing Martha Moxley.

"I just made an angel," Baldwin quoted him as having said.

"I wasted six weeks chasing it down," said Frank. "I went through everyone who knew this guy and knocked it down. There was nothing to it. Everyone I spoke to who knew him said he wasn't there that night. Baldwin had made it all up."

Over the years, people had come forward with cockamamie stories about the case. Jack Solomon had told him he had the wrong guy. Mark Fuhrman and Dominick Dunne had said he had not known what to do with their information. Now here was someone saying that he had known about the killer for 20 years and never came forward.

Here in the home stretch with the grand jury sitting, Frank snapped. He was so angry at Baldwin he subpoenaed him before the grand jury. There was no law against lying to a police officer like Frank. But if Baldwin lied before the grand jury, he could be arrested for perjury.

Baldwin testified he'd never spoken definitively and that Frank had misunderstood him. The grand jury didn't indict him, which only made Frank angrier.

When Baldwin completed his testimony, Frank escorted him out of the courthouse. "It's not over between you and me," he said. "I'm going to get you for this."

"Is that a threat?" Baldwin asked. "Are you theatening me?"

"It's not a threat," said Frank. "It's a promise that you and I will cross paths again."

Baldwin, it turned out, had been writing a screenplay about the murder in which he claimed to know the killer. A few months later, an article appeared in Mitchell Fink's gossip column in the *Daily News*, saying Baldwin had just sold his screenplay to Ben Affleck's production company, Live Planet.

Frank called Fink. "I just want you to know to be careful what you print about this guy. His information is, shall we say, less than reliable." He then called Live Planet and repeated the same.

Apparently, the calls served their purpose. Nothing more was heard about Baldwin's screenplay.

•

On the morning of January 19, 2000, Jonathan Benedict held a news conference in Bridgeport. He announced that the grand jury had found probable cause to indict Michael Skakel for Martha Moxley's murder.

The news conference was held at the Holiday Inn across the street from the courthouse, and it was packed with reporters. Benedict began by saying the case would begin in juvenile court because Michael was fifteen years old at the time of the murder but that he would seek to have it moved to adult court. This, he said, would require a series of court hearings, which he estimated would take a year. When asked about his predecessor Browne, Benedict said only, "I think Donald struggled with the case." It was the closest he would come to criticizing him.

Frank had had a special team of Florida cops in place to arrest Michael, who was living with Rushton in Hobe Sound, where he had retired. But Benedict said that Michael, who had learned of the grand jury's decision, would present himself that afternoon at Greenwich police headquarters for arrest.

•

That afternoon, Michael arrived in an SUV with his criminal attorney, Michael Sherman, at Greenwich police headquarters. Frank was ready for them. Seeing the throng of reporters outside—including me—he ducked inside the police garage, two buildings from headquarters, with Greenwich Chief Peter Robbins, the rookie officer he had broken in thirty years before.

The walkway door connecting the garage to headquarters was open, and a female reporter approached him. "Frank," I could hear her saying, "how does it feel after all these years to finally get your man?" I felt a surge of pride for him. That reporter had it right. This was his moment of triumph.

Yet Frank's face remained expressionless. I knew that look. He merely nodded his head in acknowledgment.

Moments later, as Michael arrived with Sherman, the mob of reporters closed in. "Did you do it, Michael? Did you kill her?" they screamed.

I watched Frank hustle out of the garage to guide Michael through them. He navigated him back through the garage up a rear stairway to the second floor of headquarters, past the detective bureau into the identification office. Later, he would tell me that he took out an arrest warrant, showed it to Michael, then spoke his first words to the man he'd pursued for eleven years.

"Mike," he said, "I have an arrest warrant, charging you with the murder of Martha Moxley. I have a copy for your lawyer. Obviously, you know you don't have to speak to me. You have the right to remain silent."

Sherman had primed Michael. He didn't say a word.

Frank and I had talked of having dinner at Dominick's in the Bronx the night Michael was arrested. But there was processing for Frank to do that would keep him busy at headquarters until midnight. Our dinner could wait. Twenty-five years had passed since Martha's murder. Two more would pass until Michael went to trial. There would be time to celebrate.

21

PART FIVE / CHAPTER TWENTY-ONE

# "I'm a Kennedy. I'm Going to Get Away with Murder"

CONNECTICUT
2000–2002

The Skakels' first mistake after Michael's arrest was having Sherman try his case. A local lawyer and former local prosecutor, he had grown up in Greenwich and liked to tell people during the trial that he had lived near Frank.

Frank didn't remember him. At least not then. "We may have been in school together but we never had any contact. Hell, he was on an academic track and I was on a vocational one."

Mickey, as he liked to be called, was in his fifties when the Skakels hired him, short, dark-haired, boyishly handsome, recently divorced, and dating women half his age. He had expanded his practice to include some grade-B celebrity cases when the Skakels called with the biggest offer of his life.

Michael's first cousin, Bobby Kennedy Jr.—who would emerge as Michael's most passionate defender—would later write that Mickey had marketed himself as media savvy. Indeed, his introduction to the case occurred not in a courtroom but a Los Angeles television studio. Four years earlier, Dorthy had appeared on the nationally syndicated *Leeza* show. At her urging (and on Leeza's dime) I flew to L.A. to appear with her.

As we chatted backstage, Mickey materialized.

"Who is he?" Dorthy whispered.

"Never saw him before," I answered. With no connection to the case, he had somehow talked his way onto the program as a "local expert."

But Mickey proved less media-savvy than media-friendly. A few hours after presenting Michael to Greenwich police headquarters for arrest, he was dining in New York City with the cast of *The Sopranos*. During the trial, he and Dominick Dunne—who, perhaps even more than Mark Fuhrman, the Skakels regarded as their personal enemy—appeared on CNN in New York, then arrived together at the Norwalk courthouse in a cab.

The day after the verdict, Mickey attended a Court TV party for Dominick. When Bobby Kennedy Jr. questioned the propriety, Mickey answered, "We're friends. What can I say? I'm a kiss-ass."

Six months before the trial began, Mickey spoke to a lawyer's group in Las Vegas. In his presentation, entitled "High-Profile Cases"—which was recorded on an hour-long CD and sold by the Nevada Bar Association—he acknowledged that he had forgotten the cardinal rule for trial attorneys: "This case isn't about you. It's about your client."

He then described to the group how he had traded an interview about the Skakel case with now-defunct *Talk* magazine for a ticket to the Academy Awards and "all the cool parties." *Talk*'s editor, Tina Brown, had called him, seeking an interview on his courtroom tactics. When Mickey resisted, she "started having me invited to all the 'A' parties in New York."

Finally, she agreed to interview him "anywhere you want." Mickey suggested the Academy Awards in Hollywood. "I said it as a joke and wound up doing it," he told the bar group. "Horrible, horrible," he said, as though that absolved him.

Watching Mickey in the courtroom, I sensed something in his manner that seemed all wrong. His glib and jaunty charm appeared to mock the solemnity of the proceedings. Murder is, after all, a serious business.

Later, he seemed careless, almost carefree, in his jury selection. There were six men, six women, and four alternates. Most were professionals, virtually all of them college graduates, some with advanced degrees. One of them he allowed to be seated was a cop; another was a friend of a friend of Dorthy. Cops are regarded as sympathetic to the prosecution. A friend of a friend of the victim's mother speaks for itself.

In trying the Skakel case, Mickey believed he had a lock. No physical evidence. No eyewitnesses. Twenty-seven years had passed. Many, if not most, of the prosecution's witnesses were suspect because of their pasts. In short, Mickey saw Michael Skakel as his ticket to stardom.

Frank, who had come to respect Sherman as a prosecutor, said I was being too harsh. He viewed Mickey merely as a grandstander, like all criminal lawyers. Frank saw Mickey's allowing a cop on the jury as mere flamboyance, Mickey's way of placing himself apart from everyone else and getting on TV.

After the trial, I asked Mickey about his courtroom strategy. "Classically," he said, "criminal defense attorneys don't ask their clients whether they did it. But I asked Michael. He always denied knowledge. I asked him about his admissions; about his blackouts; about the meeting at Elan with Sheridan and Father Connolly; about Sheridan's memo in the Sutton report that he and Tommy might have conspired to move Martha's body, about Julie's statement that she was scared to death of him. Michael always denied everything. The only time he made admissions, he said, was when he was pummeled at Elan."

I then asked Mickey how many other clients he had fallen in love with—a phrase that in the criminal business means uncritically accepting their stories.

"Only one other. Roger Ligron. He was a Vietnam veteran who shot and killed a drug dealer. He pleaded post-traumatic stress disorder. A jury found him not guilty. It was the first full-length trial on Court TV."

I got my first look at Mickey in the courtroom during a pretrial "probable cause" hearing in Stamford eighteen months after Michael's arrest. Frank had discovered a new witness, a second eyewitness to Michael's confession. He was a drug addict named Gregory Coleman.

Like John Higgins, he had attended Elan with Michael. "I'm a Kennedy. I'm going to get away with murder," Michael told him.

Coleman was living in Rochester when Frank found him in 1998. Coleman had seen a television program on the Moxley case and called the station.

"He was a great big teddy bear of a guy with enormous problems, but he was one of the most believable guys I ever talked to," Frank said of him. "Your worst day is a good day for this guy. He couldn't climb out of it. He had nothing. He had no future. He was sick, physically and probably mentally because he had this monkey on his back. But that didn't mean he wasn't telling the truth."

Like many kids who attended Elan, Coleman's father had money. There was a trust fund and an executor to whom Coleman came for his expenses. The executor was aware of Coleman's drug habit and insisted that Coleman appear before him in person each time to collect his money. That, said Frank, was probably what had kept him alive.

But at the pretrial hearing in Stamford, a problem developed. On the witness stand, Coleman began to sweat and twitch. He was getting sick. Mickey picked up on it. As Mickey questioned him, Coleman admitted that when he'd testified against Michael at the grand jury, he had been high on heroin.

Frank had put Coleman up in the Howard Johnson motel in nearby Darien off the turnpike. When the hearing ended, he had two Greenwich cops return him there and remain with him. Coleman had to testify again the next day.

Later in the afternoon, the cops called Frank at the courthouse. The guy is getting sick. He needs something. Maybe methadone. From the courthouse, Frank started calling local clinics. No place would take Coleman. He called Rochester, where Coleman had been in a program. Because of privacy concerns, they wouldn't talk to him on the phone.

It was growing late. The clinics were closing. Frank drove over to the Howard Johnson's. Coleman was lying in bed in his clothes. "I am dying. I have to cop," he began shouting. "You are either going to get me drugs or I'm going back to Rochester. I can fly back, get it on the street, and I'll be back tomorrow. Or I can cop around here. Just take me into New York City. Let me out somewhere in Harlem. I'll go cop and I'll be all right."

"Gregory," said Frank, "I can't do that."

Instead, Frank started driving. They drove down the turnpike toward Stamford, searching for a clinic. Desperate, Frank headed toward Greenwich Hospital. "I've been a cop here for twenty-seven years," Frank told a nurse and a doctor. "I got a guy here who is sick."

In the end, they took Coleman into a treatment room and gave him something. Instantly, Frank saw Coleman picking up. They gave Frank two pills to get Coleman through the night. The next morning he was ready to testify.

A few weeks later, Frank was driving to Bridgeport when his cell phone went off. He had been in contact with the Rochester Police Department's narcotics squad because Coleman had approached them, seeking to make some money as an informant. He had told them of his work for Frank and they had called him. Frank didn't tell Coleman of the call, or that he had asked the Rochester police not to use him. He didn't want to risk anything happening to him. He needed Coleman.

"I've got some bad news," a cop from Rochester said. "Greg Coleman is dead."

It hit Frank like a thud. It hit so hard he had to pull the car over. Yes, he'd lost a key witness, although Coleman's testimony would be read into the record at Michael's trial.

But it was more than that. "I liked this guy," Frank found himself saying out loud. "I really liked this guy."

Coleman had told Frank he had a thirteen-year-old son who was starting to use pot. Coleman had warned the kid, "Look at me, do you want to end up like me?' "

What could be worse? Frank thought. Bad enough to wreck your own life. Multiply that by a hundred, a thousand times if you have to watch your child wreck his life and you feel you are responsible for it because of how you lived.

Coleman had wanted to get a trucking license, Frank remembered.

"In his heart, I think he really wanted to pull himself together, but the monkey was too strong. There was just nothing I could do for him."

"We found him in the driveway this morning," the Rochester cop told Frank on the phone.

"Straight OD?" Frank asked.

"We've been getting some hot stuff coming in," the Rochester cop said. "Ten percent pure. He was used to the two percent kind."

# 22

PART FIVE / CHAPTER TWENTY-TWO

# "Frank Garr Is the Reason We Are All Here"

NORWALK, CONNECTICUT
April–June, 2002

Michael rose from the defense table and stalked a few feet over to Frank at the wooden railing, which separated the trial's participants from the spectators. The courtroom was emptying after the jury had just heard the testimony from Andy Pugh, a key prosecution witness.

Michael thrust his face into Frank's. "Good coaching," he said.

I was in the second row and couldn't believe what I was seeing. I caught the tension and heard Michael's next two words, "Just wait."

Was Michael threatening Frank? Was he looking to start a fight in the middle of his trial?

Frank said nothing. He made no move. Better than anyone, he knew Michael was out of control. Michael had taken every opportunity out in the hallway to brush up against Frank, to make sure his elbow struck Frank's arm. Frank had disciplined himself never to respond or retaliate, never to get into a confrontation. He had forbidden himself the luxury of even speaking to Michael.

Now inside the courtroom, just after Michael said to Frank, "Just wait," his bodyguard, a huge, bald black guy, and Michael's brother Stephen, stepped in between Michael and Frank.

"The tension is getting to him," Frank tells me later when I ask him what the hell this had been about. "Michael is probably terrified."

Later that day, I ask Mickey Sherman about the confrontation. He shrugs. "That's what Michael believes," he says. "I think he hates Frank Garr. And he is entitled to his feelings. Frank Garr is the reason we are all here."

But Mickey denies that Michael's words imply a threat. He spins them another way. " 'Just wait,' " Mickey explains, "means, 'Wait until we win.' "

This happens the spring of 2002 in the midst of Michael's month-long trial in Norwalk, Connecticut. The prosecution had wanted the trial in Bridgeport, in the State Supreme Court building where its office was located. The Skakels had wanted Stamford, which was contiguous to Greenwich.

Instead they settled for Norwalk, halfway between, with its modern courthouse and cavernous first-floor courtroom that could hold the overflow crowds. The lanky, white-haired Jonathan Benedict was at the prosecution table. Next to him was Chris Morano from the chief state's attorney's office with his mop of black hair, and a second assistant, a prim appellate lawyer, Susan Gill.

Frank, in his black pinstriped suit, his ponytail cut off, and still furious at Morano for courting Fuhrman, sat a few feet apart in a wooden chair at the railing. The Skakels filled the courtroom's far right side. But now there was a supporting cast of hundreds of spectators and reporters.

I was covering the trial for *Newsday*. That was vindication for me, considering they'd balked at running my stories of Tommy's and Michael's changed accounts. Still, resentments lingered. Before the trial, an editor called to say the paper had decided not to submit my stories for a Pulitzer prize. "You didn't write that much on it for us," he said. "Let the Connecticut papers put you up for it."

Why he felt it necessary to tell me this I had no idea. I was not even aware *Newsday* was considering me for an award. I certainly had never promoted myself. As the editor's call indicated, neither had anyone else at *Newsday.*

Dominick Dunne was covering the trial for *Vanity Fair*. He and I had made our peace. Convicting Martha's killer was more important than my hurt ego. Nurturing grudges never got anyone anywhere.

One afternoon when testimony ended, I gave him a lift to the train station and mentioned I was going to my son's baseball game. He was a junior in high school. When I'd begun this case he hadn't been born. Now he was seventeen, and I tried to catch the last few innings of his home games.

Dominick wrote in *Vanity Fair* ("Triumph by Jury," August 2002): ". . . Len Levitt of *Newsday*, who finds time to go to his son's baseball games." I liked that.

In another article he wrote that we had had our differences but that was all in the past. I liked that, too.

Mark Fuhrman was also in the courtroom, seated behind Dorthy and covering the trial for Court TV, having flown in from Idaho or wherever in the West he lived. Despite Dorthy's entreaties, Frank refused to acknowledge him. Early in the trial, he had led Dorthy away from the courtroom down the stairs to a basement office the state had arranged for its witnesses, warning her that some of the testimony might be too graphic for her to listen to. Fuhrman had tagged along. But at the top of the steps Frank stopped him. "Mark," he said, "you can't come down here. This isn't for you. Go back to the courtroom. You're only a spectator."

Yet it was Fuhrman, not Frank, who remained the focus of attention. The media regarded him as the expert on Martha's murder. During breaks in the trial, packs of reporters surrounded him. Frank and I watched, silent and ignored.

A producer from one of the networks, whose job was to ingratiate herself with anyone involved in the case, cozied up to me, saying she was interested in having me tell "my story." I made the mistake of having lunch with her and a criminal lawyer the network had brought up from New York who claimed he knew me, then picked my brain about what the producer described as "my insights."

I never heard from her again. A few days later, I spotted the two of them outside the courthouse. A camera crew was filming him while she stood to the side. I stopped to listen. The criminal lawyer was analyzing the case, offering "my insights."

"Don't feel too bad," Frank laughed when I told him the story. "No one is interested in 'my story' either."

•

I think because the Skakels felt so cocky, they made the decision to protect Tommy. I even wondered whether hiring Mickey, at Manny Margolis's behest, had come with that arrangement, to keep the focus off Tommy, whom Margolis still represented.

Instead, Margolis and Mickey decided that Michael's best defense rested with Ken Littleton. Maybe Jack Solomon had pumped them up with his stories about Littleton as a serial killer. Or maybe, as I suspected, they wanted to keep the spotlight as far away as they could from the Skakels.

"Solomon was instrumental," Mickey would say to me after the trial. "He spent hours with us. He put Littleton behind the eight ball."

Mickey or Margolis or whoever was calling the shots decided to argue that Martha's murder had occurred at 10:00 P.M., thus providing Michael with his alibi at the Terriens'.

But wouldn't Tommy's encounter with Martha just minutes before then create more suspicion than Littleton would? I asked Mickey. Wouldn't the jurors feel that Tommy had something to hide after he told the Greenwich police he had last seen Martha at 9:30 when he went inside to write his Abraham Lincoln report, omitting those twenty minutes he spent with her just before her death?

Mickey insisted that concentrating on Littleton, not Tommy, was his decision. I didn't believe him. I suspected that Margolis had influenced him to keep the focus off Tommy. I found myself wondering whether Mickey had been hired not merely to defend Michael but to protect the other Skakels. Whatever the reason, a year after the trial Mickey admitted to me that ignoring Tommy as he had done had been a tragic mistake for Michael.

Knowing that Mickey would portray Littleton as the killer, Benedict opened the trial by putting Littleton on the stand. So the trial began with a three-day sideshow—featuring a former wild man, a manic-depressive on half a dozen medications. I hadn't seen him in twenty years and had forgotten how large a man he was. In those twenty years, he had been in and out of mental institutions and attempted suicide. His hair had turned gray. No doubt because of his meds, he sounded robotic. He responded to questions in a sing-song cadence, appending the word "Mister" at the end of each response to whoever was questioning him. How would the jury view him, I wondered. Killer or victim? Frankenstein or Forrest Gump?

Mickey began by playing Mary Baker's secretly recorded, decade-old tape from the Howard Johnson motel outside Boston, where at Solomon's direction she had tried to trick her ex-husband into a confession by lying to him about what he had told her about the murder.

"Did you ever tell Mary that you stabbed Martha Moxley through the neck?" Mickey asked him.

"Yes, I did, Mr. Sherman," Littleton replied in his sing-song voice. My God, I thought, he doesn't know what he is saying. Ten years later, he still doesn't realize Mary lied to him by telling him he had said something to her that he hadn't.

Benedict jumped in to protect him. "Do you remember telling her that?" he asked.

"No, Mr. Benedict," Littleton answered.

"Do you recall ever admitting to the killing?" Benedict continued.

"No, Mr. Benedict." This poor, wounded creature. He was lost. His mind was shot.

Mickey then played a tape of Littleton's decade-old interview with Denver psychiatrist Kathy Morrall at Greenwich police headquarters, where, Mickey crowed, Littleton had confessed to killing Martha.

Repeating the lie Mary told him he had uttered in the back seat of their car after a drinking bout, Littleton said on the tape to Morrall, "This is when I said, 'I did it.' "

"And what did you tell Dr. Morrall that you said to Mary?" Mickey continued.

"I did it, Mr. Sherman."

"And when you say, 'I did it,' you are talking about that you committed the murder of Martha Moxley?"

"Correct, Mr. Sherman."

It was agonizing listening to Littleton. If people didn't know better, they would think he was actually confessing to Martha's murder when what he was referring to was what Mary had lied to him and told him he had said.

"How can you not feel sorry for the guy?" Frank said when we discussed the testimony later that day. "He's tormented by this case. It's destroyed his life."

Frank and I discovered a Dunkin' Donuts in a shopping mall across the street from the courthouse, where we could disappear and discuss each witness's testimony. Or we'd meet at nine o'clock before court began or duck out at lunch or during breaks. The coffee was pretty good and no one ever came around and disturbed us.

After his testimony, Littleton approached me. With him was a tall, attractive woman with staggeringly blue eyes, whom he introduced as his fiancée, Ann Drake. Both of them thanked me for my support. Littleton actually remembered me from twenty years before when I had interviewed him with Mary in Ottawa.

"Do you know who Ann Drake is?" said Frank. "She's heiress to a fortune." He shook his head, as though pondering why she would be mixed up with Littleton. "She must have her own problems," he said.

Later that afternoon, I bumped into Mary in the prosecution's basement office. Because of my friendship with Frank, Benedict had granted me license to wander down there.

Mary also had been brought to Connecticut to testify and was having as difficult a time as Ken but for different reasons. It had been ten years since she had seen him and when they met again, he didn't recognize her. Worse, she said, he didn't remember her.

She told me she had greeted him, the father of their two children, with a pert, "Hi, I'm Mary Baker." "Hi," he had answered. "I'm Ken Littleton."

If that was unnerving, so was her encounter with Jack Solomon. He didn't remember her either.

Solomon was next on the witness stand. Mickey asked whether he had directed Mary to lie to trick Littleton into confessing to the murder. "Absolutely not," he answered.

Absolutely not? Was that the story Solomon had been giving Mickey during all those hours he spent briefing him? I craned to look at Frank. He was in his wooden chair against the railing, motionless, expressionless. I knew he was seething. He couldn't believe Jack was saying this, he would tell me later. "My jaw was shaking. I was sitting there, furious, trying not to express anything, not wanting anyone to see what I was really feeling."

"Are you aware of any confessions or admissions Littleton made to Mary?" Mickey had continued in his questioning of Solomon.

"Many," Solomon answered.

Many confessions or admissions? Where had Jack come up with that one? He then explained he had listened to thirty tape-recorded conversations Mary had sent him from Ottawa. How could that be? If true, why hadn't he arrested Littleton? Again, I looked at Frank. He hadn't moved. Whatever loathing he felt for Fuhrman, he felt in spades for Solomon.

After his testimony, a furious Benedict summoned Jack to the office in the basement. "You show us where Kenny confessed, Jack," Benedict told him. "Go through your notes. Go through your tapes. Find it and show us where Ken Littleton said he killed Martha Moxley."

Benedict had Frank bring Solomon all his old notebooks, most notably his forty-three-page profile of Littleton, all of which were now state's evidence. Frank handed them to Benedict. He refused to acknowledge Solomon.

"He's going through them," Frank said to me later. "Benedict asks him, 'Anything yet?' 'No,' says Jack. 'But, heh, heh, heh,' and gives his little laugh. 'Something's torn out here.'" Solomon was, of course, implying that Frank had ripped out the pages.

"Typical Jack," said Frank. "That's how far he would go, saying I would tear something out of his notebook that was incriminating. To me, that was worse than anything he said on the witness stand."

Frank let it go. He didn't want to cause Benedict any problems. Not now, during the trial. When Benedict went upstairs, Frank remained with Solomon in the basement as he and Jack listened to his tapes.

"I refused to leave Jack alone with them," he said. "I wouldn't speak to him. My tongue would fall out of my mouth before I would say a word to him."

"You know," he added, "cops can go bad. They steal money. They beat up their wives or their girlfriends. But what Jack did was treachery."

Benedict, meanwhile, wasn't finished with him. The following Monday, he put Solomon back on the witness stand. Jack was forced to acknowledge he had told Mary to lie to Littleton to trick him into confessing. And, he admitted, there had never been a confession.

•

I felt Benedict had fought Mickey to at least a draw over Littleton. But what would the jury think? What would they think of the competence of the state of Connecticut, which had employed Solomon as its lead investigator? I shuddered at the possibilities.

Frank was more optimistic. "I thought Benedict was great," he said. "I thought he succeeded in shooting down what Mickey was trying to do through Solomon—to make Littleton out to be the killer."

But things did not improve when the state's first key witness, Cissy Ix, flip-flopped. Susan Gill had been preparing Cissy for her testimony in the office in the basement. In the midst of preparation, Cissy denied ever saying Michael's father feared his drunken son might have killed Martha. That meant Cissy was refuting her statement both to Frank and to the grand jury.

Susan Gill was a cautious and meticulous appellate lawyer but she had handled few murder cases, none as publicized as this. She rushed to find Frank. "You better get in there," she said to him. "Cissy is claiming she didn't say what is in your report."

Frank walked over. "Is there a problem, Mrs. Ix?" he began. He had always been formal with her. He liked her but kept a distance. She called him Frank, but to him she was Mrs. Ix. He handed her a copy of her statement to him from five years ago.

Cissy said Frank had been mistaken. Rushton had never said anything negative about Michael.

Frank turned to her husband, Bob Ix, seated next to her. "Mr. Ix, you were there that day. You said to her, 'Cissy, tell him. Tell him, Cissy.' "

"No, Frank," he answered. "That's not how we remember it."

Frank stared at him without speaking. You lying son-of-a-bitch, he wanted to say. Mister former president of Cadbury-Schweppes, you are a fucking liar. Instead, he stood up. "I have nothing further to say to either one of you," he said. He picked up his report and walked out of the room.

On the witness stand that afternoon, Cissy said that both her statements to Frank and to the grand jury were wrong. "I put into Rush's mouth what I actually thought. . . . It was my thinking as opposed to Rush's. I know Rush never heard from Michael that he ever killed anyone. . . . It was a terrible thing that I did. That was my mistake. I was wrong. I was very, very wrong. Michael never admitted anything to Mr. Skakel."

My God, I found myself thinking as I listened to her, why would Cissy change her testimony and risk committing perjury to protect the Skakels?

When she fled the courtroom, I ran after her. She and her husband were in the hallway, walking toward the courthouse's rear exit, when I caught up to them. "Cissy, why would you say that?" I asked her. "Why did you change your testimony?" She refused to acknowledge me. She continued walking with her husband out the courthouse door.

I turned around and bumped into, of all people, Dominick Dunne. Short, stocky, and gray-haired, here he was, seventy-six years old and recovering from prostate cancer, and he was hustling like a reporter fifty years younger.

"Did you hear what that woman just said?" he shouted so that everyone in the hallway could hear him. He was wearing a suit, and he stopped and placed his hands on his hips. "That bitch," he shouted again.

After court ended, I wandered down to the basement looking for Frank. "You want to know why Cissy changed her testimony?" he said. "It's simple. Because despite all that she knows about Michael, she still wants to be the Skakels' friend. She is so concerned with her neighbors, with Belle Haven, with Greenwich. She does not want to be perceived as a traitor to any of them."

•

I thought the state picked up some traction with its next few witnesses. First, there was John Higgins. Frank had read Higgins correctly from their two conversations six years before. Higgins didn't want to testify. But he was one of Frank's only two eyewitnesses to Michael's confession. He had to come.

Higgins had also testified at the probable cause hearing in Stamford the year before. An hour before his testimony, Frank showed him the transcript of their telephone conversations. It was then that Higgins realized Frank had taped him. He never forgave Frank.

"I knew he'd be pissed," Frank said. "That's why I waited until the last minute. But I wanted him in Connecticut when he got pissed."

Stocky, with light brown hair and in his late thirties or early forties, Higgins had seethed all through his testimony that day. He was so highstrung that when Mickey badgered him on cross-examination, Higgins lost his temper.

Now two years later, Higgins again resisted coming to Connecticut. "I didn't doubt he would do it," said Frank. "I felt he wanted to do the right thing. But he remained pissed off at me and pissed off at authority figures in general. He knew I needed him. And I knew he wasn't going to make it easy for me."

"I don't care about you. The only person I would do it for is Dorthy

Moxley," Higgins said to Frank. Higgins then telephoned Dorthy, saying he didn't want to testify but would if she asked him to.

"I think Frank told me he might be calling," Dorthy later remembered. "I had never spoken to him before and didn't know anything about him until Frank called me.

"When John called, he told me how he didn't want to get involved. I remember saying, 'It would be wonderful if you would. We really need you.'

"He said, 'If you ask me, I will do it.'

"It's so hard to admit your faults. I think he resisted testifying because he was ashamed that as kid he had had to go to a reform school like Elan."

After he testified, I saw him and Dorthy embracing as he left the courthouse. "I wanted him to know how grateful I am that he was there," she said. "I will always have a soft spot in my heart for John Higgins."

Here in Norwalk his testimony lasted only a few minutes. Mickey attempted to portray him as a grandstander, testifying only because he wanted his fifteen minutes of fame. But that fell flat.

This time he didn't let Mickey upset him. Or if so, he didn't show it. In a calm monotone he said what he had to. He repeated the story he had told Frank in 1996—how a sobbing Michael Skakel admitted to him he had murdered Martha Moxley.

Benedict was also able to get in the late Greg Coleman's pretrial testimony of Michael's saying, "I'm a Kennedy. I am going to get away with murder." It was read aloud to the jury with Benedict and Mickey asking the questions and Morano reading from Coleman's transcript.

Then, Michael's ghostwriter, Richard Hoffman, identified Michael's seven audiotapes, which were also played to the jury. Here was Michael in his own words, describing his going out and looking for Martha, masturbating in the tree outside her window and passing the crime scene. I watched the jurors' faces as they listened but could discern nothing. How could they not be moved by all this?

But to me it was Andrea Shakespeare Renna who provided the most damaging testimony against Michael. Unlike Cissy, she didn't flinch before the Skakels nor disavow what she had told Frank. She testified that Michael had never gone to the Terriens'.

Susan Gill was doing the questioning. This time there were no surprises. "Was Michael Skakel in the house after the car left?" Gill asked.

"Yes," answered Renna.

"From 1975 to today, have you been certain Michael was home after the car left?"

"Yes," Renna said.

"Is there any doubt that Michael was home after that car left?"

"No."

She added that she had attended the Convent of the Sacred Heart school with Julie and been called to the headmaster's office the day Martha's body was found. Both she and Julie were told to return immediately to the Skakels'. When they arrived, she said, Michael came running out to their car, telling them Martha had been killed.

"What did Michael say to you?" Gill asked her.

"That he and Tommy were the last to see Martha that night."

Mickey couldn't suggest an ulterior motive. Andrea Shakespeare Renna was no Ken Littleton, whose testimony could be manipulated. She was no ex-junkie from Elan like Gregory Coleman. Her father had gone from being a vice president at CBS to ambassador to the Vatican. She came from the Skakels' world.

But Mickey did raise questions about Andrea's testimony—specifically, her certainty that Michael had not gone to the Terriens'. Cross-examining her, he asked how she knew Michael had not gone.

"For some reason, I don't know who told me . . . I never thought Michael made the trip to the Terriens'. I thought it was the three boys."

Mickey then asked if she had ever seen in him in the house.

"No," she had answered. "Did I see him leave? No."

"Where did you see Michael after the car left?"

"I did not see Michael," she replied.

Mickey left the impression she could have been mistaken—that her memory could have failed her after all these years.

Then, in what to me seemed like a surprising and unexpected move,

Benedict subpoenaed Rushton Skakel from Hobe Sound, Florida, where he was said to be suffering from dementia. Rushton's appearance was the state's reminder to the Skakels that if they couldn't convict Michael, they could make life miserable for every member of his family.

Rushton proved useless as a witness. Not only could he not remember details of the murder, he couldn't recall what had occurred six months before—on 9/11. What struck me was what happened after he'd completed his testimony. Michael walked up to him, placed his hands on his father's shoulders, and mouthed the words "I love you."

Either Michael had had some potent therapy over the years, considering how his teenage psychiatric reports had described his feelings toward his father, or he was playing it for all it was worth.

The state also blew it with Andy Pugh. Like Andrea Shakespeare Renna, Andy Pugh was also from their world and not afraid to take on the Skakels. He had been prepared to place his old friend at the murder scene, ready to say that the pine tree Michael jerked off in was not the one outside Martha's window but "The Tree" they had climbed as teenagers—the tree under which her body was found.

Perhaps Michael sensed the potential damage of Pugh's testimony. As Pugh began testifying, he noticed Michael silently mouthing the words "You fucking liar."

But Morano, who was questioning Pugh, glossed over all this. He never made the connection between the tree where Martha's body was found and the tree he and Michael had climbed as teenagers.

"What happened?" I said to him afterwards. "What happened to 'The Tree'?"

"I was waiting for Mickey to cross-examine him before I asked about it," Morano answered. Perhaps Mickey sensed the potential damage as well, for he never asked Pugh any questions. Morano had blown it.

When I asked Benedict about this, he shook his head in disgust. But not Frank. We were again at Dunkin' Donuts. Frank was already fuming at Morano, whom he had seen slipping out the day before with Fuhrman. When I mentioned Morano's explanation for not questioning Pugh about "The Tree," Frank couldn't contain himself.

"What he told you was bullshit," he said. "Morano wasn't waiting for Mickey to cross-examine Pugh. I think he just forgot about 'The Tree.'"

Mickey also defused the testimony of the Skakels' chauffeur, Larry Zicarelli, who recounted how he'd pulled Michael down from the Triborough Bridge after Michael said he'd done something so bad he had to either kill himself or leave the country. That something was obviously Martha's murder.

Mickey suggested another explanation. "Do you know," he asked Zicarelli, "whether or not, the night before, Michael slept in his dead mother's dress?"

Outside the courtroom, Mickey provided another variation. Michael hadn't actually been sleeping in his mother's dress, Mickey said. He'd just been holding it.

Mickey's account gave me my only opportunity to talk to Michael. His bodyguard had kept reporters away from him all through the trial.

"Hey, Mike," I called to him outside the courthouse as we broke for lunch, "what's with the dress?"

He was apparently so flustered he blurted out, "I wasn't wearing the dress. I was holding it in my arms when I went to sleep. It was my mom's. She was dying for four years. She died when I was twelve. My father used to make us kneel on marble floors for hours, praying she would live. I was looking for a mom."

He spoke matter-of-factly, with no emotion, as though he'd had practice in giving this explanation. Michael had it down pat. It sounded like something right out of a psychiatrist's manual. "I was looking for a mom." Or had I become too cynical? Maybe I'd been hanging around Frank too long.

Dominick, again at my heels, overheard him. "My God," he said, "I actually feel sorry for him."

Oh, boy! I thought to myself. If Dominick—who'd pinned his reputation with the Sutton report on Michael's guilt—felt sympathy toward him, this case was in trouble.

# 23

PART FIVE / CHAPTER TWENTY-THREE

## "It's Michael. It Can't Be Anyone Else. It's Him"

In retrospect, Mickey would have been wiser not to have put on a defense, for it appeared as if each of Michael's relatives was lying to protect him. The first was his cousin Jimmy Terrien. Now forty-four years old, short, sinewy, and balding, wearing a sport jacket and open-necked shirt, he bristled when on the witness stand he was introduced as Jim Terrien.

"I'm not referred to as Jim Terrien," he said. Rather, he went by his biological father's name "Dowdle."

Mickey had called Terrien to confirm Michael's alibi: that on the night of Martha's murder, Michael and two of his brothers had gone to Terrien's house in the back-country to watch Monty Python on television. But Terrien couldn't remember details. Most questions he answered with "I don't remember."

Again, as Terrien spoke, Michael could be seen silently mouthing words to him. This time, it appeared Michael was saying "Good job."

After he completed his testimony, Michael walked over and offered him a hug. Terrien side-stepped him, avoiding his embrace. Without a word or a look back, he walked out of the courtroom, entered a waiting car, and was gone.

I was too far away to make out Michael's expression. People who saw it said he seemed stunned.

His sister Georgeann proved even less reliable. She began by saying she had seen Michael, his two older brothers, and Jimmy arrive at their home. Had she actually seen them? she was asked. She admitted she hadn't because she was closeted in the library with a "beau."

She had heard their voices, she said. But could she identify any of them as Michael's? She could not. When she left the courthouse she was in tears.

Michael's sister Julie was worse. She, too, couldn't remember details. In 1975, she told the police she had left the house at 9:30 to drive Andrea home but that when they got to the car, she realized she had forgotten her keys and asked Andrea to run inside for them. Sitting in her car, she saw Tommy saying good-night to Martha at the side of their house. A moment later, she said, she saw Tommy and Littleton answering the door for Andrea.

Just then, she testified, a figure darted by. She hadn't recognized it but had cried out, "Michael, get back here."

"You see this figure that you yell 'Michael come back' to," said Benedict, cross-examining her. "That is very shortly before you see Tom and Martha by the side door."

"I would say so," Julie said. "But," she added, "I don't think it was Michael."

One person Julie remembered seeing inside the house around 10:00 P.M. was Littleton. She recalled he had changed his clothes. But, she acknowledged, she had never mentioned this before, either to the Greenwich police or to the grand jury. How could anyone escape the conclusion that she, like Terrien and Georgeann, was lying to protect Michael?

•

Final arguments. That's when it began to turn around.

Mickey was his wise-ass self, master of the one-liner, the two-second sound-byte.

"He didn't do it," he began. "He doesn't know who did it. He wasn't there when the crime was committed, and he never confessed. That's the whole case."

The state's witnesses raised more questions than answers, he continued, noting that earlier police suspicions had rested first on Tommy, then on Littleton. "Were the Ken Littleton confessions any less compelling, any less persuasive than [Higgins's and Coleman's] garbage?" he asked. The state, he said, had played "investigative musical chairs for twenty-seven years."

Denying the Skakel family tried to cover up Michael's role in the murder, he said, "I have to tell you this is the worst-run conspiracy I have ever seen. Most importantly they forgot to find somebody to hide the golf clubs." Was he referring to the matching clubs Lunney had discovered in the Skakel home the day Martha's body was found? I assumed so. To me, his glibness—and vagueness—epitomized his entire approach to the case.

Then, it was Benedict's turn.

"Martha Moxley, a pretty, athletic, flirtatious fifteen-year-old kid, one who we learned from her diary was as any fifteen-year-old girl, just beginning to come into womanhood," he began. "Unfortunately, as we learned from the words of the defendant, from Richard Hoffman and from Martha's diary, she was also drawn into the vortex of the competing hormones of two of the young boys who lived across Walsh Lane."

He sounded folksy, colloquial. This was a side of him I hadn't seen.

Yes, he acknowledged, he did not know the time the murder occurred. Was it at 10:00 P.M. when the dogs barked? Or was it later after Michael returned from the Terriens'? It didn't matter, he said. The state only had to prove that Martha had been murdered between 9:30 and 5:30 A.M. the next morning, as the autopsy report had stated.

He then described the Moxley property, in particular, the trees, providing more detail than his witnesses had. The first tree, by the side of the house, he said, rose to permit a view into Martha's bedroom. But, he added, it was too thin to climb. Dorthy had said the only way you could climb it was if you were a monkey. Two cedar trees rose up by her brother John's bedroom, Benedict continued, but they were so thin-limbed no human could climb them either. And, of course, there is the third tree. "It is certainly climbable but that's not the point. It is a place where a body could be hidden, where a body was hidden, the place where the evidence in this trial says Michael Skakel dragged the body of Martha Moxley."

Next, he set the murder scene—the Skakels returning from dinner at the Belle Haven Club; Martha arriving with three friends; she and Michael getting into the Lincoln in the driveway.

"This was the defendant's big moment," Benedict said. "Unfortunately, they were joined by brother Thomas, Michael's nemesis, who wound up with the girl that night, at least for a little while."

He then described the trip to the Terriens'. Exactly who went there, he noted, was one of the case's controversies. "The next thing that happened is that it was time for sister Julie to take Andrea Shakespeare Renna home. As these two were stepping out the front door, a figure darted by, causing Julie to yell, 'Michael, come back here,' which was occurring at the very same time brother Thomas was parting from Martha by the side door in the driveway."

"And at that very point, the departure to Terrien's house has already taken place," he continued. "The Lincoln was already en route to north Greenwich." What was that? This was a point I had not heard made before. Where was Benedict going with it? As had Andrea, he was suggesting Michael never went to the Terriens'.

And then Benedict came to the heart of it—Michael's whereabouts the night of the murder, a story that had changed over the years as Michael told it to different people. Michael, said Benedict, had started talking about the murder within twenty-four hours. The day Martha's body was found, he had said to Andrea Shakespeare, "Martha is dead and Tommy and I were the last ones to see her."

A year later, he told the family chauffeur Zicarelli, "I have done a terrible thing. You wouldn't speak to me again if you knew it. I have to kill myself or get out of the country."

In 1978 or 1979, he told Dorothy Rogers at Elan he was in a blackout and that he might have done it. Also at Elan, he had told Coleman, "I can get away with anything" because he was a Kennedy. He told John Higgins, "I did it."

Around 1982 he confided in his father, who told Cissy Ix he might have done it while drunk.

"In 1985 he told Michael Meredith that he had climbed a tree and spied on Martha . . . and conveniently pointed his finger at Thomas coursing through the yard towards Martha's house."

In 1992 he told a similar story to Andy Pugh, although the tree, he told Pugh, was not by her window but where her body was found.

There was an edge to Benedict's voice now. He was into it, all right. My God, I found myself thinking, Benedict had put it all together. And the jury was listening. You could see them tensing, leaning forward in their seats as he spoke. Not a sound. He had them. They were into this the way he was. Yes, I'd underestimated him.

I looked over at Frank. He was watching the jury. "They were hanging on his every word," he would tell me later. "He was connecting all the dots." He and Benedict had had a running conversation about what he would tell the jury in his summation.

"Your job is to get the jury to see one big picture," Frank had said to him. To me, Frank said, "He was doing exactly what we said he had to do."

Ever since October 31, 1975, Benedict continued, either Thomas or Michael had been the case's prime suspect. "It has been one of most notorious cases in the country's history in the last twenty-seven years, not to mention that it was these people's innocent next-door neighbor, a playmate of some of them, who was murdered." And yet, no one in the family remembered anything.

He moved on to Michael, the troubled teenager. "Clearly, the defendant had a major problem. Already he was an alcoholic, a substance abuser. Already he was beyond the control of his family. He was becoming suicidal. I doubt his family was even aware of the sexual turmoil he was going through. Elan was a last resort."

Then, he returned to Andrea Shakespeare and prepared for his final assault. He began by saying she was unshakable in her conviction that Michael never went to the Terriens'. Again, he mentioned the figure Julie saw while they were out at the station wagon about to drive Andrea home and how Julie had cried out, "Michael, get back here!"

I found myself listening as intently as the jury, but for another reason. I was certain now what Benedict doing. He was indicating that the murder had occurred at 10:00 P.M. His theory was different from Frank's.

And then he launched it. His entire summation had been leading us to this point. He had planted the bomb that was now set to explode in Michael's face. As Benedict put it, "The fact that gives the lie to his entire alibi."

Yes, he had taken something from Michael's autobiography that Frank had dismissed. Frank had believed the murder had occurred later, after Michael had returned from the Terriens'. He had told me he felt Michael had gone to the Terriens' because he had given so much detail about what he had done there that night as he lay on the bed watching Monty Python and fantasizing about Martha. Now, however, Benedict was saying something else.

Quoting Michael's words from his memoir, Benedict read aloud, "I got home and most of the lights were out. I went walking around the house. Nobody was on the porch. I went upstairs to my sister's room. Her door was closed and I remember that Andrea had gone home."

Frank had dismissed this scenario, concluding that Michael was lying, that considering his relationship with his sister, he had no reason to go to his sister's room and that he never gave Andrea a thought. Benedict dismissed it as well but for a different reason.

He paused in his summation. Slowly and deliberately, he showed that it was impossible for events to have unfolded as Michael had claimed.

"On supposedly getting home from the Terriens', he goes to his sister's room and remembers that Andrea had gone home.

"But the car had departed for the Terriens' before Julie and Andrea had stepped out of the house to take Andrea home. Somebody who had actually left already would have had no idea of Julie's trip to take Andrea home."

I thought I heard the jury's collective gasp of recognition. Or perhaps it was my own.

Oh my God, I found myself thinking, Benedict had done it.

•

Dominick said Benedict's closing argument had changed everything but I wasn't so sure. Two years before, I'd covered the murder trial of four New York City cops charged with firing forty-one shots at Amadou Diallo, an unarmed African immigrant. The prosecution had not presented much of a case but gave a terrific closing argument. It didn't work because the evidence had been so weak. The cops were all acquitted.

Yet again, perhaps for the hundredth time, I found myself with Frank at our haunt, Dunkin' Donuts, trying to sort out my feelings about the evidence. This time it was evening. The courthouse had closed. Everyone had gone. Except for a waitress, we were alone.

"Let's take the worst-case scenario," I said to him. "You have no eyewitnesses, no direct evidence, no DNA."

"Okay, but he admitted it to two people."

"Yeah, but one of them, Coleman, was a junkie."

"But his testimony is believable. He was one of most believable people I've ever known."

I didn't buy it. And I worried to myself that Frank wanted to convict Michael so badly he had fallen in love with Coleman the way Mickey had with Michael.

"Zicarelli's story was strong but Mickey defused it," I said. "Michael had a history of cross-dressing. I thought the story about his mother's dress sounded plausible."

"Hey, Len, are you kidding? That's why he has to leave the country? Because he was wearing his mother's dress? I don't think so."

"And they screwed up on Pugh. The jury never heard about 'The Tree.' "

"Don't get me started on Morano."

On further examination, even Benedict's summation troubled me.

His theory, from Michael's own words in his autobiography, indicated he hadn't gone to the Terriens'. It had seemed so strong then, the icing on the cake, perhaps even the smoking gun.

But that wasn't Frank's theory. When he had listened to the tapes, he had dismissed much of what Michael had said about those last few hours. "He went to Julie's room?" Frank had said to me. "Why would he do that? Julie was scared to death of him. He thought about Andrea? Hell, he was making it up."

But when I brought that up to him now, Frank merely smiled.

Okay, so that was one side. Now Frank offered another.

"Look at it this way, Len. You begin with Martha's murder. You rule out Littleton because he had no motive, he didn't know the area. You rule out Tommy. He has an alibi—Littleton. You rule out Littleton. He has an alibi—Tommy.

"Then you take the missing golf club. Only a Skakel would care about that. And only Michael has motive. You take all his admissions, his stories about his whereabouts, his blackouts, his drunkenness, his masturbation at the crime scene. You don't want to believe Coleman? Well, what about Higgins? Michael told Higgins, who told Seigan. Neither of them had any reason to lie. And for that matter, neither did Coleman.

"Then you take Zicarelli and Michael's attempt to jump off the Triborough Bridge. You take Pugh and 'The Tree,' whether or not Morano got that in there to the jury.

"Now don't be confused about when the crime occurred. The time doesn't mean anything. Whether you accept Andrea Shakespeare's statement that Michael never went to the Terriens' or you believe Michael about whacking off in the tree and running through the crime scene around midnight, it makes no difference. What is important is that he places himself at the murder scene. The fucking murder scene, Len.

"At some point it all falls into place. It all fits. You find yourself saying, 'It's Michael. It can't be anyone else. It's him.' "

•

All I had hoped for when the jury began deliberations that Tuesday morning was that they went past the lunch break. If nothing else, that meant they would be out longer than the jurors in the O.J. case. We all agreed a quick verdict meant an acquittal. Clearly, that's what the Skakels expected. As Benedict put it, "The longer they are out, the better I think we are."

If it went longer than just a few hours, no one could slight the state of Connecticut. No one could say that Benedict, and more specifically Frank, were not legitimate in their investigation.

Outside in the hallway, I spotted Mickey and Manny Margolis. Mickey was whispering to him, smiling. But Margolis couldn't restrain himself. "The prosecution has nothing," he blurted out to me. "They've proven nothing. They haven't touched Michael."

But the jury remained out all Tuesday. Contrary to Margolis's expectation, there was no sign of a verdict.

On Wednesday, more Skakel relatives turned up. Maybe Margolis felt the jury had come to a decision Tuesday night but wanted to sleep on it until the next morning. Maybe he believed Michael would be acquitted later that day. Bobby Kennedy Jr. appeared for the first time. He'd attended the pretrial hearing two years before but had not been seen since. Later, he would write that Michael was "cold and distant," blaming him and the Kennedy family in part for his indictment.

Tommy also turned up for the first time, though only for a day, which probably tells you either that he had no use for Michael or that he was scared as hell about himself. Margolis had choreographed and stage-managed his appearance and also spoke for him. "He came because he wanted to help Michael. He is very family oriented."

The old gas-bag, I found myself thinking. Approaching eighty, he had been on the case even longer than I, surviving both heart surgery and prostate cancer. He had at various times represented the entire family—except for Michael—and, according to Frank, Margolis had earned a small fortune stonewalling the police for twenty-six years.

I saw what Manny was trying to do with Tommy. He had been hoping for a quick decision and had Tommy here for it. I could even imagine what Tommy might say. I could say it for him. All these years his family has been the target of unfair allegations. All these years he himself had been under a cloud, blah, blah, blah.

Tommy himself seemed literally to recoil before the horde of reporters that surrounded him. Margolis said it all for him. "This has been a terrible time for him. He's been living under enormous pressure and tension this whole time. But his emotional state is such that he can handle it. He's here to say, 'I'm your brother and I'm here to support you.' "

I wouldn't let Manny get away with it. I wouldn't give him this pass, parading Tommy in here at the most opportune time for himself. Not without answering the question I'd spent twenty years pursuing.

"Manny," I said in front of the reporter crowd, "why did Tommy lie to the police?"

"I'm not going to respond to that," he shot back. "What he said to police in the course of a five-hour interview—it ain't fun."

When they left the courtroom, I followed. I wouldn't let it alone. This time, I went straight at Tommy. "Tommy, can you tell us now why you lied to the police?" I knew he wouldn't answer. But I had to do it. I had to get in my shot.

Manny rushed over. "You have no right to question him," he shouted. "You go home, Len Levitt."

Margolis had shouted so loudly that Frank, standing in the well of the courtroom, heard him. He turned around. "Hey, Lenny," he called out, smiling, "You better do what he says. It's past your bedtime."

•

There was no decision Wednesday. Instead, the jury asked for readbacks of the testimony of prosecution witnesses Andrea Shakespeare, John Higgins, and Andy Pugh, which took up all day.

But now the momentum was shifting. Mickey and Margolis were stirring uneasily. Something was happening that they did not understand. They had never accepted the integrity of the state's case. Like the national media, they believed Fuhrman had discovered Michael and that the state of Connecticut glommed onto his theory. They had not counted on Frank and his witnesses.

I searched the courtroom for him. I watched as he moved about the room, always expressionless. Yet the trial had taken its toll. He had lost ten pounds. His black pinstripe suit hung on his frame.

Like everyone in the courtroom, he concentrated on the jurors as they listened to the testimony of Andrea, Higgins, and Pugh. I, too, searched their faces. Merely the fact that they were asking for the testimony of prosecution witnesses indicated something. Perhaps that they were considering Benedict's arguments. But then, maybe not.

Again on Thursday, the jury remained out all day. Strangers were turning up now at the courthouse, men and women who related Martha's murder to their own misfortunes. I refused to allow myself to think about what was becoming clear—that even I, Frank's friend and would-be partner in this case, underestimated what he had accomplished.

Here, Frank had done what no other law enforcement official—hell, what no other person in the case—had done. He had come into this in the middle—no mean feat as my old boss McCulloch, the best newsman I'd ever met, could testify to after his experience entering the Howard Hughes case in midstream. Then there was Murphy, an FBI guy, and Krebs, from the NYPD. They had seen the same information Frank had. But it was only Frank, a local detective from the muddled Greenwich Police Department, who had put it all together.

•

The end came at eleven o'clock Friday morning. The jury sent a note. They had reached a verdict. The courtroom was already full as I slipped into the second row behind Dorthy.

She was seated between her son John and her late husband's sister, Mary Jo, who had come in from Kansas. Their hands rested on each other's shoulders. Seeing me, Dorthy smiled. She leaned over and whispered, "I'll never forget what you have done. Without you and Frank, this never would have happened."

Then I saw Frank. He had been downstairs in the basement office, he told me, discussing the verdict with Benedict. If the verdict came today, they decided, they were confident it was for conviction. An acquittal would have been earlier. The worst they could expect now was a hung jury.

As the courtroom doors closed Frank made his way forward, taking his seat at the railing. As he had been for so much of the eleven years he investigated the murder, he was alone.

Despite his optimism, he had never been so nervous in his life. He sat, ramrod straight, his face expressionless. But his hands gripped his knees. His knuckles were white with tension.

Though it took only fifteen minutes before the judge and the jury emerged, it seemed forever. In those fifteen minutes, the twenty years Dorthy and I had known each other flashed before me. I remembered our first meeting at her apartment in New York, with the huge portrait of Martha on the wall; Dorthy crying through the interview. In those twenty years I never shed a tear for Martha. I did not have to. Dorthy wept enough for both of us.

In those twenty years, she had become a different person. She attributed that to her husband's death, which left her to take control. But I think there was more to it than that. Seeking justice for Martha gave her a purpose. The support she received from people like myself—strangers—helped make her whole.

And there was something more. She didn't hate. She didn't hate Michael or the Skakels. She was even able to smile at Mickey. At one television appearance, I saw them buss each other on the cheek. The Skakels saw it too. It infuriated them and they never forgave Mickey for it.

In the well of the courtroom, Michael stood and faced the entrance through which the jurors would enter any second. His jaw was clenched, his face, already florid, increasingly red. I suspected he feared the worst.

The judge, John Kavanewsky Jr., took the bench and confirmed there was a verdict. The jury, six white men and six white women, filed in and took their seats on the courtroom's left side. Some reporters said later that the jurors had smiled at Dorthy as they entered.

The court clerk read off their names. One by one, each rose and remained standing. The jury foreman, Kevin Cambra, the head of a drivers' education school, was the last. The court clerk asked him what verdict they'd reached.

"Guilty."

A collective gasp filled the courtroom. It was the sound I heard when Benedict suggested Michael had never gone to the Terriens'. Later, John Moxley would say he felt his heart stop beating.

Michael turned away and bit his upper lip, keeping his composure but on the verge of tears. Mickey closed his eyes and rubbed his hand over his mouth. He seemed about to faint. Michael's aunt, Big Ann, bolted from the courtroom, sobbing, followed by her daughter.

I saw Frank in his chair, trying not to smile. John Moxley reached over and put a hand on his shoulder. Later, Frank would say that pat was confirmation of his work for the last eleven years. "To me," he said, "that pat was worth its weight in gold."

Yet he would not open his mouth. He forced himself to remain expressionless. Instead, as he had done at Greenwich police headquarters when he formally arrested Michael, he turned in his chair and merely nodded his acknowledgment.

Judge Kavanewsky ordered Michael to stand as each juror's name was called. His family had filled each seat on the courtroom's right side but now Michael was all alone. By the time the final juror spoke, beads of sweat had broken out across his forehead.

Kavanewsky set sentencing for the following month and announced that Michael's bond would be revoked. Mickey declared he would appeal.

"I'd like to say something," said Michael.

"No sir," Kavanewsky cut him off.

He turned to the issue of bail. Susan Gill had argued that Michael's $500,000 bond be revoked and that he be taken into state custody. Mickey, in barely a whisper, urged his release, saying many issues would be subject to appeal.

"Bail is revoked," Kavenewsky ordered. "Take the defendant into custody."

Three marshals surrounded Michael and cuffed his hands behind him. His younger brother David, who was nine at the time of the murder, reached out to touch Michael's shoulder from his seat in the first row of spectators behind the defense table. A marshal swatted his hand away.

Frank noticed that Michael's smirk was gone. His arrogance, his cockiness were no more.

Mickey tried a final motion to set aside the verdict but Kavanewsky denied it. The marshals led Michael away. Twenty-seven years after Martha's death, he was in custody for the first time.

Outside the courtroom, a crowd had filled the hallway. State troopers escorted the Moxleys through them, with Frank behind. As they appeared, the crowd burst into applause. Tears streamed down John and Dorthy Moxley's faces. They hugged Benedict, Morano, Susan Gill, and Frank.

I was on the sidelines. I was a reporter now, trying to keep my emotional distance. But I caught Frank's eye and couldn't help smiling. Still expressionless, he nodded back. Watching him, you might have thought Michael had been acquitted.

"It's wonderful. Can you believe it?" I heard Dorthy saying to Dominick.

"After all this time," Dominick said, "I just want to cry."

"You did it, Frankie," I heard someone from the prosecutor's office shouting to Frank. "Shit, Frankie, you had it right all along. All those little pieces. You had the whole picture."

The television crews had assembled outside, behind the courthouse. As the Moxleys walked toward them, the crowd followed. Stepping up to the microphones, Dorthy said that before coming to court she had repeated a familiar prayer that was finally answered: "Dear Lord, again today, like I have been doing for twenty-seven years, I'm praying that I can find justice for Martha. This whole thing was about Martha."

At her side, John Moxley was asked what message the verdict sent. "I think one message is, 'You've got to be responsible for your actions.'"

A few minutes later, it was Mickey's turn. "Yes, I am bitterly disappointed," he said. "This is the most upsetting verdict I have ever had or will ever have in my life. But I will tell you as long as there is a breath in my body, this case is not over as far as I am concerned. I'm not bitter. I'm determined. I believe in Michael Skakel. He didn't do it. He doesn't have a clue who did it. He wasn't there. He never confessed."

Benedict spoke to the media next. Michael, he said, was convicted by his own words. "Hoist by his own petard," he added, quoting Shakespeare.

Was there a break in the case? someone asked him. A single event that broke it open? Yes, Benedict said. "It was Frank Garr's goofy idea in early 1996 to present the case on a segment of the television program *Unsolved Mysteries*."

Two alternate jurors, Anne Layton and Gary Shannon, were telling reporters it was Coleman who provided the most believable testimony against Michael.

"I believed Coleman," Layton said. "Just because he's a drug addict doesn't mean he can't give truthful testimony." So Frank had been right about that too. The jurors had believed him.

Finally, the Skakels appeared. They were, all of them, grim-faced. All four brothers were there but Tommy, who did not return to court after his first and only appearance.

David spoke first. "We all know each other so very well and we all stand behind our brother Michael, not out of loyalty but from an intimate understanding." Michael, he said, was a person of "love and integrity. Michael is innocent. I know this because I know Michael like only a brother does."

Stephen, the youngest brother, said there were two Michaels. "The one you know is that arrogant, rich kid with no self-control. But that is not the real Michael. He is generous and compassionate. I love my brother. I believe in him 100 percent. I will fight until my last breath. There is no way on earth he would have done this."

I wondered what it meant that the two brothers who spoke up for Michael were the youngest, who knew him the least growing up. Nothing from Rush Jr. Nothing from Johnny, who as a teenager fought brutally with him. And, of course, nothing from the missing Tommy.

•

"I'll tell you what it means," said Frank. "It means the Skakels know what he is and none of them can stand him."

We were standing in the courthouse hallway an hour later. Everyone had gone and the building was nearly empty. It was as though a storm had passed through. A hurricane. The courthouse was returning to its normal routine, the slow pace of a Friday afternoon in spring.

We both felt empty, drained. We had talked about celebrating at Dominick's restaurant in the Bronx after the verdict but somehow neither of us felt like it yet. The enormity of what had occurred hadn't sunk in.

•

"I think he should spend the rest of his life in jail. I think his sentence should be life." That was Dorthy speaking. She stood before Judge Kavanewsky four months later, on August 29, 2002, the day of Michael's sentencing, to give what is known as a "victim impact" statement. It was the first and only time I'd seen her let go and express her bitterness at the Skakels.

Again the courtroom was packed. Everyone who had attended the trial was present except Mickey. The Skakels had already replaced him.

Again, the Skakel family filled the rows on the courtroom's far right side. In her seat in the first row sat Michael's aunt, Ann McCooey—Big Ann—with her daughter next to her. When John Moxley rose to speak about his sister, he passed them. Big Ann could not restrain herself. "You son-of-a-bitch," she muttered to him.

When I asked her about it later, she smiled. "I'm a convent girl," she said. "Do you think a convent girl would talk like that?"

Then it was Michael's turn. Friends and family members—including his aunts, cousins, and in-laws—spoke on his behalf. They sounded alike, as though they had been advised or instructed together. All of them mentioned his motherless childhood and his alcoholic father; his two torturous years at Elan; his recovery and support for other alcoholics, including his Kennedy cousins and his own brothers. All of them attested he had been with them that night at Terrien's. That meant, they said, that he was innocent of Martha's murder.

The court also received ninety letters, including a single-spaced, four-page typewritten letter from Bobby Kennedy Jr. and an eight page, handwritten letter from Bobby's mother, Michael's aunt Ethel. It was her first public acknowledgment of Michael since his indictment more than two and a half years ealier.

I was curious how Ethel Kennedy, Bobby Kennedy's widow and an American icon, would describe her nephew. I wondered whether she harbored him any ill will for the death of her own son Michael. Whatever she may have felt did not make its way into her letter. Ethel Kennedy wrote only in clichés.

"With a heavy heart yet with hope born of the morning sun, I write to ask that your compassion will tip the scales in your decision regarding my nephew, Michael Skakel," she began. The letter ended: "I pray that you will season justice with that twice blessed attribute of God, mercy, and let him continue to enrich our lives."

Finally, Michael spoke. Despite his conviction, he was unrepentant. "I have thought every day, 'Why has my life come to this?' " he began. Then, his voice breaking, he said, "I've been accused of a crime I'd love to be able to say I did, so they [the Moxley family] can sleep. So that the Moxleys can finally find peace. But I can't. Because that would be a lie. To do that is a lie before my God.

"I cannot bear false witness against anyone or myself. I cannot tell a lie before my God. Jesus Christ told people as he walked around the world that he loved them. Should he go to jail for that?"

Was Michael comparing himself to Jesus Christ? Is that how he saw himself? Frank would say afterward I was overreacting, that Michael was simply repeating the standard refrain of reformed alcoholics who like to cry "victim."

Judge Kavanewsky was as unmoved as I. He sentenced Michael to twenty years, making him eligible for parole in eleven.

# 24

PART FIVE / CHAPTER TWENTY-FOUR

## "You and I Will Still Be There"

NEW YORK CITY
2002–2004

With the trial over, I returned to my job at One Police Plaza in New York City. Frank returned to his in Bridgeport. Although our paths were diverging, we continued to meet. We spoke regularly on the phone. Except for Michael's conviction, the most rewarding part of the Moxley case for me had been our friendship.

I regaled Frank with my problems at Police Plaza. There was a new police commissioner, Ray Kelly. As usual, he didn't like what I was writing about him. His predecessors had taken my knocks in silent fury. Kelly took an afternoon off from fighting crime to brave the Long Island Expressway and meet with my editors at *Newsday* to complain. As my boss, Les Payne put it to me, "He wants your head on a platter."

Frank, meanwhile, had the possibility of a promotion. The supervisor of inspectors was about to retire. That had been Solomon's job under Browne. Frank wasn't sure who Benedict would choose. Frank thought it might go a colleague with more seniority but he refused to lobby. In the end Benedict chose Frank. It was his final vindication.

Not long after the verdict, I called Dominick. I had a last piece of unfinished business to settle with him.

We met for lunch at Michael's, a writer's spot in midtown that he selected. As I took the subway uptown from Police Plaza, I realized I was looking forward to seeing him. Say what you will of him—and over the years Frank and I had said plenty—he was always entertaining, replete with gossip and sometimes even real news.

He was being sued by former California Congressman Gary Condit over an article he had written in *Vanity Fair*. Condit had had an affair with Chandra Levy, a young intern in his Washington office, who disappeared. Dominick had written that he had overheard someone say at a cocktail party that Condit was at the heart of a Middle East call girl ring that had dropped Levy's body from a plane over the Atlantic Ocean. After her body was subsequently discovered in a Washington park, Condit sued Dominick for libel.

Dominick said he wanted to settle but that *Vanity Fair* wanted him to fight it. I couldn't figure out why he had ever printed something so obviously libelous based on cocktail-party chatter. Better he had stuck to fiction.

But my reason for seeing him had nothing to do with Condit. Although we had made our peace, I had never quite forgiven him for the fax he'd sent me years before. I brought it to our lunch. Over dessert, I handed it to him.

"Oh my," he said as he read it. "Did I hurt you? Please forgive me. I was so wrapped up in the case because of my daughter. And," he added, "I just love Frank. He and I are very close now. It's funny, isn't it? You never know how life will turn out."

I smiled. I found myself thinking of Frank's mother Beatrice, who had taught her son never to forgive a slight.

Dominick looked up at me and smiled too, sheepishly, I thought. "But you know, Len, it's true what I wrote about giving the Sutton report to Mark Fuhrman. That was brilliant."

This time, I burst out laughing. I couldn't help myself. It was impossible to remain angry at him.

Meanwhile, the Skakels had filed notice of Michael's appeal and turned on Mickey. Just weeks after the verdict, their new lawyers, appellate specialists from Hartford, charged that he had failed to make a basic argument, based on what they said was the case's strongest legal point—that in 1975 there was a five-year statute of limitation on murder. They suggested he had intentionally failed to pursue that theory. In the *Atlantic Monthly*, Bobby Kennedy Jr. wrote that an early appeal "would have deprived Sherman of the nationally publicized trial he expected would boost his career." In the article, Kennedy also continued to maintain that Littleton was more likely Martha's killer than Michael.

Unfair as this may have been to Mickey, I shed no tears for him. Such family anger, he jauntily explained, "came with the territory." I suppose he could afford to be magnanimous. The Skakels had paid him plenty for his services. The figure heard was over $1 million.

And despite Michael's conviction, Mickey's practice flourished. Liza Minnelli hired him. So did local residents. His draw now was less that he would get a client acquitted than that he could draw media coverage.

He also became a regular on Court TV and the talk show circuit. I bumped into him a couple of times in New York. He had a new girlfriend and was hanging out at Elaine's, another spot frequented by writers.

"People come up to me now," he said to me. "They say, 'Hey, you're that guy from the O.J. case.' I say, 'No, try the Michael Skakel case,' They say, 'Oh, yeah, I saw you on television.' "

"How do you feel about the Skakels turning on you?" I asked.

"Devastated," he said, glancing over my shoulder, checking out the celebrity crowd. Clearly, he had moved on.

There was one last thing I felt I had to do, one more person I had to see. And I had to do it alone, with no help from Frank or anyone else. I wanted to see Tom Sheridan, Michael's first attorney. He knew more about Michael than anyone else, even more, I felt, than Frank, though whether Sheridan would talk to me about Michael was another question.

He lived in a brownstone in the 50s off Tenth Avenue, where he also had his law office. I hadn't seen him in years and was taken aback at how he had aged. The last time I'd visited him we'd had lunch at a pub around the corner that was pretty good. Now, he was seventy-seven years old and suffering from emphysema. He carried a bottle of liquid oxygen that he breathed whenever he became fatigued, which was often. I brought in sandwiches because he could barely walk.

But there was nothing wrong with his mind. He remembered in detail events that had occurred twenty-five years before.

I began by saying that with Michael's trial over, I was writing a book.

"You should," he said. We'd always gotten along. I think he appreciated that I'd helped him and Murphy out years before, when I'd given them my copy of the Greenwich police report.

But hiring Murphy had proved his undoing with the Skakels. Despite his fifty-year friendship with Rushton and his decades of service to his family, they had turned on him as they later would on Mickey. They never forgave him for the troubles the investigation had caused when word of Tommy's and Michael's lies to the police leaked out. And Michael had never forgiven him for literally having had him kidnapped and sent to Elan.

There were also the children's trust funds from their grandparents. Sheridan had been in charge of them. The children wanted their money and pleaded with their father to keep Sheridan out of their affairs.

"Rush Jr. called and said the kids had petitioned to keep me away," Sheridan said. "To tell you the truth, it was a burden removed from my life."

Then he said something startling. "Going to prison is probably the best thing that could have happened to Michael."

That was a strange remark from a lawyer who over the years had professed Michael's innocence. I asked what he meant.

"It might do him a world of good," he said. "Things happen in this life. It might be the making of him. I do feel badly. A sick person has been wrongly accused. But I think it is for his own good that this happened. He is not the first person to be wrongly accused. He'll probably do lots of good work there as a counselor with other inmates and their addiction problems. He's very good at that."

I couldn't figure out what Sheridan meant. Was he saying that while he believed Michael did not murder Martha, his conviction was divine retribution for other transgressions?

"Michael is a sociopath and a sick personality with a mental disorder but he did not do it," Sheridan said. "He did not kill Martha Moxley."

He then described his visit to Elan with Father Connolly shortly after Michael had been admitted. There was more to the story than what Connolly had told Frank. Far more. According to Sheridan, Connolly reported that a counselor at Elan told him Michael said that on the night of the murder he'd been covered in blood. Sheridan added that Michael also told him he thought he might have killed Martha.

"When we went up to Elan, two, three weeks later, they were giving him a real grilling," Sheridan said. "I spoke to Michael alone. Michael said, 'I was out that night. I might have done it, Mr. Sheridan. If she caught me whacking off, I might have whacked her.' "

" 'What about the bloody clothes, Michael?' " Sheridan said he had asked. " 'Michael, how did you clean the blood off yourself?' Michael just stared at me. He didn't know."

Sheridan said that when he discussed this with Father Connolly, who was also a psychologist, the priest told Sheridan that because of Michael's behavior disorder, he could have been "fantasizing." Despite all Sheridan knew about him, he refused to believe that his best friend Rucky's son was capable of murder. Fantasizing. That's what it was. That's what Michael had done. He was having a "guilt trip," Sheridan decided.

Two years later, Sheridan continued, "Michael graduated from Elan with hugs and kisses from his family. For years, he was in and out of treatment. He couldn't get a job. He said the Moxley case was hanging over him and he was forever asking his father for money. I felt he was using this to extort money from his old man. I wouldn't let him come home. He stayed at his cousin Terrien's."

Through the years, said Sheridan, Michael's fear that he may have killed Martha became a recurrent theme. "He spent years thinking he did it. He told me he didn't know when Martha was killed but that if it was after 12:30, he would be in deep shit. I went through two sessions like this with him after he got out of Elan. Two flashbacks: 'Could I have done this?' he asked."

Sheridan brought him to Dr. Lesse, who tested him with sodium Pentothal. "Lesse told me, 'No way.'" At another point, Lesse's associate had Michael tested and hypnotized. "He said Michael had no involvement in the murder but recommended he be hospitalized and given psychotherapy."

The years passed. "Everything seemed fine," Sheridan said, until the Krebs interview.

"During the questioning, which occurred in my office, Michael was reliving it. Afterwards, he came down to see me. He said, 'Do you think I could have done it? I had a load on.' I felt he was having another guilt trip. He was saying he believed he may have murdered Martha but couldn't remember. I thought, 'Here we go again.'"

Sheridan then fired Murphy and Krebs. "I didn't think it was necessary to spend any more money," he said. "It was not my duty to do what the Greenwich police should have done at the beginning. And if Martha was killed at 10:00 P.M., as the police said, Michael was in the clear because he was at the Terriens'."

We had been talking more than two hours. I still did not know what to make of what he was saying. He had provided more damning information about Michael than anything that had come out at his trial. I couldn't get out of my mind what he had said about Michael's virtually confessing to him at least twice. That and what Michael had told the counselor at Elan about the blood. How could Sheridan continue to maintain Michael was innocent?

I had one more question. It was about Margo, Sheridan's niece, who had married Michael and was divorcing him. "Knowing all you did about Michael," I asked, "did you warn her about him?"

Sheridan said he hadn't.

"Why not?" I asked.

"Lawyer–client privilege," he answered. I stared at him an extra second, waiting for him to smile at what I assumed was a joke. He did not.

•

On a cold January morning in 2003, I attended the funeral of Rushton Skakel. He had died the week before in Hobe Sound but the service was held at St. Mary's Church on Greenwich Avenue. The church was packed. Not a seat went unfilled.

The family sat in the front rows on the left. They were all there but Michael. Although his brothers each wore coats and ties, I noted that none of them wore a suit. Only the rich can indulge in such informality. Jimmy Terrien, tieless, sat a few rows behind them.

Ethel Kennedy was said to have appeared, although I didn't see her. I did see Andrew Cuomo, the son of New York's former governor, who at the time was married to Ethel's daughter Kerry. My first thought was one of surprise that Andrew had known Rushton.

Tommy was listed in the program to read a verse from the Book of Wisdom but for reasons I never learned, Rush Jr. took over for him. David also read from the book of Matthew. As he reached the portion: "For I was hungry and you gave me something to eat, I was thirsty and you gave me something to drink," his voice broke. He collected himself and continued, "I needed clothes and you clothed me. I was sick and you looked after me. I was in prison and you came to visit me."

No fewer than nine priests sat on the stage. The mass was led by Father Aidan Hynes, who had been Rushton's priest in Hobe Sound.

"I bless the body of Rushton Skakel," he began in a brogue. There was something reassuring about that brogue. It was as though the mourners were getting the real thing, the true old-time Irish Catholicism.

As the priest spoke, I imagined Rushton as a boy. Yes, the silver spoon had been in his mouth but there had been all that chaos with his absentee parents. He was not particularly intelligent, nor effectual in business, but he was not unkind. As Sheridan had said, there was nothing in him of the double-cross.

Yet the chaos of his childhood had followed him as a parent. As a father he had been a disaster. Sheridan had said something else to me about him: He should never have had children.

Rushton "had an abiding faith. God is not interested in ends. It is how you strive. He had terrible difficulties in his last years," the priest intoned, "but he had charity. I never heard him utter an unkind word. Rush tried to see things as God sees them. He tried."

He then cited a litany of names Rushton had known and lost: his father, George Skakel Sr.; his mother, Big Ann; his older brother, George Jr.—all of them killed in plane crashes; George's wife Pat Caroon, an alcoholic who died at the dinner table when she choked on a piece of meat; Rushton Sr.'s brother Jimmy and his wife Virginia, both of them also alcoholics; his sister Georgeann and his brother-in-law, George Dowdle, Jimmy Terrien's biological father, who had drunk himself to death the day Terrien was born; and Senator Robert Kennedy, RFK, Ethel's husband (whom I knew Rushton and the other Skakels had despised).

His old friend Victor Ziminsky then told the gin rummy story from the company plane, the Great Lakes Convair, when one of the two engines had conked out and Rushton had ambled up to speak to the pilot, then made three short stops, chatting with other guests before he sat down and knocked with three points. "We were all calm," Ziminsky said, "because Rushton had been calm."

John Skakel, Johnny—the boy who according to Andy Pugh, had had murderous fights with Michael—also spoke. "Dad loved many people," he began. "He reserved a special spot for all his children."

Again, I recalled the trial. Rushton, in the last stages of dementia had come up to testify. At the end of his testimony, Michael had mouthed the words "I love you."

Of course, it had all been for show. In pleading for leniency for Michael, everyone had made a big deal of how Rushton had abused him. Now, it was love that served their purpose.

Then, Johnny cited his mother's illness, what he called, "God's plan to take her from this life." Referring to Michael's conviction, he said of his father, "In his last years, he faced the indignity of having his son wrongly accused. He chose not to get down on the level of those who have attacked the family."

So there it was again. No responsibility. No accountability. This was

Michael Skakel's brother John speaking. He was throwing down the family gauntlet. Their denial would continue. They would never admit it. They would never acknowledge what Michael had done, and we would never be certain of exactly what had occurred that night.

I was sitting on the aisle toward the rear of the church. A woman and a little boy sat down next to me. He was perhaps three or four, and the woman did not appear to be his mother. He held a plastic toy and was fidgeting in his seat, fighting to stay quiet. "Shh, Georgie," the woman whispered. I realized this was Michael's son. In his plea for leniency, Michael had asked the judge to consider little Georgie so that he would not grow up without a father.

Georgie had Michael's fair coloring and round face but he was adorable. His mother Margo, Sheridan's niece, had also come to the funeral, though for some reason, she was not sitting with Georgie.

"Are you going to the toy store?" I heard him ask the woman he was sitting with.

"Not yet," she whispered. Little Georgie made a face, then broke into a smile.

As I watched him, tears came to my eyes. I, too, had been the father of a little boy who was now grown. Yes, Michael had pleaded for no jail time so that he could raise his son and for the first time I felt pity. Not for Michael. He had had his chance. He could have come forward years before and accepted responsibility. Had he done so then—had his family done so—Michael would have served perhaps a few years in a juvenile facility and would now have been free.

No, it was not for him that I grieved. It was for this little boy, who would not only grow up without a father, but who would learn someday that his father was a murderer.

•

I was on vacation in Colorado in September 2003, when Dominick called. Susan and I were visiting her brother, my closest friend at Dartmouth of forty years before. He'd built himself a house on top of a mountain outside Aspen on 110 acres with spectacular views. Up on the ridges you could see elk. Bears also lived in the area. I hadn't seen any up close, thank God, although their droppings were everywhere.

"Did you hear the latest?" Dominick said when I answered my cell phone. I was outside, taking in the vistas, staring up at Mt. Sopris, which even in September was snow-capped.

Michael's appeals lawyer, Hope Seeley, claimed to have discovered two new suspects in Martha's murder—two black men from the Bronx. As teenagers in 1975, Seeley said, they had admitted being in Belle Haven on Halloween eve, picking up a golf club lying on the ground at the Skakels', then using it to murder Martha "caveman style"—whatever that meant.

As bizarre as her story sounded, I had heard something about it a few months earlier, from, of all people, Cissy's daughter, Helen Ix Fitzpatrick. Not long after the verdict, Helen's husband had telephoned me, saying, as Sheridan had years before, that because my articles on the case had been fair, Helen and her parents felt they could talk to me about the case. Specifically, they felt they might be helpful in sharing information about the Skakels for this book.

I drove over to Helen's house one Friday night after work. She and her husband lived in Belle Haven just down the street from her parents. He was a Wall Street guy. She also had a corporate job and they had young children, one of whom attended Greenwich Academy, the sister school of Brunswick. Whatever help she offered was tailored to benefit Michael. That was how she mentioned the two black suspects.

She said she had learned of them through Bobby Kennedy, who had learned of them through Tony Bryant, who had attended Brunswick years before. Tony was now a prosecutor in Florida, she said. After all these years, he had come forward.

It turned out that Gitano "Tony" Bryant happened to be a cousin of the Los Angeles Lakers basketball star Kobe Bryant. His story was that on Halloween eve, 1975, he had been in Belle Haven with the two black teenagers from the Bronx and that the next day they admitted killing Martha.

Helen added that Tony Bryant had recently told this story to another Brunswick classmate, a television writer named Crawford Mills. Mills had contacted Bobby Jr. after reading his article in the *Atlantic Monthly*.

"Dominick, you have got to be kidding," I said when he told me of the two new suspects. I had dismissed what Helen had told me as preposterous. I had never seen anything about two black teenagers in the Greenwich police reports. How had they gotten past the guards at the Belle Haven police booth without being stopped? Why had nobody reported seeing them at the time? And why would they have taken the missing part of the golf club handle with Anne Skakel's name on it and risk being apprehended with the murder weapon?

In fact, pinning the murder on two unnamed blacks seemed to me not just ridiculous but ludicrous. Seeley appeared to be playing to the meanest of American racial stereotypes. Two blacks from the Bronx. "Caveman" style.

"Where do you suppose she came up with this?" Dominick asked.

"I think it was from Bobby Kennedy Jr.," I said.

I immediately called Frank. When I asked him about Crawford Mills, Tony Bryant, and the two black guys, he exploded. "It's all bullshit. How can people believe this crap? Remember Tad Baldwin? I almost indicted him for perjury. I tell you, Len, when I hear this kind of stuff I have to laugh." I couldn't tell whether he was more amused or disgusted.

Frank said he had already checked out Tony Bryant. First, he wasn't a prosecutor or even a lawyer. In 1993, he'd been convicted as an accomplice in a burglary in Beverly Hills, California. According to that trial testimony, thieves had entered a woman's home pretending to deliver flowers, then threatened her with a gun, tied her up, and stole her jewelry.

More recently, Bryant had started a tobacco distribution company. It went out of business because he underreported sales and failed to pay $5 million in state taxes.

As for Crawford Mills, before the trial he had contacted Mickey Sherman, who dismissed his information. Like Baldwin, Mills had been writing a TV script about the murder, and Mickey—who knew something about getting himself on TV—questioned whether Mills's story was fact or fiction.

Frank added that when Benedict had asked Seeley for the names and addresses of the two suspects so that the state could interview them and perhaps clear Michael, she refused to provide them. "They say they are saving it for their appeal," he said. "Benedict thinks they'll use this to claim Mickey was incompetent for not pursuing the lead."

"Why did Bryant wait all this time to come forward?" I asked Frank.

"Why don't you ask Michael's lawyers?" he replied.

"What about Littleton? Does this mean the Skakels have given up on him as Martha's killer?"

"Why don't you ask Bobby Kennedy?" Eighteen months had passed since Michael's conviction. Frank hadn't lost his sense of humor.

Coincidentally, I was supposed to meet with Bobby Kennedy Jr. the following week. He had written to me at *Newsday*, although he had gotten my name wrong, addressing the letter to "Larry Leavitt." Because of his relationship with the Skakel family, he wrote, he felt he could provide me with information for this book, like the Ixes had. For reasons that I didn't understand, he was under the mistaken impression that I didn't want to meet with him.

Of course, I jumped at the opportunity. We agreed to meet at his office at Pace University in Westchester. But the day of the meeting, he canceled. Frank had warned me that would happen.

"Circumstances have changed," Kennedy said. Specifically, he said he had changed his mind because of my relationship with Frank.

Then he offered some advice. Or perhaps it something other than advice.

"It would be silly and foolhardy not to rethink your thesis," he said. "I think it will be obvious to a lot of people that many of your presumptions about the Skakels are wrong. Your presumption is that Michael Skakel is guilty. I think this evidence [that he had developed to clear Michael] is strong enough and will emerge over time that if you go ahead and write your book on that earlier theme, it will not look accurate."

At the same time, Seeley's partner, Hubert J. Santos, sent a letter to Benedict, with a copy to the newly appointed chief state's attorney—who was none other than Frank's nemesis, Chris Morano.

"It is our understanding that Mr. Garr serves as the main character and hero in Mr. Levitt's book," Santos wrote, "and that he has been actively involved with Mr. Levitt in this book project."

Because of this, Santos said Frank had a conflict of interest and urged Benedict to drop him from the case.

"Do you see what the Skakels are doing?" said Frank. We were back at the Lakeside at our usual table by the water. Spring was coming. The ice was melting and ducks were paddling about.

"First, they went after Littleton," he said. "They hired Murphy and Krebs to ruin him. Instead, when Murphy and Krebs discovered that Tommy and Michael had lied to the police, Sheridan fired them.

"Because the information got out, they turned on Sheridan. Next, they fired Mickey, saying he was incompetent. Now with your book, they're coming after us."

Could this be true? That now it was Frank and me in the Skakels' crosshairs? For a moment, I tried to imagine how the Skakels could attack me. As far as I could see, they couldn't. I worked for a top news organization. I'd been a reporter for thirty years. In his article in the *Atlantic*, even Bobby Kennedy Jr. had written that my articles had been the most thorough about the case.

Then I realized what they were doing. In his letter to me, Bobby Jr. had written, "I suspect that your alliance with Officer Frank Garr may have caused you after many years of aggressive yet unbiased reports on the Moxley murder to adopt his bias towards the Skakel family."

To the Skakels, Frank was the weak link. To them, he was the local detective from the discredited Greenwich Police Department. They would attack me through him.

"What happened to Santos's letter to Benedict, saying you should be taken off the case?" I asked him.

"Benedict said he wouldn't dignify it with a response," he answered. That was reassuring at least.

I began discussing my meeting with Sheridan. I had told Frank of it before, of course, but I couldn't get out of my mind what Sheridan had said of Michael, of his two virtual confessions. That and what Michael had told the counselor about the blood.

"Len," he said, "why do you sound surprised? They all know he did it. What Sheridan said makes no sense and no difference. That old windbag did everything he could to protect Rucky and the Skakel family. That's all he cares about. He tells you Michael confessed to him at least twice and he still doesn't believe he did it? Just remember, he is not a stupid man."

"Jesus, Frank," I said, "this still isn't over." The subject of the appeal and Kennedy's letter were depressing me. The Skakels, I realized, would never let it die. They were like the forces of evil and they just kept coming. Not only that. Despite the conviction, Frank and I still questioned whether Michael had acted alone.

I happened to think of Dorthy. Like Frank and me, we had remained in touch since the verdict. She'd come into the city a couple of times and we'd had lunch. I'd found a place downtown near my office that she enjoyed and we had a fine old time reminiscing.

"You know, Frank," I said, "she's somehow different now." I had to ponder a moment to figure out how, and then I hit on it. For the first time since I'd known her, she seemed, well, almost happy. She'd never get over Martha, of course. No parent could. But with Michael's conviction, she had finally found a kind of equilibrium.

"But here's where you're wrong, Len," Frank answered. "For the Skakels, it is over. They just don't know it.

"And remember this. If I am wrong and their appeal is somehow granted, and even if Michael gets a new trial, you and I will still be there. We'll be there to stop them. Sometimes I think that's what we are meant to do in this world."

# List of Names

### THE MOXLEYS

MARTHA MOXLEY, fifteen years old at the time she was murdered (in 1975).
DORTHY, Martha's mother.
DAVID, Martha's father.
JOHN, Martha's older brother, seventeen years old at the time she was murdered.
JOHN MCCREIGHT, friend and colleague of David Moxley.

### THE SKAKELS

RUSHTON SR., brother of ETHEL SKAKEL KENNEDY (wife of the late SENATOR ROBERT KENNEDY).
ANNE REYNOLDS SKAKEL, his wife, who died in 1973.

#### Their Children

TOMMY, seventeen years old at the time of Martha's murder. For years he was the prime suspect.
MICHAEL, fifteen years old at the time of the murder. He became a suspect in 1995 when it was reported that he placed himself at the murder scene the night of the murder.
DAVID, JOHN (JOHNNY), RUSH JR., STEPHEN, JULIE.

### Skakel Relatives, Supporters, Acquaintances

JIMMY TERRIEN, Skakel first cousin. Michael said that he and his brothers were at Terrien's home at the time of the murder. Terrien's whereabouts later that night are unknown.

GEORGEANN TERRIEN, Jimmy's mother, Rushton Sr.'s sister.

TOM SHERIDAN, Skakel family friend and lawyer who became Michael's criminal attorney after a drunken-driving accident in 1978.

MICKEY SHERMAN, Michael's attorney at his trial.

EMANUEL "MANNY" MARGOLIS, Tommy's attorney.

KEN LITTLETON, Skakel family tutor. He moved into the Skakel house the night of Martha's murder and later became a suspect.

FATHER MARK CONNOLLY, Skakel family priest. He visited Michael shortly after his arrival at the Elan school in Poland Springs, Maine, and was told by a guidance counselor that Michael said that on the night of the murder he had been covered in blood.

ANDREA SHAKESPEARE, family friend of Julie Skakel, who was at the Skakel house the night of the murder and testified that Michael never went to Terrien's.

### Neighbors and Friends

ROBERT AND CISSY IX, whose daughter HELEN was Martha's age. In front of the grand jury, Cissy said that Rushton told her Michael had confided to him he thought he might have killed Martha. At Michael's trial, she renounced her grand jury testimony.

EDWARD HAMMOND, a neighbor, who became the murder's first suspect.

## LAW ENFORCEMENT

### From the Greenwich Police Department

STEPHEN BARAN, chief of the department at the time of the Moxley murder.

TOM KEEGAN, chief of detectives and head of the Moxley investigation, who succeeded Baran as chief.

DETECTIVE JIM LUNNEY, lead investigator on the Moxley case.

DETECTIVE STEVE CARROLL, Lunney's partner.

DETECTIVE FRANK GARR, who took over the case when it was reopened.

### From the Fairfield County State's Attorney's Office in Bridgeport

DONALD BROWNE, Fairfield County state's attorney.

DETECTIVE JACK SOLOMON, Browne's chief investigator.

JOHN BENEDICT, Browne's successor as Fairfield County state's attorney.

SUSAN GILL, assistant state's attorney.

CHRIS MORANO and DOMINICK GALLUZO, assistant state's attorneys sent from the chief state's attorney's office outside Hartford

### From the Detroit Police Department

HOMICIDE CHIEF GERALD HALE, who came to Greenwich to look into the case at the request of John McCreight.

### Private Investigators for the Skakels, Hired by Sheridan

JIM MURPHY, former FBI supervisor.

WILLIS [BILLY] KREBS, Murphy's associate, former New York City Police Department lieutenant. When their investigation revealed that both Tommy and Michael had lied about their whereabouts the night of the murder, they were fired.

## FROM THE TIMES-MIRROR CORPORATION

KEN BRIEF, editor-in-chief of the *Stamford Advocate* and *Greenwich Time.*

JOE PISANI, Ken's deputy and editor of the *Greenwich Time.*

STEVE ISENBERG, publisher of the *Stamford Advocate* and *Greenwich Time* and later associate publisher of *New York Newsday.*

DAVE LAVENTHOL, editor, then publisher of *Newsday* on Long Island and later the head of Times-Mirror's East Coast newspapers.

TONY INSOLIA, Laventhol's successor as editor of *Newsday.*

DON FORST, editor of *New York Newsday.*

# Index